"This new book is a vital correc
that immigrants 'take jobs' from
careful historical research shows
degradation on the one hand and rising inequality on the other
are the key drivers of rising low-wage immigration over the past
half-century – not vice versa. Understanding that employers and
political elites – not immigrants – are to blame for the plight of
U.S.-born workers can help to build bridges across racial and
ethnic lines to mount a unified challenge to the toxic politics of
right-wing populism."

Pramila Jayapal, member of the U.S. House of Representatives
and co-chair of the Congressional Progressive Caucus

"Ruth Milkman addresses the central claim of contemporary
nativism, that immigrants 'take' the jobs of 'Americans.' She
persuasively shows that immigrant labor is not the cause of wage
degradation but its consequence. An important and timely book."

Mae Ngai, Columbia University

"This carefully documented and forcefully argued book shows
that low-wage immigration is rooted in deteriorating wages
and working conditions. A convincing counter to conventional
immigration narratives."

Michael J. Piore, Massachusetts Institute of Technology

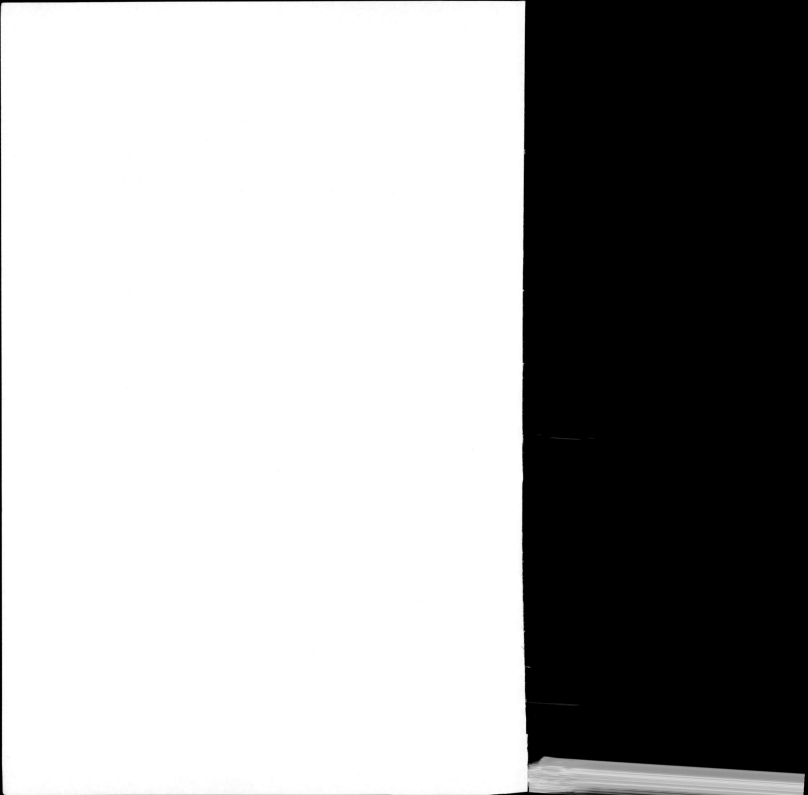

Immigrant Labor and
the New Precariat

Immigrant Labor and the New Precariat

Ruth Milkman

polity

The right of Ruth Milkman to be identified as Author of this Work has been asserted in accordance with the UK Copyright, Designs and Patents Act 1988.

First published in 2020 by Polity Press

Polity Press
65 Bridge Street
Cambridge CB2 1UR, UK

Polity Press
101 Station Landing
Suite 300
Medford, MA 02155, USA

ISBN-13: 978-0-7456-9201-2
ISBN-13: 978-0-7456-9202-9 (pb)

A catalogue record for this book is available from the British Library.

Library of Congress Cataloging-in-Publication Data

Names: Milkman, Ruth, 1954- author.
Title: Immigrant labor and the new precariat / Ruth Milkman.
Description: Cambridge, UK ; Medford, MA : Polity Press 2020. | Series:
    Immigration & society | Includes bibliographical references and index. |
    Summary: «Why immigrants aren›t to blame for the erosion of the US labor
    market»-- Provided by publisher.
Identifiers: LCCN 2019052457 (print) | LCCN 2019052458 (ebook) | ISBN
    9780745692012 (hardback) | ISBN 9780745692029 (paperback) | ISBN
    9780745692050 (epub)
Subjects: LCSH: Foreign workers--United States. | Precarious
    employment--United States. | Unemployment--United States. | Labor
    market--United States. | United States--Emigration and
    immigration--Economic aspects.
Classification: LCC HD8081.A5 M545 2020 (print) | LCC HD8081.A5 (ebook) |
    DDC 331.6/20973--dc23
LC record available at https://lccn.loc.gov/2019052457
LC ebook record available at https://lccn.loc.gov/2019052458

Typeset in 11 on 13pt Sabon
by Fakenham Prepress Solutions, Fakenham, Norfolk NR21 8NL
Printed and bound in Great Britain by CPI Group (UK) Ltd, Croydon

The publisher has used its best endeavours to ensure that the URLs for external websites referred to in this book are correct and active at the time of going to press. However, the publisher has no responsibility for the websites and can make no guarantee that a site will remain live or that the content is or will remain appropriate.

Every effort has been made to trace all copyright holders, but if any have been overlooked the publisher will be pleased to include any necessary credits in any subsequent reprint or edition.

For further information on Polity, visit our website:
politybooks.com

Contents

Acknowledgments

Jonathan Skerrett kindly solicited this book from me on behalf of Polity several years ago, and he has been extraordinarily patient in awaiting its completion. I am deeply indebted to the Center for Advanced Study in the Behavioral Sciences (CASBS) at Stanford University, where I was privileged to have a nine-month residential fellowship in 2018–19. Freed from all my other duties, I was able to concentrate during that period on writing this book. The ideas in it have been germinating for some time. They were influenced by comments and criticisms from colleagues who attended my presentations of the work in progress at the Advanced Research Collaborative at the CUNY Graduate Center; the Center for Global Migration Studies at the University of Maryland; the University of California, Davis; the University of Massachusetts, Amherst; the University of Kansas; the University of Massachusetts, Boston; the University of Hong Kong; the University of California, Berkeley; the University of California, Santa Cruz; and CASBS itself. I am also grateful for the helpful suggestions of three anonymous reviewers who read an earlier draft of the manuscript at the publisher's request, and to Deepak Bhargava, who provided invaluable comments at the eleventh hour as I completed the final revisions. Many thanks to all.

RM
New York City, October 2019

Permissions Acknowledgments

For epigraph to Introduction:
From Greig de Peuter, "Universities, Intellectuals, and Multitudes: An Interview with Stuart Hall," in *Utopian Pedagogy: Radical Experiments Against Neoliberal Globalization* edited by M. Cote, J. F. Day, and G. de Peuter. © University of Toronto Press. Reproduced with permission.

For epigraph to chapter 1:
From *Birds of Passage: Migrant Labor and Industrial Societies* by Michael J. Piore. © Cambridge University Press. Reproduced with permission of Cambridge University Press through PLSclear.

For epigraph to chapter 3:
From *What do Unions Do?* by Richard B. Freeman and James L. Medoff, copyright © 1984. Reprinted by permission of Basic Books, an imprint of Hachette Book Group, Inc.

For epigraph to chapter 5:
Used with the permission of *The American Prospect*, "Immigrants and Unions Make America Great," by Hector Figueroa and Cristina Jimenez Moreta. © The American Prospect, Prospect.org, 2018. All rights reserved.

gender neutral plural

Latinx

Introduction

These people are doing the shit work of global capital: they are
servicing it, feeding it, washing its windows late at night, cleaning its
offices, and looking after the children of the global entrepreneurs. ...
Du Bois once said, 'The color line will be the central problem of the
twentieth century.' I think migration will be the central issue of the
twenty-first century.

Stuart Hall (de Peuter 2007: 128)

The United States is home to more immigrants than any other
country in the world. Its 44.4 million foreign-born inhabitants
made up 14 percent of the nation's population in 2017, a higher
proportion than at any time since 1910 (Radford 2019; Tavernise
2018; Carter 2006). The foreign-born component of the U.S. labor
force was even larger: 17 percent in 2017, more than triple the
level in 1980 (Zong et al. 2019). A large and growing share of the
nation's foreign-born workforce is made up of college-educated
professionals and white-collar workers, disproportionately of
Asian origin. Yet public debate (and this book) focuses primarily
on the less-educated immigrants concentrated at the bottom of
the labor market, most of whom are Latinx. Although they
are widely believed to be doing "jobs Americans don't want,"
low-wage immigrant workers, disproportionately from Mexico
and other parts of Latin America, have become the third rail of
American politics in recent years. The "illegal aliens" among them
are especially controversial, notwithstanding the fact that less

than 5 percent of the nation's workforce was undocumented in 2017 (Passel and Cohn 2019).

Immigration has been a contentious issue for decades, but in the twenty-first century it moved to center stage, helping to catapult Donald Trump into the U.S. presidency and upending traditional political alignments around the world. Although nativism has been resurgent in many other contexts as well, the "native" population of the United States is distinctly different from that of most other wealthy nations in that until the late twentieth century it consisted almost entirely of descendants of European immigrants, on the one hand, and African slaves, on the other. But Americans have notoriously poor historical memories, and recent immigration debates have unfolded not in relation to the legacy of settler colonialism and slavery but, rather, against the backdrop of the exceptional period of low immigration that began after World War I. Two shifts in U.S. immigration law demarcate that era: the establishment in 1924 of nationality-based quotas designed to sharply restrict immigration from Southern and Eastern Europe; and the lifting of those quotas in 1965, which spurred a massive new immigrant influx from the global South (Ngai 2004).

Because the overwhelming majority of post-1965 immigrants are people of color, their incorporation into American society has been mediated by pre-existing racial hierarchies; yet the growing immigrant presence itself has also gradually reconfigured the U.S. racial order. The Latinx ("Hispanic" in official statistics) population exemplifies this dialectic. In 2017, 44 percent of the nation's total immigrant population was Latinx; among the undocumented the share was much higher, estimated at 75 percent. Although nearly twice as many Latinxs are U.S.-born as foreign-born (Zong et al. 2019), in practice few Americans differentiate between those whose families have resided in the United States for generations and those who arrived recently. Latinxs can be of any race, and they span the class spectrum, but those differences too are increasingly blurred. Similarly, variations in Latinx citizenship status and national origin have become less salient over time, as a single "panethnic" category has taken shape (Mora 2014).

By the twenty-first century, indeed, most Americans considered "Latinos" to be a racial rather than an ethnic group. And that group, however understood, is at the center of the increasingly heated debates over immigration – debates that fuse racial, cultural, and economic concerns. In recent decades conservative advocates of immigration restriction have elaborated a powerful "immigrant threat narrative," according to which the Latinx influx, and especially its undocumented component, not only has hurt American workers economically but also has contributed to the nation's cultural decline. More specifically, in this view, the U.S.-born have suffered as a result of "immigrants' use of welfare, health and educational services, their propensity to turn to crime, and their tendency to displace native citizens from jobs" (Abrajano and Hajnal 2015: 5). The origins of this narrative can be traced back several decades, to the mid-1970s (Minian 2018: ch. 2). Over the years since, it has been amplified by media outlets such as Fox News and conservative talk radio and by right-wing websites and organizations such as the Tea Party.[2] More recently Donald Trump has become the most prominent proponent of the immigrant threat narrative. If immigration were summarily curtailed, border security established, and the estimated 10.5 million "illegal aliens" residing in the country as of 2017 (Passel and Cohn 2019) removed, his rhetoric suggests, the American Dream and the living standards it once delivered to working people would be restored – helping to "Make America Great Again."

The Immigrant Threat Narrative and the Politics of Resentment

Nearly all experts on the subject agree that the economic benefits of immigration for the United States outweigh its costs. Immigration contributes positively to overall economic growth and to techno-logical innovation. It reduces the costs of many goods and services, benefiting consumers; it also increases demand in key sectors such as housing, stimulating the real-estate industry and other economic activities tied to it. The fiscal impact of immigration is typically negative at the local and state levels, mainly because the cost of providing education to new arrivals and their children is not fully recovered in state and local taxes paid by immigrants. But this is offset by a positive fiscal impact at the federal level, not only because immigrants are disqualified from many government benefits but also because they are disproportionately prime-age workers, contributing more to Social Security and Medicare than they receive (Blau and Mackie 2017).

However, the expert consensus regarding the economic benefits of immigration is not shared by the larger public (Schuck 2007). On the contrary, as a large body of data demonstrates, Americans are deeply divided on this question (Gallup 2018a, 2018b). For example, as figure 1 shows, 45 percent of respondents to a Pew Research Center survey conducted in mid-2016, when the attacks of then candidate Trump on Mexican immigrants were riveting public attention, agreed that "the growing number of immigrants working in this country hurts American workers." Almost as many respondents to this survey (42 percent) endorsed the opposite view, namely that growing immigration helps American workers. (The remaining 13 percent said that there was not much effect, didn't know, or refused to respond.)

Anti-immigrant sentiments have become increasingly visible thanks to Trump's presidential campaign and the policies his administration has promulgated since he took office, but the issue long pre-dates his entry onto the political stage. Nativism has been a feature of American politics from the earliest period, and at many points in the recent past negative attitudes toward the foreign-born were *more* prevalent than they were in 2016. Ten years earlier, for example, a wave of May Day protest marches by immigrants and their supporters sparked an intense backlash among the U.S.-born (Wong 2017). As figure 1 shows, in a mid-2006 Pew survey that included the same question asked ten years later, a *higher* share of respondents than in 2016 – 55 percent – agreed that immigrants hurt American workers. (In 2006, 28 percent of respondents said that immigration helped U.S. workers, while 17 percent said it did not have much effect, didn't know, or refused to answer.)

Figure 1 Percentage of respondents saying that the growing number of immigrants working in the U.S. hurts American workers, by race, education, household income, and political identification, 2006 and 2016[3]

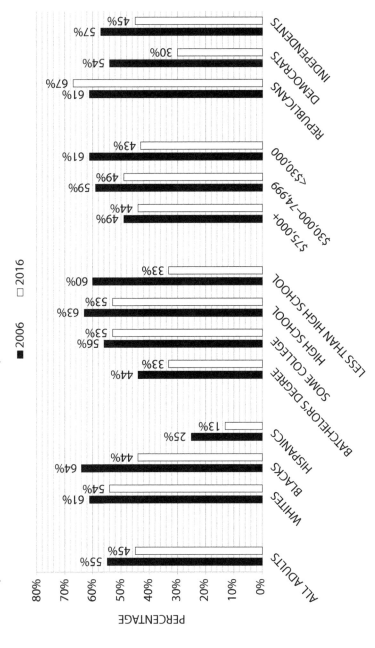

■ 2006   □ 2016

ALL ADULTS: 55% / 45%
WHITES: 61% / 54%
BLACKS: 64% / 44%
HISPANICS: 25% / 13%
BATCHELOR'S DEGREE: 44% / 33%
SOME COLLEGE: 56% / 53%
HIGH SCHOOL: 63% / 53%
LESS THAN HIGH SCHOOL: 60% / 33%
$75,000+: 49% / 44%
$30,000–74,999: 59% / 49%
<$30,000: 61% / 43%
REPUBLICANS: 61% / 67%
DEMOCRATS: 54% / 30%
INDEPENDENTS: 57% / 45%

PERCENTAGE

Source: Pew Research Center (2016).

As these data suggest, attitudes about immigration are extremely volatile. They fluctuate not only over time (see Gallup 2018a) but also across space, with hostility generally more pronounced in new immigrant destinations than in areas with a long-established foreign-born population (Enos 2017). Attitudes also are affected by the way in which the immigration issue is framed (Bloemraad et al. 2016). Amid all these variations, however, one consistent pattern in recent years is that non-college-educated workers are especially receptive to the immigrant threat narrative. The data shown in figure 1 illustrate this: in both 2006 and 2016, non-college-educated respondents, as well as those with lower household incomes, disproportionately endorsed the view that immigrant employment hurts American workers.

Some commentators explain this in terms of economic self-interest, arguing that less-educated, lower-income workers are those most likely to feel threatened by labor market competition from immigrants. Indeed, the economic dividends from immigration are unequally distributed, with less privileged U.S.-born workers benefiting far less than their more affluent counterparts. Some studies find that high-school dropouts, especially African-American and Latinx males, experience wage declines as a result of immigration, although these effects are very small – less than 2 percent for each 1 percent increase in the labor supply as a result of immigration (Blau and Mackie 2017: 241–3). Other analysts point to heightened economic anxieties among the non-college-educated, especially in the wake of the Great Recession.

However, most recent scholarship suggests that ethnic and racial resentments far outweigh economic concerns in shaping working-class anti-immigrant attitudes (Hainmueller and Hopkins 2014). As one analysis of survey data on attitudes toward immigration over the period from 1992 to 2016 concluded, "an ounce of racial resentment is worth a pound of economic anxiety" (Miller 2018: 23; see also Zolberg 2006: 386–7). Moreover, as political scientists John Sides, Michael Tesler, and Lynn Vavreck have shown, racial anxiety is itself a critical driver of economic anxiety. Their analysis of the 2016 presidential election highlights Trump's success in activating non-college-educated "whites' own group identity" and harnessing it to economic concerns. "The important economic sentiment underlying Trump's support," they argue, "was not 'I might lose my job' but, in essence 'People in my group are losing jobs to that other group'" (Sides et al. 2018: 7–8; see also Gimpel and Edwards 1999; Haney López 2019: 58).

Justin Gest's fieldwork in the U.S. Rustbelt led him to a similar view. "Working-class people [are] consumed by their loss of social and political status in social hierarchies, particularly in relation to immigrant and minority reference groups," he concludes. "Their politics are motivated and pervaded by a nostalgia that reveres, and seeks to reinstate, a bygone era" (Gest 2016: 16). Gest's research focused on what he calls "post-traumatic cities" in deindustrialized Ohio, Michigan, and Pennsylvania. Other scholars have documented a parallel "politics of resentment" (Cramer 2016) among non-college-educated whites in small towns and rural areas. Frustrated by rising taxes and convinced that their communities have been abandoned by government, they are deeply anti-statist, mistrustful of urban elites, and hostile to racial and ethnic minorities. Workers in rural areas who (not without reason) fear the extinction of their traditional way of life see immigrants as an especially salient threat (Wuthnow 2018: 144–6). Arlie Hochschild's ethnography of rural Louisiana vividly captures this mentality:

> Look! You see people *cutting in line ahead of you*! You're following the rules. They aren't. As they cut in, it feels like you are being moved back. How can they just do that? Who are they? Some are black. Through affirmative action plans, pushed by the federal government, they are being given preference for places in colleges and universities, apprenticeships, jobs, welfare programs, and free lunches …
>
> And now Filipinos, Mexicans, Arabs, Indians and Chinese on special visas or green cards are ahead of you in line. Or maybe they snuck in … You see the Mexicans work hard – and you admire that, but they work for less, and lower American pay … Blacks, women, immigrants, refugees, brown pelicans [a formerly endangered species] – all have cut ahead of you in line. But it's people like you who have made this country great … You've suffered a good deal yourself, but you aren't complaining. (Hochschild 2016: 137–9)

diploma divide

Introduction

In recent years, U.S.-born Latinxs and African Americans have been less receptive to the immigrant threat narrative than their white working-class counterparts, but that was not always the case. Negative views of immigrants have declined sharply among African Americans, perhaps reflecting the open racial hostility directed at them by the same conservative groups who regularly attack immigrants. As figure 1 shows, in 2006 a slightly higher proportion of black (64 percent) than white respondents (61 percent) said that immigrant employment hurts U.S. workers, but ten years later their positions were reversed, with 44 percent of blacks and 54 percent of whites endorsing that view.

Meanwhile, the growing prevalence of mixed-status Latinx households that include both U.S. citizens and undocumented immigrants, along with the unifying effects of Latinx panethnicity, has eroded hostility to the undocumented among U.S.-born Latinxs. This is one reason why Latinx voters increasingly have exited the Republican Party, joining their African-American counterparts who did so decades ago. Thus Latinx Democrats outnumbered Latinx Republicans by 36 points in 2016, up from 23 points in 2002. College-educated whites also shifted toward the Democratic Party in this period, while less-educated whites moved in the opposite direction. This "diploma divide" among whites was strongly tied to attitudes about race and immigration (Sides et al. 2018: 25–9).

Political Polarization and the Populist Upsurge

The nation's growing political polarization is inextricably intertwined with attitudes toward immigration as well. As recently as 2006, 61 percent of Republicans and 54 percent of Democrats endorsed the view that immigration is harmful to American workers; as figure 1 shows, ten years later the gap had widened dramatically, with 66 percent of Republicans but only 30 percent of Democrats doing so. Another 2016 survey found that 70 percent of white Trump voters wanted immigration reduced, compared to only 20 percent of whites voting for Clinton (Kaufmann 2019:

8

122). "No other factor appeared as distinctively powerful in 2016," Sides, Tesler and Vavreck (2018: 156) conclude, "as attitudes about racial issues and immigration."

Only a few decades ago, moderate Republicans in the business wing of their party actively opposed restrictive immigration policies, as did market fundamentalists who opposed economic regulation more generally. Indeed, with the support of these elements within his party, Ronald Reagan presided over the last major immigration reform, the 1986 Immigration Reform and Control Act (IRCA), which famously granted amnesty to nearly 3 million undocumented persons. Two decades later George W. Bush tried to build consensus in support of a follow-up immigration reform measure; the failure of that effort both reflected and reinforced the declining influence of moderates in the Republican Party. That decline gained momentum during the Obama presidency and was further consolidated after Trump's unexpected 2016 victory.

As the influence of the far right has grown, and as political moderates have been marginalized, Republican rhetoric has become increasingly xenophobic. Although the hardening of their anti-immigrant stance is a relatively recent development, Republican efforts to woo white working-class voters began over half a century ago, when Democratic support for the civil rights movement led Southern whites to exit that party *en masse*. That was the first crack in the legendary New Deal Democratic coalition anchored by unionized blue-collar workers, white Southerners, and African Americans. That coalition was subsequently eroded further by deindustrialization and the accompanying crippling of private-sector labor unions, which led many white workers in the North and Midwest to defect, most notably the "Reagan Democrats" who surfaced in the 1980 presidential campaign. Unable or unwilling to effectively address the growing economic distress in the nation's former industrial heartland, Democrats embraced the "identity politics" of the civil rights movement, the environmental movement, women's rights, LGBTQ rights, and, most recently, immigrant rights. That shift further alienated many white non-college-educated workers who had once been stalwart Democrats, deepening their resentment not only of urban cosmopolitan elites but also of racial minorities and immigrants. Over time, more and more working-class whites either stopped voting entirely or moved into the Republican column.

Trump's 2016 presidential campaign shrewdly capitalized on these developments. His strident criticism of the offshoring of jobs and of "free trade" marked a radical break with mainstream Republicans and Democrats alike and resonated deeply among blue-collar workers whose communities had been ripped apart by plant closures – including many union members and even some union officials. Trump famously embraced the "poorly educated," and his campaign speeches regularly celebrated manual labor in factories and on construction sites while heaping scorn on college-educated workers laboring at desks or in cubicles (Berezin 2017). The "diploma divide," indeed, provided Trump with a crucial source of support (Sides et al. 2018: 156).

Insofar as he championed the "forgotten man" and criticized the "rigged" political system and the powerful elites who run it, Trump shared common ground with left-wing presidential candidate Bernie Sanders, who also won extensive support from white workers in 2016. From opposite ends of the ideological spectrum, both populist candidates criticized the rich and vowed to help "the people." The crucial difference was that Trump's idea of "the people" was strictly confined to U.S.-born whites, excluding – indeed vilifying – Muslims, African Americans, and especially Latinx immigrants. "Leftwing populism is dyadic," John B. Judis points out. "Rightwing populism is triadic. It looks upward, but also down upon an out group" (Judis 2016: 15; see also Mouffe 2018). In the case of the United States, demonizing immigrants became a hallmark of the Trump brand.

In 2014, the conservative journal *National Review* published an essay by Alabama Senator Jeff Sessions, who would later become Trump's first attorney general. The essay articulated the political reasoning behind the anti-immigrant populism that became Trump's signature campaign issue two years later. Pointing out that both business elites and the Democrats favored more open immigration policies, Sessions wrote, "Republicans can either join the Democrats as the second political party in

Washington advocating uncontrolled immigration, or they can offer a principled alternative and represent the American workers Democrats have jettisoned." He added, "The last 40 years have been a period of uninterrupted large-scale immigration into the U.S., coinciding with increased joblessness, falling wages, failing schools, and a growing welfare state. Would not the sensible, conservative thing to do be to slow down for a bit, allow wages to rise and assimilation to occur, and help the millions struggling here today?" (Sessions 2014: 20–1).

Sessions, with help from his youthful communications director Stephen Miller, had been promoting these views relentlessly throughout the Obama years. In 2013, Sessions and Miller met with Steve Bannon, then head of Breitbart News and a leader of the alt-right, who urged Sessions to run for president and to promote his immigration platform. Sessions demurred, but soon afterward all three men emerged as early supporters of Trump's presidential candidacy, at a time when it was widely considered a fringe phenomenon. All three would become part of Trump's inner circle, playing key roles in his campaign and then in his administration. In January 2016, Bannon persuaded Miller to leave Sessions's staff and become Trump's main speechwriter; a month later Sessions formally endorsed Trump's candidacy; and in August 2016 Bannon left his position at Breitbart to head up Trump's campaign. After the election Bannon was appointed as the president's "chief strategist," Sessions became his attorney general, and Miller took a position in the White House as a senior policy advisor and rapidly took on the role of chief architect of immigration policy. Bannon departed in August 2017, and Sessions was forced to resign in late 2018; at the time of writing Miller remains in the White House (Davis and Shear 2019).

With their help, as *New York Times* reporters Julie Hirschfeld Davis and Michael D. Shear have documented in rich detail, "Trump's assault on immigration became the beating heart of his administration" (Davis and Shear 2019: 10). The immigrant threat narrative was now no longer a mere narrative but instead was systematically weaponized into official policy. This involved ramping up deportations, banning nationals from several majority-Muslim countries from entering the United States, sharply limiting refugee admissions, and notoriously separating thousands of immigrant children from their parents at the border. The Obama administration also had conducted large-scale deportations, but those primarily targeted immigrants with criminal records and those who had just crossed the U.S.–Mexico border without authorization. Under Trump, the focus shifted to "internal removals," which led to the deportation of thousands of law-abiding immigrants who had lived in the United States for long periods of time. The administration has also taken steps to restrict *legal* immigration, a move with no precedent in the post-1965 period, but one that Sessions had long advocated (Davis and Shear 2019: 164).

Immigration, Inequality, and Labor Degradation

Is immigration really a key driver of the reversal of fortune experienced by U.S.-born workers since the 1970s, as Trump and other promoters of the immigrant threat narrative claim? The timing seems to suggest as much. Soon after the passage of the 1965 law that ended four decades of highly restricted immigration, the economic status of non-college-educated workers, most of whom had prospered during the post-World War II years, began to spiral downward. In 2018 the real (i.e. controlling for inflation) median hourly wage of male wage and salary workers aged eighteen to sixty-four was lower than it had been in 1973 (Economic Policy Institute 2019). In the same period, moreover, inequality in income and wealth grew dramatically.

Correlation is not causation, but there *is* extensive evidence that the deteriorating situation of the U.S. working class and the growth of low-wage immigration after 1965 are tightly interconnected. However, the line of causality runs in the opposite direction from that implied by the immigrant threat narrative. The central thesis of this book is that immigration was not the *cause* either of the massive economic restructuring that began in the 1970s or of the accompanying growth of

12

economic inequality and labor degradation; rather, the influx of low-wage immigrants was a *consequence* of those developments. As American employers sought to externalize market risk through various forms of subcontracting and took steps to undermine organized labor, their demand for low-wage labor exploded. That, in turn, led millions of immigrants, both authorized and unauthorized, to enter the bottom tier of the U.S. labor market. As chapter 3 documents, immigrants entered low-wage jobs in substantial numbers largely *after* pay and conditions had been degraded to such a degree that U.S.-born workers exited the impacted occupations *en masse*.

A key premise underlying this argument is that the primary driver of labor migration, past and present, is economic demand. (Refugees fleeing war, violence, ethnic cleansing, political perse-cution, climate change, or natural disasters are another matter.) Certainly "push" factors within sending countries can help to spur emigration, and in some contexts those have become more significant in recent years. But, as Douglas Massey, Jorge Durand and Nolan J. Malone put it in their influential study of Mexican immigration to the United States, "If there were no demand for their services, immigrants, particularly those without documents, would not come, since they would have no means of supporting themselves" (Massey et al. 2002: 145).

To be sure, political forces and state policy in receiving countries can and often do limit the volume of immigration. But, in the case of the United States from the 1940s up until the start of the Trump administration, immigration policy largely catered to the needs of employers, which meant that, as Michael Piore argued long ago, "The strategic factor in initiating the migration and controlling its evolution appears to be the search of American employers for new sources of labor." Moreover, Piore added, "the migrants appear to be coming to take a distinct set of jobs, jobs that the native labor force refused to accept" (Piore 1979: 3). The 2008 financial crisis was a revealing illustration of the demand-driven character of labor migration in this era. As employment in sectors such as construction and manufacturing collapsed, unauthorized migrants abruptly stopped crossing the border. Other forms of (legally authorized) migration, such as for purposes of family reunification, continued in this period, however (Blau and Mackie 2017: 78).

Before the Great Recession, from the neoliberal turn of the early 1970s onward, migration to the United States, including unauthorized migration, grew in direct response to rising employer demand for low-wage labor. In this period of intensified international competition, new business strategies emerged to drive down labor costs through outsourcing, deregulation, and concerted efforts to weaken or eliminate labor unions. Whenever and wherever they could, U.S.-born workers voted with their feet to reject the newly degraded jobs, and many employers responded by hiring immigrants to replace them. In industries where migrants did not enter the country on their own in sufficient numbers to meet the demand for low-wage labor, recruiters were routinely dispatched to Mexico and other parts of the global South to find them, typically with blatant disregard for immigration laws and regulations (which until very recently were notoriously poorly enforced).

The construction industry illustrates this dynamic. In the 1980s, after a concerted employer assault on trade unions depressed pay, benefits, and working conditions in residential construction, many U.S.-born workers abandoned it for the commercial construction sector, which was still unionized and was booming at the time. Employers then recruited immigrants from Mexico and elsewhere to fill the vacancies in the residential sector. Similarly, in industries such as truck driving, where deregulation led to union decline and wage degradation, as well as in many de-unionized manufacturing and service industries (for example, meatpacking and building services), employers increasingly turned to immigrants from across the global South to fill the jobs abandoned by U.S.-born workers in the late twentieth century.

This process can be understood in terms of a shift in "job queues" that rank jobs by their relative attractiveness to workers. As Barbara Reskin and Patricia Roos note, "Any change that reduces an occupation's financial rewards, mobility opportunities, or job security can depreciate its ranking in a job queue" (Reskin and Roos 1990: 29, 44; see also Lieberson 1980). Job queues are especially likely to shift when labor markets are subjected to economic shocks like the rapid deregulation and de-unionization of the 1970s and 1980s. When this occurs, the most privileged workers (men, whites, or in this case the U.S.-born) reject jobs whose rankings in the queue have declined.

Crucially, employers' preferences can also change, transforming not only *job* queues but also *labor* queues – which "order groups of workers in terms of their attractiveness to employers" (Reskin and Roos 1990: 29). Indeed, once they grew accustomed to hiring immigrant workers, initially in a search for cheap labor (to fill the vacancies created by the shift in the job queue), many employers came to prefer them to the U.S.-born (Waldinger and Lichter 2003). This was reinforced by immigrant self-selection: the low-wage immigrants who came to work in the United States from Mexico and elsewhere in the 1970s and 1980s were, relative to non-migrants with similar levels of education, disproportionately young, healthy, skilled, and eager for economic advancement (Chiquiar and Hanson 2005). Once employers' preferences shifted decisively, a new equilibrium was established in the labor queue, and the boundaries defining "brown-collar" jobs performed by immigrants were naturalized, taken for granted by workers and employers alike.

Demand for immigrant labor expanded not only in male-dominated industries degraded by the neoliberal restructuring that began in the 1970s but also in the predominantly female domestic and personal services sector. Here the key driver was not employment restructuring and job degradation but instead a mix of demographic pressures and rising income inequality. The increasingly prosperous professional and managerial classes began to devote a significant part of their disposable income to purchasing services from housecleaners, nannies, home-care and eldercare providers, as well as gardeners, manicurists, and other service workers. In this period, such affluent households often included two adults with long working hours, thanks to the feminist movement's success in opening the doors of the professions and the corporate suite to upper-middle-class women in the 1970s – even as changing expectations of parenting and the aging of the population stimulated growing demand for paid carework inside the home. Yet, in the same period, the traditional labor supply for domestic work was evaporating, as the civil rights movement opened up lower-level clerical and service jobs and other options to African-American and Mexican-American women. In another case of a shifting job queue, these U.S.-born women of color began to shun paid domestic work just as demand for it began to soar, leading households to hire immigrants instead. Soon these jobs too became "brown collar."

These dynamics have remained largely invisible to the public, as the immigrant threat narrative has effectively distracted attention from the actual causes of declining working-class living standards and from the forces driving migration itself. Non-college-educated American workers have every reason to be enraged and alienated by rising inequality and the degradation of employment, but their anger has been profoundly misdirected. It was not the influx of immigrants that generated these changes but, rather, employers' deliberate efforts to degrade formerly well-paid blue-collar jobs and to promote public policies that widened inequality.

Overview of the Book

The following chapters elaborate this counterargument to the immigrant threat narrative in more detail and present supporting evidence. Chapter 1 provides a brief profile of the twenty-first-century U.S. immigrant workforce, both authorized and unauthorized, emphasizing the concentration of low-wage immigrants in a limited number of occupations and industries and critically interrogating the popular claim that they are taking "jobs Americans don't want." The key point here is that direct competition between low-wage immigrants and U.S.-born workers is rare, as the latter reject most "brown-collar jobs" as unacceptable.

Chapter 2 sets the twenty-first-century immigration debate in historical perspective, arguing that, in the past as in the present, labor migration into the United States was spurred primarily by employer demand. As the rise of capitalism transformed the nation in the nineteenth century, foreign-born workers were actively recruited for low-skill, poorly paid jobs that most U.S.-born workers shunned. That process took place not only in industries such as manufacturing or construction but also in capitalist agriculture, which recruited immigrant workers from countries across the globe. Indeed, the labor contractor-based system that growers used to recruit Mexican farm workers in California and the Southwest starting in the late nineteenth century would set the template for low-wage immigrant employment in many urban industries later on. Similarly, the farm worker union drives that emerged in the 1960s and 1970s in many respects prefigured the low-wage immigrant labor organizing that blossomed in the late twentieth century.

Chapter 2 also briefly explores both the historical relationship of immigrant workers to the U.S. labor movement and organized labor's gradual shift from an exclusionary to an inclusionary stance. In part because employers regularly used immigrant workers as strikebreakers, most early trade unions embraced immigration restriction, especially in regard to Chinese workers, who were barred from entry to the United States by the Chinese Exclusion Act of 1882. At the end of World War I, when not only organized labor but also far more powerful political actors rallied to it, the broader restrictionist cause triumphed, inaugurating a forty-year interregnum of low immigration. That overlapped with a highly exceptional period in U.S. history, the New Deal era that emerged from the shock of the Great Depression (Cowie 2016). Indeed, starting in the mid-1930s, U.S. capitalism became highly regulated, unionization surged, and inequality declined sharply. Immigrants from Southern and Eastern Europe and their children, previously relegated to the bottom of the labor market, now moved into the economic and social mainstream, a process facilitated by the revitalized labor movement, which organized foreign-born workers and their descendants on a massive scale.

When the New Deal order unraveled in the closing decades of the twentieth century, however, demand for low-wage immigrant labor reemerged. That historical shift is the focus of chapter 3.

It explores the transformation and degradation of employment in the late twentieth century and the accompanying increase in undocumented migration that IRCA sought to curtail but instead unintentionally exacerbated. This chapter documents the ways in which deindustrialization, union decline, deregulation, and subcontracting combined to erode high-wage, stable, unionized jobs in construction, building services, meatpacking, and trucking. Male workers predominated in all these industries, although the building services and meatpacking workforces had significant female components. The chapter documents the processes through which, starting in the 1970s, as real wages declined and inequality surged in each of these industries, U.S.-born workers abandoned them and were then replaced by immigrants. In many cases they were recruited by labor contractors through human supply chains (J. Gordon 2017) similar to those long established in commercial agriculture. As a result, foreign-born workers came to be overrepresented in low-wage job. They were also far more likely than their U.S.-born counterparts to be victims of wage theft and other violations of labor and employment laws. Yet precarity and degradation have diffused across the labor market, affecting many U.S.-born workers as well – many of whom nevertheless have embraced the immigrant threat narrative.

Chapter 4 turns to the parallel set of economic dynamics generating demand for low-wage immigrant labor in the predominantly female-employing service sector. It documents the exodus of African-American women from paid domestic labor just when growing income inequality, rising maternal employment, and the aging of the population led to a surge in labor demand in that field. Domestic work soon became a primary gateway occupation for newly arriving Latinx and Caribbean immigrant women, especially those without legal authorization. As income inequality continued to rise, a variety of other services also became increasingly affordable for the affluent, including high-end restaurants, leading to expanding employment in that sector. Latinx immigrants soon came to dominate low-wage "back of the house" restaurant work, some of which previously had been the domain of African-American women. Other types of low-wage personal

18

service work also grew explosively in this period, such as the nail salon industry, which employed mostly low-wage immigrant women from Southeast Asia.

Chapter 5 turns to the ways in which immigrant workers themselves have struggled to improve their pay and working conditions. Although most employers (and others) presumed that immigrants generally, and the undocumented in particular, would be reluctant to assume the risks involved in union organizing or other types of workplace protest, they turned out to be mistaken. Instead, in the late twentieth and early twenty-first century, foreign-born workers often were *more* engaged in the labor movement activity than their U.S.-born counterparts, both in traditional unions and in "alt-labor" organizations such as the worker centers that burgeoned starting in the 1990s. This chapter also explores the impact of the immigrant rights movement on low-wage worker organizing and the challenges presented by the changed political climate after the 2016 presidential election, both for labor struggles and for efforts to advance immigrant rights.

The book's final chapter lays out the broader implications of this analysis, arguing that the U.S.-born workers who have suffered as a result of de-unionization and other aspects of neoliberal economic restructuring should reject the immigrant threat narrative and instead direct their anger at the employers who have degraded once-desirable jobs and at the political system that has been increasingly subservient to business interests. In contrast to some progressives who have recently embraced immigration restriction, this concluding chapter makes the case for a left-wing populism targeting the beneficiaries of the spectacular growth in economic inequality since the 1970s. That political approach, I argue, is not only more humane than the alternatives but also represents the interests of working people far more effectively than the right-wing populism that propelled Donald Trump into the U.S. presidency.

1

Brown-Collar Jobs: Low-Wage Immigrant Workers in the Twenty-First Century

> Migrants provide a way in which workers in the native labor force are able to escape the role to which the system assigns them.
>
> Michael Piore (1979: 42)

This chapter profiles the immigrant labor force in the twenty-first-century United States – both the unauthorized "illegal aliens" who are the focus of contemporary political controversy and the larger population of immigrant workers with legal status. It highlights the concentration of foreign-born workers in particular occupations and industries and the limited extent to which they compete directly with the U.S.-born. At the bottom of the labor market, this pattern of occupational segregation involves the overrepresentation of foreign-born workers in poorly paid, physically demanding, menial, and often dangerous jobs with limited requirements for English-language proficiency – jobs that most U.S.-born workers seek to avoid. Indeed, this is the basis of the frequent claim that low-wage immigrants are doing "jobs Americans don't want." In the past, U.S-born workers had held some of these jobs, but increasingly rejected them in the wake of employers' deliberate efforts to cut wages and degrade working conditions in the course of the economic restructuring that began in the 1970s. In other instances, such as paid domestic labor, the jobs always had been undesirable but were abandoned by U.S.-born workers – especially workers of color – when the civil rights movement opened up better opportunities.

Occupational segregation between U.S.- and foreign-born workers also helps explain why the influx of low-wage immigrants in recent decades has had little or no effect on the economic status of less-educated U.S-born workers. Although the real (i.e. controlling for inflation) earnings of the latter group *have* declined dramatically since the 1970s, immigration was not the cause of that wage suppression but, rather, its result. As chapter 3 details, attacks on unions, deregulation, subcontracting, and other forms of restructuring transformed many formerly well-paid blue-collar jobs with decent working conditions into poorly paid, precarious positions that U.S.-born workers then exited. As employers turned to immigrants to fill the resulting vacancies, they created a new category of low-wage "brown-collar" jobs, racially stereo-typed as best suited to Latinx immigrants (Catanzarite 2002). Less-educated U.S.-born workers now moved into better-paying, less onerous positions that required English-language proficiency, but which often fell short of the labor standards set in the era of strong unions and state regulation.

Immigration and Occupational Segregation

Because public debate about immigration focuses disproportion-ately on the unauthorized, it is easy to forget that they constitute less than 5 percent of the nation's workforce. Foreign-born workers with legal status, most of whom are permanent residents or naturalized citizens, make up a far larger share – about 12 percent in 2017 (Radford 2019). Immigrant workers are also more ethnically diverse than many Americans realize: in 2008, 17 percent were white, 25 percent were Asian, and 1 percent were black, while just under half (48 percent) were Latinx. (That year the U.S.-born labor force was 72 percent white, 2 percent Asian, 12 percent black, and 11 percent Latinx.)[1] Belying the stereotype that they are poorly educated, in 2018, 37 percent of immigrant workers aged twenty-five years and older held a four-year college degree, only slightly below the 41 percent of U.S.-born workers in the same age group with that level of education (U.S. Bureau of Labor Statistics 2019). In contrast, only 15 percent of unauthorized immigrants aged twenty-five or more held a four-year college degree (Migration Policy Institute 2018).

The geographic dispersion of immigrants has increased in recent years, in contrast to the earlier pattern of concentration in traditional gateway areas such as New York, California, and Florida (Blau and Mackie 2017: 77). Yet the regional distribution of foreign-born workers remains markedly uneven: in 2018, 24 percent of the labor force in the West and 20 percent of that in the Northeast was foreign-born, compared to only 9 percent in the Midwest and 16 percent in the South (U.S. Bureau of Labor Statistics 2019). There is also substantial variation *within* each region. In general, immigrant workers are disproportionately concentrated in geographical areas where economic growth (and thus labor demand) is most robust.

The foreign-born are unevenly distributed not only across regions but also across occupations. They are overrepresented in certain professional fields, such as science and engineering, and as owners of certain types of small businesses, such as dry cleaners and nail salons, whereas in other professional and business occupations their presence is far more limited (Blau and Mackie 2017: 94). Overall, 33 percent of immigrant workers held professional and managerial jobs in 2017, compared to 42 percent of the U.S.-born (U.S. Bureau of Labor Statistics 2019); this reflects the slightly lower average educational attainment of the foreign-born population, as well as language barriers and the fact that most professional credentials obtained in other countries are not recognized in the United States.

At the other end of the labor market – of primary concern here – immigrants are strongly overrepresented in fields of employment with the greatest risk of occupational injury and on-the-job deaths. One study found an average of 31 more occupational injuries per 10,000 workers among foreign-born workers than their U.S.-born counterparts, and about 1.8 deaths per 100,000 workers among immigrants for each death among the native-born. Injury and death rates were even higher for immigrants with little or no English-language proficiency. These are conservative estimates, since occupational injuries and deaths tend to be underreported in industries employing large numbers of immigrants, such as construction and meatpacking (Orrenius and Zavodny 2009).

Figure 2 shows the distribution of unauthorized immigrants, authorized immigrants, and the U.S.-born across ten major occupational groups in 2016. Foreign-born workers were a majority in only one of the ten groups, "services," which includes a wide variety of occupations. Even among these highly aggregated occupational categories, however, the extent of immigrant concentration is striking, especially for the unauthorized. Two-thirds of unauthorized immigrant workers were employed in only four of the ten occupational groups shown in figure 2: service, construction, production, and transportation. Those four groups accounted for a much smaller share – 40 percent – of authorized immigrant workers, and even fewer (34 percent) of U.S.-born workers. By contrast, nearly one-fourth (24 percent) of authorized immigrants were employed in professional occupations in 2016, a slightly higher share than among the U.S.-born (23 percent), and nearly triple the share among the unauthorized.

Just as women workers make up the vast majority of the workforce in gender-stereotyped "pink-collar" jobs such as clerical work, child care, and nursing, so too working-class Latinx immigrants make up the bulk of those employed in ethnically segregated brown-collar jobs (Catanzarite 2002). In such sectors foreign-born workers are often presumed to be unauthorized, although in fact many have legal status. Brown-collar jobs are themselves internally gender-segregated: for example, women are the vast majority of immigrant nannies, housecleaners, and home-care aides, while men are overwhelmingly predominant in the ranks of immigrant construction workers. In recent decades the overall extent of occupational segregation by gender has declined somewhat in the United States, but segregation between native- and foreign-born workers has actually increased, especially among women (Blau and Mackie 2017: 95–8).

Figure 2 understates the degree to which employment patterns differ between U.S.-born and foreign-born workers, as there is further segmentation *within* each of the broad occupational

Figure 2   Major occupational groups, by nativity and immigration status, 2016

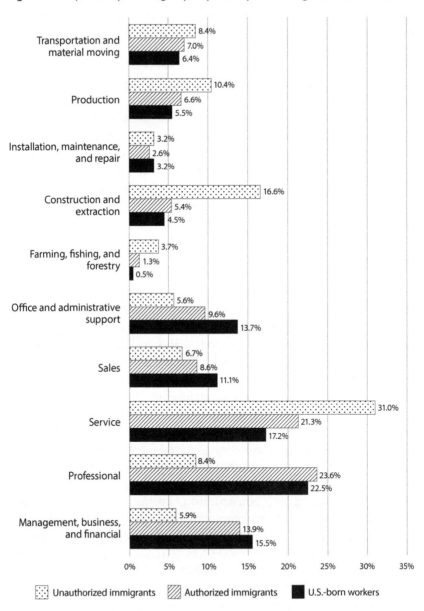

Source: Passel and Cohn (2018: 74).

groups shown. Data on more detailed occupational classifications are limited, but the analyses that are available offer a glimpse of far more extensive segregation. For example, one study found that, in 2010, 58 percent of all "graders and sorters" in agriculture, 56 percent of assemblers in high-tech manufacturing, 53 percent of maids and housekeeping cleaners, 52 percent of janitors and building cleaners, and 50 percent of roofers were foreign-born (Singer 2012). Other research shows that, in 2011, 68 percent of dishwashers were foreign-born (Zavodny and Jacoby 2013); and in 2014, almost two-thirds (63 percent) of "miscellaneous personal appearance workers" (including manicurists), 59 percent of plasterers and stucco masons, and 52 percent of sewing-machine operators were foreign-born (Passel and Cohn 2016).

Even these data fail to capture the full extent of occupational segregation between immigrants and U.S.-born workers, however, because the figures are averages for the entire United States, collapsing together regions where immigrants are few and far between with those where a large share of the labor force is foreign-born. In regions of the latter type, such as southern California, immigrants are the vast majority of garment workers, housecleaners, taxi drivers, hotel housekeepers, car-wash workers, janitors, and residential construction workers – among many other brown-collar occupations (Milkman 2006).

The aggregate data in figure 2 reveal the distinctive occupational profile of unauthorized immigrants; but here too more detailed data expose more pervasive segregation. Although unauthorized immigrants were just under 5 percent of the overall U.S. labor force in 2016, they accounted for 31 percent of roofers, 30 percent of drywall installers, 30 percent of farm workers, 27 percent of construction painters, 24 percent of maids and housekeeping cleaners, 22 percent of sewing-machine operators, and 19 percent of grounds maintenance workers (DeSilver 2017). Again, these are national data and therefore, given the uneven geographical distribution of unauthorized workers, understate the degree of occupational segregation.

Unauthorized immigrant employment patterns are also distinctive in other respects. In contrast to the more diverse overall foreign-born population, this group is overwhelmingly Latinx: in 2014, 71 percent of the unauthorized were born in Mexico or Central America and another 8 percent in South America. Fully half lack a high school diploma (Migration Policy Institute 2018). Moreover, the unauthorized are disproportionately vulnerable to illegal employment practices, such as being paid less than the statutory minimum wage or being denied legally mandated overtime pay. Authorized immigrants experience such violations more frequently than their U.S.-born counterparts, but prevalence is far greater for the unauthorized (Bernhardt et al. 2009). In addition, wages and working conditions for unauthorized immigrants have deteriorated significantly since 1986, when "employer sanctions" – penalties for hiring workers without legal documents – were introduced under the Immigration Reform and Control Act (IRCA). Among the unintended effects of that legislation was that it led many employers to pass on the added risks and costs involved in hiring unauthorized workers to subcontractors or to the workers themselves (Phillips and Massey 1999).

But the central feature of low-wage immigrant employment is the extensive degree of occupational segregation described earlier, which means that immigrants and natives are rarely competing directly for the same jobs. And, crucially, this form of occupational segregation is racialized, sharpening the boundaries between brown-collar jobs and those considered – by employers and workers alike – as the preserve of U.S.-born white workers. Another dimension of occupational segregation involves educational attainment: immigrants make up about one-sixth of all U.S. workers, but more than half of those who lack a high-school diploma are foreign-born, and many immigrants in this group also have limited English-language skills. Indeed, U.S.-born workers without a high-school diploma are disproportionately employed in less-skilled jobs that require English proficiency, while their immigrant counterparts (who are also younger, on average) are concentrated in labor-intensive manual jobs demanding physical strength and stamina. The latter are the brown-collar jobs shunned by even the least educated U.S.-born workers (Zavodny and Jacoby 2013; Peri and Sparber 2009). Direct competition is further constrained by the geographical unevenness of immigration, which in turn reflects the fact that the foreign-born tend to be more willing than the U.S.-born to relocate to areas where demand for labor is strong, as noted earlier (Blau and Mackie 2017: 5).

"Jobs Americans Don't Want"

Occupational segregation, reinforced by the racialization of brown-collar jobs, means that the employment patterns of foreign-born workers, especially the unauthorized, are distinctly different from those of their U.S.-born counterparts, especially white U.S.-born workers. But are low-wage immigrants really "doing jobs Americans don't want," as is so frequently asserted? Many employers seem to think so, regularly complaining that they cannot find U.S.-born workers willing to perform the physically demanding, poorly paid jobs that immigrants eagerly accept. Agriculture is an iconic example. In California, over 90 percent of farm workers are foreign-born, and most are undocumented (Kitroeff and Mohan 2017). Although farm workers' wages grew twice as fast as average pay in the state between 2010 and 2015, even growers who offered 401(k) plans, health insurance, subsidized housing, and profit-sharing bonuses reportedly found it almost impossible to attract U.S.-born workers. For example, a fourth-generation California farmer, who advertised in local newspapers and tried to recruit through the state employment agency to fill jobs in his vineyards paying an average of $20 per hour, declared that he could not retain U.S.-born workers. "We've never had one come back after lunch," he told the *Los Angeles Times* (ibid.).

Agricultural employers in other parts of the country recount similar experiences. For example, from 1998 to 2011, jobs were offered to 97 percent of the U.S.-born unemployed workers referred to the North Carolina Growers' Association, but attrition was enormous. In 2011, only 173 of the 245 U.S.-born workers hired by the Association showed up for the first day of work, and only seven remained by the end of the growing season

(Matthews 2013). Similarly, interviews with Wisconsin dairy farmers conducted in 2010–11 yielded complaints "that U.S-born workers would insist upon only doing non-milking tasks, refuse the shifts that were available, and quit coming to work after a week or two" (Harrison and Lloyd 2013: 290). A website offering agricultural jobs to both citizens and legal residents across the country in 2010, in the depths of the Great Recession, generated 12,000 applications, but only twelve citizens or legal residents showed up, and not one stayed longer than a single day (Greenberg 2018: 91). More recently, as unemployment rates have fallen over the recovery and fewer new immigrants have arrived, agricultural employers report that they are often forced to leave jobs unfilled. "They want to send all these people back," a tomato farmer told the *New York Times* in 2019, referring to workplace raids and deportations. "Who the hell is going to do all this work?" (Cohen 2019).

Accounts of U.S.-born workers rejecting work that immigrants eagerly accept are by no means limited to agriculture, however. Urban employers testify to the same phenomenon in a wide variety of brown-collar occupations. For example, an Atlanta restaurant owner told a researcher that U.S.-born workers never applied for jobs as dishwashers. "Only immigrants want these jobs," he declared, "and they work hard." Similarly, a Colorado resort owner confessed that he had not hired an American housekeeper for decades, explaining that "this is unglamorous work that many U.S. workers look down upon" (Zavodny and Jacoby 2013: 6, 12). The owner of a restaurant chain in Miami, about 80 percent of whose employees are foreign-born, declared that the idea that "immigrants are taking jobs away from residents of the U.S. is just not reality. That's the armchair view of somebody who doesn't run a business" (Cohen 2019).

In 2005, when the Las Vegas Ironworkers union publicized 150 apprenticeships, they received only a handful of applications at first. But once the positions were advertised in Spanish-language newspapers, they were all quickly filled. "It's gotten harder and harder to recruit American-born workers to construction," a union official declared (Kitroeff 2017). Additional examples abound: "Meatpacking companies have tried recruiting white and African American workers in Minneapolis, Chicago and Kansas City, and most don't last longer than a week," the *Dallas Morning News* reported in 2018 (Corchado 2018). "In every market that we're in, we're dealing with staffing shortages," an executive who manages several assisted-living centers in Florida lamented the following year, adding, "Thank God we have immigrants coming in. We're hiring them as fast as they come" (Cohen 2019).

At a meatpacking plant in rural Illinois, when in 2007 immigration raids decimated the largely Mexican workforce, a local Republican politician declared that, "the day after the raids, Americans were lined up to get their $18 an hour jobs back." However, that did not occur. Hourly wages for the jobs in question were actually $12 at the time, reflecting the elimination of unionism two decades earlier, when U.S.-born workers abandoned the jobs and immigrants were hired in their place. Facing a sudden labor shortage after the raids, the company made no effort to hire local workers but instead dispatched recruiters to other parts of the country in search of immigrants who were legal residents, as well as to Puerto Rico (Miraftab 2016: 67–8).

As later chapters in this book document, many urban brown-collar jobs dominated by low-wage immigrants *were* once performed primarily by U.S.-born workers.[2] But when wages, benefits, and working conditions were degraded as a result of de-unionization, subcontracting, and related changes, these positions were rapidly transformed into "jobs that Americans don't want." If that process could be reversed and the jobs newly upgraded, perhaps some U.S.-born workers would return, but that scenario seems unlikely at best. The vast majority of U.S.-born workers have no interest in entering brown-collar, immigrant-dominated occupations that are poorly paid, physically demanding, dirty, and dangerous. Moreover, employers themselves have come to prefer immigrants for such jobs, reinforcing occupational segregation and helping render direct labor market competition between U.S.- and foreign-born workers conspicuous mainly by its absence (Moss and Tilly 2001: 116–17; Waldinger and Lichter 2003).

Although Latinx immigrants, and especially the unauthorized, are largely confined to brown-collar jobs at the bottom of the U.S. labor market, over time some of them have managed to move up. Labor market mobility is especially feasible for those with English-language proficiency, above-average formal education, and/or legal status (Massey and Magaly Sánchez 2010: 106–11). Such mobility is apparent in data on immigrant unionization rates, which are much higher for those who have lived in the United States for long periods of time. Union members, on average, have higher earnings and more benefits and employment security than their non-union counterparts. By 2019, 8 percent of all immigrant workers and 12 percent of naturalized citizens were union members – in the latter case exceeding the 11 percent unionization rate for U.S.-born workers (Milkman and Luce 2019).

The Impact of Immigration on U.S.-Born Workers

Both among scholars and in the public square, another major focus of debate concerns the effect of the influx of foreign-born workers on the economic situation of U.S-born workers. It is well documented that American workers have experienced substantial job degradation in recent decades as a result of union decline, economic globalization, new technologies, and deregulation. But the consensus among researchers who have attempted to isolate the impact of immigration (both authorized and unauthorized) on average wages and employment is that the net effect has been minuscule and is confined almost entirely to previous immigrants and U.S.-born high-school dropouts (Blau and Mackie 2017: 5, 266–8).

In theory, one might expect that, since immigration increases the overall labor supply, it would intensify job competition and drive down wages, to the detriment of U.S.-born and foreign-born workers alike. But, in practice, such competition is severely limited because of the occupational segregation between immigrants and U.S.-born workers described earlier. Even at the bottom of the labor market, less-educated U.S.-born workers tend to "respond to low-wage immigration by leaving physically demanding jobs for language-intensive ones" which typically have higher pay, as economists Giovanni Peri and Chad Sparber (2009: 136) have demonstrated.

Moreover, insofar as immigrants spend their earnings to buy food, clothing, shelter, and other goods and services inside the United States, they contribute to increased economic demand, which in turn generates jobs that would not otherwise exist. Complicating the picture further, insofar as low-wage immigrant labor lowers prices for goods and services such as restaurant food, child care, gardening, or housing construction, it improves the buying power and living standards of U.S.-born workers (Cortes 2008). In addition, because immigration expands the nation's supply of younger workers, it reduces the negative economic effects typically associated with an aging population (specifically, a declining base of active workers supporting growing numbers of retirees). Immigration inflows also have positive effects on economically stagnating cities, reviving commercial districts, raising home values, and reducing crime (Sandoval-Strausz 2019).

In short, belying the assumptions embedded in the immigrant threat narrative described in the Introduction, most U.S.-born workers accrue economic benefits from immigration, and even the least educated are largely cushioned from any negative wage effects stemming from potential labor market competition by occupational segregation and the racialization that accompanies it. But while occupational segregation itself is an enduring phenomenon, the specific jobs that are marked as "brown collar" can change over time, especially in periods of rapid economic change. The dynamic processes through which "brown-collar" jobs took shape within the U.S. low-wage labor market over the late twentieth century are analyzed in detail in chapters 3 and 4. But, first, it is crucial to recognize that those processes are not unprecedented; on the contrary, there are many parallels to previous periods of labor migration, especially during the nineteenth and early twentieth century, when entry to the United States was largely unrestricted. That earlier history is the subject of the following chapter.

2

Immigration and Labor in Historical Perspective

American labor has to bear the burden of competition with an immigration that in the last decade has brought to the population a net increase of at least five million laborers, of whom an enormous percentage was totally illiterate, the great majority ignorant of the English language, and nearly all so poor on arrival that a month's idleness would have brought them face to face with starvation. To this class has been mostly due the undermining of American labor in certain industries ... and much of the hostility to the American Federation of Labor.

Samuel Gompers, president, American Federation of Labor
(1910: 486)

Apart from descendants of African slaves and of the few Native Americans who survived European conquest, the U.S. population is comprised entirely of immigrants and their progeny. Throughout the nation's history, the primary magnet attracting immigrants has been economic opportunity, although some newcomers were refugees from religious or political persecution, war, or famine, while others came to join family members already settled in America. In the colonial era, hundreds of thousands of Europeans crossed the Atlantic Ocean to work as indentured servants in what would later become the United States. But the volume of immigration grew far larger as demand for labor expanded with the rise of industrial capitalism, starting half a century after the nation's independence and accelerating rapidly after the Civil War. In that period, millions of European immigrants flocked to the nation's burgeoning mines and factories and to jobs as domestic servants or construction laborers in the growing cities of the Northeast and Midwest. Some workers made the journey to America on their own after having learned that jobs were abundant; others were recruited directly by employers.

During the late nineteenth and early twentieth century, the foreign-born share of the U.S. workforce rose to well over 20 percent, higher than ever before or since (Carter 2006). By 1920, over half of the nation's manufacturing workers were immigrants or the children of immigrants (Hirschman and Mogford 2009). Europeans made up the vast majority of the foreign-born population in this period, but it also included hundreds of thousands of Chinese immigrants employed as miners, as contract laborers building the transcontinental railroad, and later as farm workers. With the rise of large-scale capitalist agriculture, especially in California and the Southwest, farm workers were also recruited from around the world.

This history gradually faded from public memory after the 1920s, when restrictive legislation rapidly reduced immigration to a trickle. Yet the dynamics of contemporary U.S. immigration in many ways resemble those characteristic of the first massive influx of new Americans that ended a century ago. In both periods, immigration was driven primarily by labor demand, simultaneously reflecting and intensifying the disruptive effects of capitalist development. In both periods, the bulk of immigrants were young adults, whose countries of origin had borne the costs of raising them to adulthood and of any formal education they had obtained. In both periods, many U.S.-born workers disdained the newcomers as ethnic or racial "others," a view galvanized by populist demagoguery that generated political pressure for immigration restriction. Yet, until World War I, immigrant entry to the United States was largely unrestricted, reflecting tacit state recognition of the vast need for labor to fuel the nation's explosive economic growth.

Although employers welcomed this policy approach, organized labor was often critical of it, and at times unions mobilized in support of limiting immigration, most prominently in promoting the 1882 Chinese Exclusion Act. As illustrated in the epigraph to this chapter, labor leaders who feared that unrestricted immigration could undermine their hard-won wage and employment standards also wanted to limit European immigration in the late nineteenth and early twentieth century. Over time, however, unions gradually abandoned restrictionism and increasingly sought not to exclude but instead to organize foreign-born workers, who often proved eager to join their ranks. Indeed, in the twenty-first century the labor movement became one of the most prominent forces supporting liberal immigration policies and immigrant rights (see chapter 5).

Immigrants in the U.S. Labor Market before 1920

Global inequality, past and present, has often spurred labor migration from economically less developed to more advanced regions. But this process is far from continuous. Rather, it tends to be activated when demand for labor in a given location exceeds the available supply, leading employers to expand the geographical scope of their search for workers. Once they do so, as Michael Piore notes, they discover that "the supply of labor available to industrialized areas from underdeveloped regions or countries appears to be virtually unlimited ... [so that] employers were able to find labor quickly and easily when they needed it." Piore adds a crucial caveat, however, underscoring the demand-driven character of migration: "Labor, which responded so readily when actively recruited, exhibited little tendency to move spontaneously on its own initiative before the initial recruitment efforts were made" (Piore 1979: 25).

There is a broad consensus among U.S. economic historians that the "Great Atlantic Migration" of the late nineteenth and early twentieth century was demand-driven in precisely this way (Blau and Mackie 2017: 45; Hirschman and Mogford 2009). Although some migrants were refugees, and others crossed the ocean to join family members who had preceded them, for the vast majority jobs were the key magnet. "Swings in immigration were a response to corresponding swings in the demand for labor," Richard Easterlin concludes in his authoritative review of the historical data, noting that the timing "is difficult to explain in terms of conditions in the originating areas." Instead immigration fluctuations closely tracked rates of wage growth and unemployment (Easterlin 1968: 30–1).

From the outset, chronic labor shortages plagued the American colonies and, after independence, the new nation as well. Initially, the shortages fueled demand for indentured servants as well as the large-scale importation of African slaves. But, as early as the 1810s, labor brokers began to recruit European immigrants as wage workers; soon after that shipping companies also took on this role (Zolberg 2006: 114, 132). In the nineteenth century most newcomers hailed from Northern and Western Europe, although farm workers from other parts of the world were drawn to California and the Southwest in this period, while Chinese immigrants were strongly represented among Western miners and contract workers hired to build the transcontinental railroad.

After the Civil War, as urbanization and industrialization rapidly transformed the U.S. economy, employer demand for wage laborers swelled to new heights. It was met partly by internal rural-to-urban migrants but far more often by Europeans who crossed the Atlantic to work in American mines, factories, or construction sites. The rate of immigration accelerated in the 1880s, as large corporations formed and employment mushroomed in the nation's burgeoning factories; it finally peaked in the decade before World War I. Known at the time as the "new immigration," the post-1880 influx was not only greater in volume than those that preceded it but also different in composition. The proportion of immigrants who were unskilled laborers and servants grew from 16 percent in the 1820s to 55 percent in the 1890s (Hatton and Williamson 2005: 79), and the share of Southern and Eastern Europeans grew as well.

Young adult males dominated this wave of immigration. Between 1868 and 1910, 76 percent of those who entered the United States were between fifteen and forty years old, at a time when only 42 percent of the total U.S. population was in that age range. Over three-fifths of the newcomers were male, although the gender balance became more even over time (Hatton and Williamson 2005: 78–9). Many were sojourners who intended to work in America for a few years and then go back to Europe. Some did indeed return, although most of these "birds of passage" would eventually settle in America permanently (Morawska 1990: 195).

In contrast to the post-1965 wave of immigration to the United States, driven by economic restructuring that involved *de*-industrialization (along with de-unionization and other shifts), the late nineteenth- and early twentieth-century immigration wave was driven by the *rise* of industrial capitalism. Moreover, while the post-1965 immigrant influx took place in the context of *declining* real wages for male U.S.-born workers, in the pre-World War I period real wages for male U.S.-born workers *rose* in the sectors that employed the largest numbers of immigrants (Hirschman and Mogford 2009: 899). In recent decades, most low-wage foreign-born workers were hired to perform jobs that had long been part of the labor market but in which pay and conditions were degraded to the point that U.S.-born workers had abandoned them. By contrast, in the earlier period, male immigrants were typically employed either in unskilled factory jobs that had been newly created with the rise of mass production or as wage workers in capitalist agriculture, which also had no historical precedent in a nation originally built on family farming and plantation slavery. Female immigrants who became domestic servants, on the other hand, entered a longstanding, highly traditional occupation in both periods.

There are additional contrasts between past and present. Whereas a large proportion of recent immigrants work in professional occupations (see figure 2), in the earlier era only about 2 percent of the foreign-born were professionals; the overwhelming majority were manual laborers (Morawska 1990: 193). In that respect, the class composition of the post-1965 foreign-born population is far more heterogeneous than its counterpart of a century earlier. Heterogeneity is also greater today in regard to race and ethnicity, at least in twenty-first-century terms. Most of those who participated in the Great Atlantic Migration before

World War I were Southern and Eastern Europeans whose descendants would be assimilated into the larger Euro-American "white" population, although at the time they were often seen as racially distinctive from – and inferior to – the Northern and Western Europeans who had preceded them. Even if one rejects the claim that the Southern and Eastern European immigrants of this era were "white on arrival" (Guglielmo 2003), obstacles to this type of assimilation are far more formidable for today's Latinx, African, and Asian newcomers.

Another critical difference between the two periods is that the large undocumented population that is currently concentrated at the bottom of the U.S. labor market had no counterpart in the earlier era. Before World War I, only 1 percent of the 25 million European immigrants who landed at Ellis Island were rejected, usually for health-related reasons. Statutes of limitation of one to five years meant that even those who did enter the country illegally lived with fear of deportation for a relatively short time. To be sure, Asian immigrants faced a far different situation after the passage of the 1882 Chinese Exclusion Act and subsequent restrictive laws, but their numbers were relatively modest in this period, when the vast majority of immigrants were of European origin (Ngai 2006).

In the manufacturing centers of the Northeast and Midwest, employers relied on chain migration along with a variant of what recent commentators call "referral hiring," in which current workers draw on their social networks to help fill job openings. Not only did most of the "new" immigrants cross the Atlantic with direct assistance from family members or friends from home who had already settled in America, but most also had job offers in hand before they embarked. "In order to secure much needed labor, American employers deliberately relied on ethnic-based hiring," historian Ewa Morawska notes. "Even before they left their villages in Europe, the migrants knew not only to what American city they were going but usually ... where they would work, with whom, and for what wages" (1990: 204).

Employers welcomed the newcomers enthusiastically (with the notable exception of those who became involved in labor unrest).

Andrew Carnegie famously referred to immigration as a "golden stream which flows into the country each year" (Calavita 2010: 5). In 1907, the National Association of Manufacturers launched what would become a long-term effort on the part of employer groups to promote liberal immigration policies and to lobby against proposals for restrictive legislation (Higham [1955] 1968: 116). Progressive reformers such as Jane Addams and others in the settlement house movement also supported the newcomers and opposed restriction (Hahamovitch 1997: 61). However, this welcoming attitude was not always widely shared and, indeed, became increasingly unpopular in the early twentieth century amid an upsurge of nativism. The social Darwinist doctrine of "survival of the fittest," highly influential in this period, helped fuel a wave of unapologetic xenophobia that was especially hostile to the growing numbers of immigrants from Southern and Eastern Europe.

Intellectual elites, including academic social scientists, helped to shape the nativist narrative of this era, which in many respects parallels the immigrant threat narrative described in the Introduction. A prize-winning essay by University of Chicago economist Edward Bemis in 1888 lambasted immigration as a "moral evil," claiming that the newcomers were overrepresented in poorhouses and among convicted criminals, and that they were "illiterate and ignorant in the extreme." Bemis declared that the influx of immigrants would "lower the standard of living and wages" for Americans and increase unemployment (Zolberg 2006: 209). Using explicitly racial language, MIT president Francis A. Walker, who had supervised the 1870 and 1880 U.S. censuses, characterized immigrants from Italy, Hungary, and Russia as "vast masses of peasantry, degraded below our utmost conceptions ... Beaten men from beaten races, representing the worst failures in the struggle for existence." Walker argued that, in regard to immigration, natural selection operated in reverse, so that the "fittest" stayed in Europe while the unfit emigrated to America (Higham 1968: 143).

Laying the groundwork for the subsequent shift in government policy toward immigration restriction, nativist ideology also penetrated official government bodies such as the U.S. Immigration Commission, which conducted a wide-ranging, multi-year study of the foreign-born population starting in 1907. Its final report stated matter of factly that the new immigrants, "unskilled laboring men … from the less progressive and advanced countries of Europe," were "far less intelligent" and "actuated by different ideals" than their predecessors from Northern and Western Europe had been (cited in Hatton and Williamson 2005: 81). Asian immigrants were viewed in an even more negative light, not least by organized labor. At the turn of the twentieth century a union publication lambasted Chinese workers as "more slavish and brutish than the beasts that roam the fields. They are groveling worms" (Higham 1968: 25). Many middle-class Americans also felt threatened by the foreign-born. "Masses of immigrants intensified their insecurity," historian Linda Gordon observes of those who were drawn to the xenophobia platform of the Ku Klux Klan (KKK) in the 1920s. The influx of Catholic and Jewish immigrants from Southern and Eastern Europe "threatened a dominance that many white native-born Protestants considered a form of social property" (L. Gordon 2017: 183).

The issue of whether immigrants "rob jobs" or lower wage standards for the U.S.-born was as hotly debated in this era as it is today (Hatton and Williamson 2005: 97). Then, as now, many saw the foreign-born as a threat, including many labor leaders and their Progressive allies. The KKK too blamed immigrants for "stealing jobs from 'true' Americans." Imperial Wizard Hiram Evans declared in 1926, "While the American can outwork the alien, the alien can so far underlive the American as to force him out of all competitive labor" (L. Gordon 2017: 3, 54).

Economic historians have amassed extensive evidence suggesting that such claims had no foundation in reality. In regions with large-scale immigration, employment among U.S.-born workers did not decline but instead increased during the late nineteenth century, while their wages either rose or remained the same – largely because immigrants were disproportionately drawn to the very areas where economic growth was strongest (Carter and Sutch 2007). The historical data also suggest that, much like today, the newcomers entered a segmented labor market in which direct competition with natives was extremely limited. Immigrants from Southern and Eastern Europe were relegated to the bottom of the labor market, where wages were lower and employment more unstable than in the jobs held by U.S.-born workers and earlier immigrants. The "new" immigrants were disproportionately employed in newly created jobs, such as the unskilled factory work that burgeoned with the rise of mass production industry, which most U.S.-born workers and earlier immigrants disdained.

In 1791, anticipating just such a division of labor, Alexander Hamilton's "Report on Manufactures" declared that the employment of immigrants as wage laborers would "leave Americans free to engage in more dignified pursuits" (cited in Zolberg 2006: 70). That prediction was repeatedly realized as the massive transformation of manufacturing unleashed by the industrial revolution radically reshaped the nation's labor market. A job queue (see p. 14) developed in which unskilled industrial labor was ranked below most other jobs, and "new" immigrants were typically relegated to the bottom of the queue.

The U.S. Immigration Commission found that, in 1910, nearly three-quarters of Slavic and Hungarian male immigrants were concentrated in only four industries: coal, iron and steel, metalworking, and meatpacking. Similarly, three-quarters of Italian male immigrants were clustered in the coal, iron and steel, construction, and clothing industries; and nine-tenths of the East European Jewish immigrants employed in manufacturing were in the garment, wool, silk, fur, and leather trades (Morawska 1990: 196–7). While these newcomers dominated the ranks of the unskilled, U.S.-born workers and earlier immigrants were typically found in the more skilled positions. For example, the Commission reported that, in 1910, among foundry workers, 32 percent of the laborers, but only 4 percent of the machinists, were Southern or Eastern European immigrants; while, in the building trades, the share of new immigrants among painters and masons was only half their share among unskilled laborers (Goldin 1994: 241). In other cases, wage differentials were applied to similar jobs to set new immigrants apart from their co-workers. In the steel mills of Johnstown, Pennsylvania, for example, in departments where 80 percent of the workers were Southern and Eastern European immigrants, common laborers were paid $1.25 to $1.35 per day in 1908–9; but in departments where those groups were less than 20 percent of the workers, laborers' wages were $1.45 to $1.65 (Morawska 1990: 200).

The U.S.-born also were overrepresented in better-paid sectors such as transportation and communication, education, and the emerging professions (Hirschman and Mogford 2009). Nativist intellectual Madison Grant was alarmed to note that the U.S.-born apparently disdained blue-collar labor. "A race that refuses to do manual work and seeks 'white collar' jobs," he warned in his 1916 book *The Passing of the Great Race*, "is doomed through its falling birth rate to replacement by the lower races or classes" (cited in Ngai 1999: 75). Such fear of "race suicide" was widespread among patrician intellectuals – none of whom did manual work themselves – fueling President Theodore Roosevelt's infamous opposition to birth control as well as the era's eugenics movement (Higham 1968: 147–51). Roosevelt would later align himself with opponents of immigration restriction, but among the wider population, as well as in organized labor, nativism and xenophobia were on the rise.

Immigrant Labor and the Rise of Agricultural Capitalism

After the Civil War, capitalist development transformed not only U.S. manufacturing but also the nation's agriculture. That transformation was inexorable, yet its impact was extremely uneven, affecting the nation's regions in distinctly different ways. Even in the twenty-first century, the iconic status of the family farm as a pillar of American democracy remains an object of popular nostalgia. Although their longevity is sometimes exaggerated in the public imagination, many family farms dating from the colonial era in fact did remain largely intact well into the twentieth century, especially in New England. As late as 1910, 25 percent of the nation's population was based in the farm sector, down from 44 percent in 1880 but still substantial (Olmstead and Rhode 2006). In the South, sharecropping became the dominant mode of agricultural production after the abolition of slavery; it became prevalent in much of the Midwest as well. By 1920, half of the farms in the South and a third of those in the North Central United States were tenant-operated, compared to only 7 percent of those in New England (Wright 1988: 186).

In this period, wage labor and full-fledged capitalist "agribusiness" emerged only in California, the borderlands of the Southwest, and parts of the Atlantic coast. Initially, these were also the only regions where growers recruited immigrants as farm laborers. The pioneering case was California, where a production regime predicated on both extensive mechanization and the exploitation of immigrant wage labor took shape in the late nineteenth century. This created a template for immigrant employment in agriculture in other parts of the country that would later be adopted in low-wage urban industries as well, as chapter 3 documents. That template was defined by a human supply chain staffed by labor contractors who recruited immigrants on behalf of employers while effectively shielding the latter from accountability for labor abuses.

A distinct class of U.S.-born hired farm laborers, often stigmatized as "tramps" and "hobos," also emerged in the late nineteenth century, but it was modest in size and later became even smaller as itinerant native-born Americans increasingly gravitated to the more attractive job opportunities available in construction and other urban industries (Wright 1988: 201). A 1901 government report found that agricultural jobs were "the lowest paid of all the great groups of occupations" in this era (Hahamovitch 1997: 214 n.5). Family farming remained widespread among the U.S.-born, but for them agricultural wage labor was increasingly rare. In the early twentieth-century Northeast and Midwest, historian Gavin Wright points out, most farm owners were middle-class "small businessmen ... with substantial investment in land and equipment, established credit relationships, and an interest in passing their class status on to the next generation" (Wright 1988: 198). Although many farmers did assume mortgage debt to finance equipment purchases and keep up with rising land values, as late as 1920, 35 percent of the nation's owner-operated farms, and 54 percent of those in New England, remained mortgage-free (ibid.: 186, 190). Moreover, in this era even farm owners with mortgages typically retained control over their daily work lives and that of their families, relying minimally on hired labor.

California, in contrast, developed a distinctly proletarianized form of agriculture starting in the second half of the nineteenth century. "I should be very much pleased if you could find me something good (meaty) on economic conditions in *California*," Karl Marx wrote in 1880 to an American correspondent. "California is very important for me because nowhere else has the upheaval most shamelessly caused by capitalist centralization taken place with such speed" (Mins 1938: 226). By 1900, indeed, family farming in the state "survived only as a marginal appendage of a rural economy dominated in fact and in spirit by agribusinessmen as single-minded in their pursuit of profits as the most unwavering urban capitalist," observes historian Cletus Daniel (1981: 43). Land grants under the Spanish and then the Mexican government were vast, typically 50,000 acres or more. When California gained statehood in 1850, the average farm size was a much smaller 4,466 acres, but that was still far greater than elsewhere in the nation (Martin 2018: 4–5; Olmstead and Rhode 2018: 18; Fuller 1991: 1). The unusually large size of its farms was among the conditions stimulating the state's rapid capitalist development in agriculture.

As early as the 1870s, California wheat growers and cattle ranchers began to recruit immigrant wage laborers, although on a limited scale at first. Grain production in the West was highly mechanized from the outset, reflecting the economies of scale that could be realized on the region's large "bonanza ranches," as well as its chronic labor shortages. Starting in the 1890s, labor-intensive fruit and cotton cultivation increasingly replaced cattle ranching and grain farming, and demand for wage labor exploded (Fuller 1991; Olmstead and Rhode 2018: 2–3). Slavery had been banned in California, and sharecropping never developed on a significant scale there, so growers turned to wage labor from a variety of sources.

The first recruits were Chinese immigrants, almost exclusively single males. After the transcontinental railroad was completed in 1869, the state's farmers hired both former railroad workers and other Chinese workers who were being driven out of San Francisco and other Californian cities at the time (Fuller 1991: 10–12). Growers were effusive on the subject: "White men who claim to be competent farm hands," they lamented in 1872, "are positively not as intelligent as regards the prosecution of ordinary farm labor as are the darker colored 'heathen Chinese'" (ibid.: 10). The passage of the 1882 Chinese Exclusion Act sparked renewed anxieties about farm labor shortages. But three years later Japan legalized emigration, and by 1905 half of the state's seasonal farm workers were Japanese (Martin 2003: 39). They proved unexpectedly militant, regularly demanding higher wages (Daniel 1981: 74–5; Martin 2003: 39). In addition, Japanese immigration was subjected to legal restriction in 1907, so growers once again shifted their labor recruitment efforts – this time to immigrants from South Asia, the Philippines, and Mexico (Fuller 1991; Martin 2018: 5; McWilliams 1939).

In the borderlands of the Southwest (especially West Texas, Arizona, and Colorado), early twentieth-century agricultural capitalists also relied heavily on Mexican immigrant labor to harvest cotton, sugar beets, fruits, and vegetables. The region's growers recruited tens of thousands of workers with the assistance of labor contractors, most of whom were bilingual Mexican Americans who in turn engaged Mexican-based *coyotes* (smugglers) to ensure their recruits' safe passage across the border. Through these human supply chains Southwestern growers, along with railroad and mining employers in the region who also employed Mexican immigrants, easily evaded the 1885 law prohibiting the immigration of contract workers (Zolberg 2006: 198; McWilliams [1948] 1990). Similar arrangements developed in California. Reliable statistics are scarce, but between 1900 and 1930 about a million Mexicans – almost 10 percent of Mexico's population at the time – emigrated to the United States, mostly to work in agriculture in California and the Southwest (McWilliams 1990: 128). Like the European "birds of passage" in the industrial Northeast and Midwest, some Mexicans were "sojourners" who returned home after the harvest season, but many more settled permanently north of the border with their families – unlike the predominantly male Asian immigrant farm workers who had preceded them. By 1940, according to that year's census, California alone had 416,000 Spanish-speaking residents (Galarza 1964: 32).

Starting in the 1870s, wage-labor-based capitalist agriculture also developed on the Atlantic coast, especially in New Jersey and Florida, where truck farmers (so named because they grew fruits and vegetables to "truck" in the industrial cities of the East) proliferated. Like their counterparts in California and the Southwest, East Coast commercial farmers depended greatly on migrant labor to harvest their crops. But their sources of labor supply were distinctly different: in New Jersey, Italian immigrant women from nearby cities – recruited through labor contractors known as *padrones* – along with itinerant African Americans from the South; and, in Florida, immigrants from the Bahamas and African Americans from nearby states (Hahamovitch 1997).

Farm workers of all races and nationalities tended to exit the fields whenever they had the opportunity, and most took care to ensure that their children did so. As scholar-activist Ernesto Galarza noted, "not more than one generation of newcomers could be counted on to accept farm employment on any terms" (1964: 35). By the early twentieth century, indeed, many Mexicans and Filipinos already had gained a foothold in urban occupations in California; Japanese and South Asian immigrants more often stayed on the land, but many had managed to become small landowners rather than wage workers (Martin 2003: 39–40). As historians Alan Olmstead and Paul Rhode conclude, "Over the span of decades, agricultural labor in California has not been a dead-end pursuit creating a permanent class of peasant laborers." Instead, for immigrants who remained in the United States, as well as for U.S.-born whites such as the dust-bowl refugees of the

1930s, "agricultural labor offered a stepping stone into the robust, high-wage [California] economy ... few of the descendants of the earlier generations of agricultural laborers toil in the fields today" (Olmstead and Rhode 2018: 18). Similarly, in 2018, a journalist's report on farm workers in California's San Joaquin Valley noted that "fruit and vegetable picking is a one-generation job" (Greenberg 2018: 91).

Indeed, agricultural labor consistently has been at the very bottom of the job queue for U.S.-born whites and immigrants alike. Not only did growers make every effort to keep wages low, particularly for more labor-intensive crops, but also the work itself "was usually less attractive to workers than city jobs because it was seasonal, and typically involved very long hours, working conditions that were harsh, and living conditions that were at best primitive" (Daniel 1981: 25–6). Of course, it was precisely because farm work was anathema to most white U.S.-born workers that growers recruited immigrants in the first place, alongside far smaller numbers of transient white "hobos" and "tramps" whose availability was confined mostly to the nation's grain farming regions in the early twentieth century (Martin 2003: 41).

Yet the shape of the job queue was not entirely fixed; it could change with business conditions. "Whites won't turn a hand to menial [farm] labor during good times," an employment agency manager in California's Imperial Valley declared in the 1920s (Ngai 2004: 106). Similarly, a Chamber of Commerce spokesperson explained in 1926 that Mexicans were employed in Californian agriculture "because there is nothing else available. We have gone east, west, north, and south and he is the only man-power available to us" (Martin 2003: 43). Whereas, during such boom periods, growers recruited immigrants with few impediments, when U.S.-born workers faced high unemployment in other occupations and wanted to return to farm work, organized opposition to immigrant labor often emerged, sometimes accompanied by violence. As late as the 1950s, "industrial workers, many of them former field hands, continued to regard farm work as a filler during layoffs or a stop-gap during strikes" (Galarza 1964: 221).

The most dramatic illustration of this cyclical aspect of the job queue was the Great Depression. Mexicans and Filipinos comprised the bulk of California farm workers when the economic crisis erupted, but, just months after the 1929 crash, anti-Filipino riots broke out. They were "the target of resentment among unemployed white workers, for whom Asiatics were familiar and convenient scapegoats," notes Mae Ngai (2004: 108–9). Later in the 1930s, hundreds of thousands of Mexicans – many of them U.S. citizens – were repatriated, in some cases forcibly (McWilliams 1939: 129; Fuller 1991: 47). There were also efforts to repatriate Filipinos, but for various reasons that was more difficult to achieve (Ngai 2004: 120–2).

As the Depression continued, immigrant farm workers were increasingly replaced by white U.S.-born dust-bowl and drought refugees, as John Steinbeck famously chronicled in his 1939 novel *The Grapes of Wrath*. Growers in the West saw these migrants as "a providential dispensation," wrote Carey McWilliams. "The circumstances of their misery made them admirable recruits. They came in without expense to the growers; they were excellent workers ... they were so impoverished that they would work for whatever wage was offered." Although they were U.S.-born whites, these "Okies," "Texicans," and "Arkies" were widely despised by Californians, who considered them "another minority alien racial group." They were therefore "treated in exactly the same manner as their predecessors, the Mexicans and the Japanese" (McWilliams 1939: 306, 323).

Just a few years later, with the World War II-driven economic boom, the labor glut of the Depression gave way to an acute labor shortage, and the job queue returned to its earlier shape. "Agriculture was being continuously drained of manual labor ... by the growth of war industry – shipbuilding, aircraft, steel and oil refining" (Galarza 1964: 41–2). As white workers abandoned agriculture in droves, growers rapidly reverted to their former dependence on immigrant labor – but this time with an unprecedented level of state assistance. As it had done on a smaller scale during World War I, the U.S. government intervened to ensure a labor supply for the nation's agriculture for the duration of the war, launching the *bracero* program in the spring of 1942. By agreement with the Mexican government, which negotiated minimum wage rates and other basic labor protections for its citizens, the program supplied over 200,000 Mexican contract workers to farmers in twenty-four states during the war, with the lion's share going to California (Calavita 2010: 22). *Braceros* also worked on the railways, although those contracts were terminated shortly after the war came to an end in 1945 (Galarza 1964: 54). The much larger agricultural component would endure until 1964. A total of 4.6 million Mexican *braceros* were employed as U.S. farm workers over the life of the program (Martin 2003: 47).

Agricultural employers were unreservedly enthusiastic. "Any nation is very fortunate if it can, from sources near at hand, obtain the services on beck and call of labor, adult male labor," a grower declared in 1951, underscoring the especially convenient "condition that when the job is completed the laborer will return to his home." In tacit recognition of the fact that agricultural work was at the very bottom of the job queue, *braceros* were explicitly barred from pursuing more attractive job opportunities: they were "indentured to agriculture and prevented by law from listening to the siren call of the shipyards" (Calavita 2010: 22–3). Moreover, the terms of the program facilitated labor discipline, with mechanisms in place to exclude "undesirable" or "subversive" workers from continued participation. Initially justified by the severe wartime labor shortages, the *bracero* program was repeatedly extended in response to oft-repeated employer claims that U.S.-born workers were not willing to perform agricultural "stoop labor."

Even as they welcomed *braceros* with open arms, growers also continued to recruit unauthorized Mexican immigrants (Galarza 1964: ch. 7). As Kitty Calavita explains, "Plentiful, cheap, unencumbered by the red tape of the government program, and for the most part tolerated by the Immigration Service, undocumented workers provided growers with an inviting alternative" (Calivita 2010: 40). Although precise data are elusive, by all accounts the number of farm workers who entered the country illegally in the 1940s exceeded the number recruited as *braceros*. Border enforcement was conspicuously lax, especially during harvest seasons, and until the early 1950s the U.S. immigration authorities regularly granted legal status to undocumented farm workers who were already in the country by converting them into *braceros*, a maneuver known as "drying out the wetbacks" (ibid.: 29–30; Galarza 1964: 63–4).

In 1954, however, as controversy over mushrooming illegal immigration began to mount, the U.S. authorities launched "Operation Wetback" and deported tens of thousands of undocumented Mexicans. During the decade that followed, the vast majority of agricultural workers were recruited through a revamped and rationalized *bracero* program, and "domestic" workers (mostly U.S.-born Mexican Americans) were increasingly outnumbered by *braceros* – a phenomenon industry insiders called "crop domination." By 1957, no major crop in California's Imperial Valley was less than 70 percent "dominated"; in sugar beets the figure was 95 percent, and the levels in Ventura and San Diego counties were similarly high (Galarza 1964: 156–7).

In 1964, the *bracero* program was finally terminated as a result of the combined effects of agricultural mechanization, growing opposition from organized labor, and the changed political climate of the 1960s. A year later, the passage of the Hart–Celler Act radically altered U.S. immigration law, eliminating the national quotas enacted in 1924 and introducing an annual limit of 120,000 admissions from the western hemisphere, from which immigration had previously been unrestricted. In 1976, a country quota for that hemisphere was established, limiting annual legal admissions for immigrants from Mexico to 20,000. This represented a substantial decline: Mexican admissions for legal permanent residency (not including the massive inflow of *braceros*) had averaged 35,000 a year in the early 1960s (Ngai 2004: 261).

The stated purpose of abolishing the *bracero* program was to put an end to the dependence of agribusiness on Mexican immigrants, but that goal was never realized. Waged agricultural work was as unappealing as ever to U.S.-born whites, for whom employment opportunities had expanded enormously in the preceding quarter-century. Lacking access to *braceros*, growers returned to their previous practice of recruiting workers from south of the border through labor contractors. Most came without authorization, although some were legal guest workers on H-2A visas.[1] Border apprehensions of adult male Mexican farm workers rose by 600 percent between 1965 and 1970, and deportations rose sharply as well – despite the fact that immigration enforcement was notoriously poor at the time. Alongside the undocumented migrants and H-2A workers, a smaller population of circular Mexican migrants with legal status, known as "green card commuters" or "*viseros*," became part of the farm labor force in the immediate post-*bracero* period, as did some Mexican Americans who had settled permanently in the United States, with or without legal status (Calavita 2010: 164–8; Galarza 1964: 250; Ngai 2004: 261).

Growers hired some farm workers directly, but more often they relied on labor brokers or contractors, especially for temporary or seasonal work. These intermediaries, a longstanding presence in Western agribusiness, assembled and supervised work crews, typically comprised of single males recruited directly from Mexico. The contractors, most of whom were bilingual Mexican Americans, also arranged workers' housing, food, and transportation, deducting charges for such items from already meager pay – a system that incentivized super-exploitation:

> By the terms of the labor contract, the contractor is tied to the interests of the grower. The contractor is required to have a specified set of tasks (e.g. harvest operations) completed by a specified date. The contractor assumes full responsibility for recruiting, transporting and supervising the work crew. The majority of contractor income is derived from the difference between the contract payment and the wages paid out to workers. In other words, the contractor and grower have a joint interest in low wages. The balance of contractor income derives from providing special services to workers – transportation, housing, food, etc. ... As assimilated residents regulating seasonal migration, contractors have at most weak loyalties to crew members. Pursuing their own economic advantage, contractors tend to recruit the most dependent workers available – illegals. (Jenkins 1978: 526–7)

Most recruits were unauthorized immigrants with little or no previous U.S. work experience; but even those with visas were vulnerable to abuse by unscrupulous labor contractors. Legal violations were widespread, including payment below the statutory minimum wage, illegal payroll deductions, fees charged for securing jobs, and sometimes outright failure to pay workers for labor they had performed. Growers, however, were conveniently able to disavow all knowledge of and responsibility for the abuses committed by labor contractors and, similarly, to distance themselves from immigration- and employment-law violations (Jenkins 1978; Linder 1987).

Mexican migrant farm workers often arrived in the United States with no intention of staying permanently, and many did return home, but others set down roots north of the border. Some continued to work in agriculture, but many others were drawn to nearby cities as the postwar economy boomed (Jenkins 1978: 518). Mexican Americans "mostly lived in rural and agricultural areas in 1950 [but had] migrated in large numbers to cities such as San Jose and Los Angeles by 1960" (Martin 2003: 49). By the 1970s, many Mexican migrants were heading directly to cities rather than to rural areas, with Los Angeles the most popular destination (Minian 2018: 36). The progression "from field to town was a natural one, although attended by greater risks of arrest and deportation … The Wetback soon was found in restaurants, hotels, laundries, garages, building construction, domestic service, mills, brick factories and railway maintenance" (Galarza 1964: 31). Between 1965 and 1985, the share of migrants leaving Mexico for agricultural work in the U.S. fell from 45 to 25 percent (Massey et al. 2002: 61). As the next chapter shows, employment practices typical of agriculture in the post-*bracero* period – including labor contracting, the accompanying violations of wage and hour laws, and other abuses – would soon appear in immigrant-employing urban industries as well. Ironically, however, the farm workers' movement that developed in the 1960s and 1970s aimed to achieve precisely the opposite goal: to elevate the pay and conditions of agricultural workers to the level of unionized urban workers.

Immigrant Workers and the Labor Movement

The farm workers' union movement was at one end of a century-long historical arc of immigrant worker organizing in the United States. From the earliest period, immigrants and their offspring made up the bulk of the nation's working class, so that successful unionizing was often predicated on recruiting them. Yet ethnic divisions among immigrants were a longstanding and formidable challenge for American labor organizers. To bridge those divisions, as historian Richard Oestreicher put it in one influential formulation, "new institutions had to be created, and a new moral code developed that convinced workers that they owed the same kinds of loyalties to workers of other nationalities that they owed to people of their own" (1986: 61). Throughout its history, the U.S. labor movement wrangled internally over immigration, and the policies that it adopted shifted over time (Fine and Tichenor 2009; Minian 2018). By the end of the twentieth century, the AFL-CIO would become an ardent champion of immigrant rights, asserting that "the labor movement is strongest when we are open to all workers, regardless of where they come from" (Kazin 2013). But, in earlier decades, most unionists had favored immigration restriction – presenting a steady counterpoint to the eagerness of employers to ensure the continued flow of the "golden stream" of labor from abroad. Unions were especially vociferous advocates of the 1882 Chinese Exclusion Act, the nation's first piece of restrictive legislation (Mink 1986), and of the 1885 Foran Act, which prohibited the immigration of contract workers (Zolberg 2006: 194).

Yet, even in the nineteenth century, a few labor organizations successfully organized across lines of skill and nativity, most notably the Knights of Labor, which flourished in the 1880s. Like the rest of the labor movement, the Knights supported the 1882 Chinese Exclusion Act, but unlike other unions it welcomed the "new" Southern and Eastern European immigrants, recruiting skilled and unskilled workers alike into its local organizations under the legendary slogan "An injury to one is the concern of all." Yet, by the 1890s, the Knights had virtually disappeared and the American Federation of Labor (AFL) had become the nation's dominant labor organization. With only a few dissenters, AFL leaders supported immigration restriction.

Ironically, U.S. labor leaders in this era, including AFL president Samuel Gompers, were disproportionately foreign-born themselves (Sorokin et al. 1927). Gompers acknowledged that "the labor movement approached the problem of immigration restriction reluctantly" and with "mixed feelings" (Gompers 1925, vol. 2: 153, 158). But ultimately he became convinced that the availability of unskilled "new" immigrants facilitated employers' efforts to degrade skilled labor.

> This flood of immigrant workers drifted to so called "unskilled work." Practically all of the basic industries were revising their production methods to substitute machine work in the place of previously indispensable craft skill. In the early years of this period of transition, the idea developed that the workman should be only a machine tender and, hence, an unskilled workman. For this sort of work the immigrants were considered desirable. (Ibid.: 158)

This stance was reinforced by the fact that employers often used foreign-born workers as strikebreakers in this period. Moreover, the craft unions that dominated the AFL were committed to an organizational logic based on the notion that their power depended primarily on their ability to control the supply of labor, which they typically aimed to accomplish by tightly restricting the number of skilled workers. In this context, unskilled immigrants were considered inherently "unorganizable."

Edna Bonacich characterizes the result as a "split labor market," in which higher paid workers "see a large concentration of cheaper labor in a few industries which could easily be used to undercut them in their own" and seek to prevent such undercutting by establishing an exclusionary organization. "The higher paid group controls certain jobs exclusively and gets paid at one scale of wages, while the cheaper group is restricted to another set of jobs and is paid at a lower scale" (Bonacich 1972: 554–5). Bonacich's theory usefully highlights the economic divisions underlying what might otherwise appear as purely ethnic or nativist antagonism. Yet she seems to regard exclusionary unionism as an inevitability, ignoring the possibility that labor unions could organize low-wage workers alongside the more privileged, creating inclusionary organizations such as the Knights of Labor. Bonacich's deterministic approach also tends to take the power of higher paid workers vis-à-vis employers for granted, while at the same time presuming that "cheaper labor" passively submits to its own exploitation.

In the U.S. case, at least, such assumptions are problematic. Skilled workers were often outmaneuvered by employers, who systematically undercut their power through deskilling. At the same time, many of the "new" immigrants responded enthusiastically when opportunities to unionize arose. In 1912, economist Isaac Hourwich declared that "immigrants from Southern and Eastern Europe are the backbone of some of the strongest labor unions," including the miners and garment workers. During the massive steel organizing drives of World War I, "the great initial response came from the immigrant steelworkers. They were the first to crowd the mass meetings and sign up for membership," notes David Brody (1960: 223). "In contrast, the natives were, according to all reports, an unenthusiastic lot." In meatpacking, too, "organizers found the foreign-born much easier to organize than the native-born" in this period (Barrett 1987: 195).

Ethnically based social networks among the new immigrants, and in some cases left-wing ideology as well, helped propel the World War I union upsurge. "Not only were foreign-born workers prominent among the strikes in the coal, steel, textile, clothing oil, lumber and maritime and other industries, but their patterns of collective mobilization were usually based on ethnic communities," observes David Montgomery, adding that "both commitment to trades unionism and a heavy sprinkling of revolutionary rhetoric were easy to detect" (1986: 329, 346). Similarly, in the needle trades, especially among Eastern European Jews, "it was within the immigrant working-class community that the roots of labor militance took hold and spread" (Glenn 1990: 178). It was no accident that the garment workers' unions were among the few AFL affiliates to oppose restrictive immigration policy in this period (Haus 2002: 51).

Receptivity to unionization among old and new immigrant workers alike was often rooted in prior experiences with strikes and labor organization in Europe (Hourwich 1912: 349–51; Glenn 1990: 178–85). Selig Perlman attributed the very existence of the nineteenth-century U.S. labor movement to the influence of immigrants who brought "an important socialistic class-consciousness" from across the Atlantic (Perlman 1928: 192–3). Not all immigrants were veterans of labor or radical movements at home, however, and ethnic parochialism and fragmentation did inhibit unionizing efforts in many contexts. But organized labor confronted far more formidable obstacles, most importantly the era's intransigent employer anti-unionism, bolstered by strong state support.

For most AFL officials, support for immigration restriction was unwavering, and the notion of recruiting unskilled workers into their unions remained anathema. But a decade after the advocates of restriction triumphed with the passage of the 1924 Johnson–Reed Act, the economic and political context would be radically altered by the Great Depression and the New Deal. In the late 1930s, the fledgling Congress of Industrial Organizations (CIO) began a decades-long growth surge, and the membership of pre-existing AFL unions also expanded rapidly. Like the Knights half a century earlier, the CIO unions explicitly welcomed immigrant workers, who made up the bulk of the workforce in the mass production manufacturing sector they targeted for organizing.

As Lizabeth Cohen has shown, the homogenizing effects of popular culture and consumerism in the 1920s, along with the CIO unions' deliberate efforts to build a "culture of unity" that transcended ethnic and racial divisions, yielded powerful results in the 1930s. The industrial unions were committed to organizing workers at all skill levels, without regard to race, ethnicity, or gender, and their spectacular successes soon rendered anachronistic the notion that immigrant workers were "unorganizable." Instead, Southern and Eastern European immigrants and their children were the main source of CIO membership growth (Cohen 1990: 324–5).

Paradoxically, the union upsurge of the 1930s and 1940s also served as a major vehicle for immigrant assimilation. Not only did the economic gains won by organized labor lift large numbers of immigrant union members and their families into the middle class for the first time, but the growing labor movement also offered opportunities for individual mobility, as first- and second-generation immigrant activists with leadership skills took up careers as secondary union officials. As Mexican-American historian George Sánchez notes, 1930s unionism involved "at its core an attempt by the children of the immigrant generation and those who had arrived in the United States as youngsters to integrate themselves into American society." Sánchez argues that, despite the labor movement's well-earned reputation as a challenger to the status quo, "labor and political activity often served as the greatest 'Americanizing agent' of the 1930s and 1940s" (Sánchez 1993: 249). This assimilationist dynamic involved Southern and Eastern Europeans in the East and Midwest as well as Mexican Americans in California.

However, the situation of those two groups diverged sharply in another critical respect. The descendants of Southern and Eastern European immigrants were incorporated into the nation's "white" population in this period, a process that was largely complete by the end of World War II. In contrast, Mexican Americans remained racial "others," along with African Americans (Lieberson 1980). After the passage of the Johnson–Reed Act in 1924, as Mae Ngai (2004) has shown, Mexican immigrants were discursively and administratively constituted as "illegal aliens," a group that previously was almost nonexistent. In the years that followed, some unions did organize Mexican-born workers, for example in the L.A. garment industry in the 1930s (Sánchez 1993; Milkman 2006: 42–5). But, far more often, organized labor considered them, especially the undocumented, as a threat to hard-won labor standards. For example, the AFL-CIO stated in a 1976 U.S. Senate hearing that "illegal immigrants have for years been taking jobs from American citizens and legal immigrants in increasing numbers, often work for substandard wages and accept substandard working and living conditions" (Minian 2018: 69).

The post-1924 regime regulating Mexican labor migration was tailored largely to the needs of agricultural capitalists in California and other parts of the Southwest (Fuller 1991: 46–7). As the previous section of this chapter noted, although temporarily disrupted by the Great Depression, that regime was rapidly reestablished, at first alongside the *bracero* program and then more comprehensively after that program ended in 1964. Despite dramatic strikes and other sporadic expressions of farm worker militancy over the previous century (Daniel 1981), no lasting labor organization had developed in agriculture, in part because the sector was explicitly excluded from coverage under the 1935 National Labor Relations Act, which guaranteed most other U.S. workers the legally protected right to unionize. Organized labor did not make serious efforts to recruit farm workers until the 1950s, when the civil rights movement began to focus public attention on the plight of workers of color generally and the low pay and appalling working conditions of farm workers in particular.

The AFL-CIO played a leading role in efforts to abolish the *bracero* program, as did a series of farm worker strikes in California from 1959 to 1962 (Bardacke 2011: 105). Starting in 1959, the AFL-CIO also sponsored farm worker unionization drives under the auspices of the Agricultural Workers Organizing Committee (AWOC). Three years later, Cesar Chavez had launched the Farm Workers Association, later called the National Farm Workers Association (NFWA). When the termination of the *bracero* program created a farm labor shortage, organizing finally gained traction; in 1966 the AWOC and NFWA merged into the United Farm Workers Organizing Committee, an AFL-CIO affiliate, later to become the United Farm Workers (UFW). The rival Teamsters union (at the time independent of the AFL-CIO) also successfully organized farm workers in this period, although in a more traditional, less confrontational fashion that often involved undercutting the UFW (Ganz 2009).

In many respects, the Chavez-led UFW was a model of pro-immigrant unionism. As Jennifer Gordon observes:

It had a decidedly immigrant "feel": Spanish was the language of daily work, and the culture and religion of its largely Mexican and Mexican- and Filipino-American members played important roles in its organizing model. The union's membership included recent immigrants from Mexico and elsewhere, both documented and not. When undocumented immigrants were working on a ranch where the UFW was organizing, the union sought to include them, offering help with immigration issues and treating them like any other member.

(J. Gordon 2005: 29)

With support from churches, students, and other allies, and high-profile consumer boycotts, the UFW flourished, peaking in 1973 with membership of 67,000. As Marshall Ganz (2009) has shown, its success reflected a unique strategic repertoire, deeply influenced by the community organizing tradition in which Chavez had been schooled and in many respects departing from established union traditions (Bardacke 2011: 110). Most UFW leaders were drawn from the same ethnic communities as the workers (Mexican or Filipino) and received minuscule salaries. The union provided a wide range of social services to dues-payers, offered assistance with immigration problems and other legal matters, and sponsored credit unions and food cooperatives. It drew on workers' pre-existing social networks to build grassroots strength and assiduously cultivated relationships with outside allies – student groups, faith leaders, and civil rights organiza- tions – to build public support. It also built relationships with elected officials, locally and at the national level. In short, it was not only a union but also a social movement, known to many in the Mexican-American community simply as *La Causa*.

In California, the passage of the Agricultural Labor Relations Act, which became law in 1975, appeared to herald an era of stable farm worker unionization. Ultimately that proved illusory; by the end of the century UFW membership had plummeted to fewer than 6,000, a decline from which the organization would never recover (Martin 2003: 70–81; Ganz 2009: 240). The UFW nevertheless had an enormous impact. It was the first labor organization to demonstrate that undocumented workers could be successfully unionized, defying widespread beliefs to the contrary. The strategic repertoire it developed would influence many subsequent immigrant organizing campaigns (Shaw 2008), some of which adopted the slogan *Sí Se Puede!* (Yes, We Can!), later popularized by Barack Obama, which had originated in a UFW campaign (Bardacke 2011: 413).

Organizing the undocumented posed challenges that previous generations of labor organizers had rarely encountered, since nearly all the immigrant workers they recruited had full legal status and were not at risk of deportation. At first, the UFW concentrated its organizing on farm workers who had legal status and had settled permanently in the United States, while lobbying for strict border control and endorsing legislative proposals for immigration restriction in the 1970s (Gutiérrez 1995: 197; Minian 2018: 161). Complaining that growers were recruiting undocumented workers as strikebreakers, Chavez and others in the union also put pressure on the U.S. government to deport the workers involved. The union went so far as to supply the names of undocumented immigrants working in struck fields, which at times led to deportations of UFW members as well as strikebreakers (Thomas 1985: 160–1; J. Gordon 2005: 29–30). Similarly, the Teamsters' union tried to block the hiring of undocumented workers to protect its members both in the fields and the adjacent packing plants (Thomas 1985: 208).

Just as earlier generations of unionists had believed that unskilled immigrants from Southern and Eastern Europe (also regularly used as strikebreakers) were a threat to the hard-won labor standards of its U.S.-born members, so too the UFW feared that undocumented immigrants posed a threat to its efforts. "I have to be honest. We cannot get anywhere – with the contracts, with seniority, with good representation – until the *indocumentados* are out of the fields," one UFW activist told a researcher. "As long as you have guys trembling because they are afraid of being deported, you can't expect to protect jobs or make the work more human" (Thomas 1981: 16). In 1974, Chavez announced a "massive campaign to get the recent flood of illegals out of California." He claimed that undocumented workers were taking jobs from legal residents and citizens, undercutting strikes, and even bringing disease into the fields. The union also sponsored a shadowy operation known as "the wet line" in the Arizona desert in 1975. Wearing "UFW Border Control" armbands, a group of union-paid men camped out near the border, apprehending "illegals" and in some cases physically abusing them (Bardacke 2011: 488–506).

The UFW's anti-illegal efforts provoked bitter criticism inside the union, as well as from outside supporters, and especially from Mexican-American activists (Gutiérrez 1995: 197–8) and other farm worker organizations (Thomas 1981: 16–17; Martin 2003: 53). "We must urge you to stop all actions that would create greater division among documented and undocumented workers," wrote an organizer for the Maricopa County Organizing Project in Arizona to Chavez in 1979. "If the United Farm Workers Union has problems with undocumented workers being brought in as scabs [strikebreakers], the answer is to organize those scabs" (Thomas 1985: 165; Minian 2018: 159–67). Others noted that not only strikebreakers but also a large share of ordinary farm workers – by one estimate more than half of those in California in the mid-1970s – were undocumented (Bardacke 2011: 490).

Chavez continued to complain publicly about both the U.S government's failure to enforce immigration law and the growers' use of undocumented strikebreakers (Bardacke 2011: 628). But gradually he began to soften his view. As early as 1974, in response to pressure from Mexican-American civil rights groups, he promised to advocate for "amnesty for illegal aliens" (Gutiérrez 1995: 199). A decade later, the UFW was among the many unions that supported IRCA, the 1986 law that provided amnesty to about 3 million undocumented workers, many of them farm workers. Because IRCA also mandated increased border enforcement, it was controversial among Mexican-American civil rights activists and immigrant rights groups. But Chavez believed that the new law's amnesty provision would facilitate unionization. "I think they'll always support, if not our union, the idea of a union," he declared. "When a work force is not afraid, it bargains for itself" (Shaw 2008: 198). As chapter 5 shows, that prophecy would eventually be fulfilled, although not in the agricultural sector. In later years, after Chavez's death in 1993, the UFW allied itself more closely with the immigrant rights movement, for example strongly supporting the massive 2006 immigrant rights marches, and in the Trump era providing legal services to undocumented farm workers threatened with deportation (Greenberg 2018: 92).

At its peak, the UFW won contracts for its members that boosted wages to more than one and a half times the minimum wage, and some crews earned far more (Bardacke 2011: 2). Those contracts also established seniority rights, union-run hiring halls to reduce the power of labor contractors, grievance procedures, and medical insurance benefits (Ganz 2009: 194). These achievements would prove fleeting, but they embodied the union's aspiration to elevate the pay and working conditions of farm workers to match the standards won by unionized workers in other sectors. As the UFW's power unraveled, however, that goal became increasingly elusive. Instead, by the late twentieth century, immigrant workers in urban industries – especially the undocumented – would regularly face degraded pay and conditions that resembled those long entrenched in non-union agriculture. Indeed, as chapter 5 recounts, immigrant unionization drives in that period would revive many elements of the UFW's strategic repertoire; not coincidentally, the organizers involved included many UFW veterans (Shaw 2008). Thus just as agricultural employers created a template of immigrant labor exploitation that later spread to urban sectors, so too the UFW created a template for immigrant organizing that would eventually move from the country to the city.

3

The Eclipse of the New Deal:
Labor Degradation, Union Decline,
and Immigrant Workers

In the absence of unionism, the worker has limited responses to orders that he [*sic*] feels are unfair: the worker can quit, or ... engage in quiet sabotage or shirking, neither of which is likely to alter the employer's actions. In the union setting, by contrast, the union constitutes a source of worker power, diluting managerial authority and offering members protection through ... the grievance and arbitration system, under which disputes over proper managerial decision-making on work issues can be resolved.

Richard Freeman and James Medoff (1984: 11)

Forged in the crucible of the Great Depression and World War II, the New Deal was a unique era in U.S. history. Franklin Delano Roosevelt, the nation's longest-serving and widely beloved president, pursued an egalitarian legislative and policy agenda that profoundly transformed the American political economy. At its center was the 1935 National Labor Relations Act (NLRA), which guaranteed most U.S. workers the right to unionize and bargain collectively for the first time, helping to spur a massive labor upsurge that generated record levels of union membership and power. The New Deal also expanded state regulation of the economy and institutionalized a broad array of new social protections, from minimum wage and overtime laws to social security. These initiatives led to a sharp decline in inequality between rich and poor; indeed, the era would later be dubbed the "Great Compression" (Goldin and Margo 1992). And yet, after only four decades, all these changes would be reversed. In the neoliberal era that began in the late 1970s, unionization declined sharply, deregulation swept across the economy, and inequality surged.[1]

The shift toward immigration restriction that began during World War I, culminating in the passage in 1924 of the Johnson–Reed Act, has traditionally been understood by scholars as entirely independent of the New Deal transformations that began a decade later. But some recent commentators have questioned that view, arguing that limited immigration was a crucial precondition for the growth of unionism and the broader egalitarian turn of the 1930s. "Only after a century of mass immigration ended during the 1914–1924 era was the labor movement able to take root," declares economist Vernon Briggs. "From the early 1930s to the mid-1960s, unionism flourished ... The same was true for the pioneering governmental policies, enacted over these same years, which sought to protect and to enhance the well-being of workers" (Briggs 2001: 173). For Briggs, this simply reflected the laws of supply and demand. "Immigration has the power to influence the size of the labor supply and, thereby, both wage and employment conditions," he argues, adding the corollary that "the labor movement would flounder during periods of high immigration and flourish during periods of low immigration" (ibid.: 170). Briggs cites data like those at the top of figure 3 in support of these claims.

Historian Jefferson Cowie advances a similar perspective in his book *The Great Exception* (2016). In his view, as the book's title signals, the New Deal marked a unique deviation from the United States' long-term historical trajectory. Although focusing on political and cultural dynamics rather than economics, Cowie, like Briggs, argues that the restriction of immigration in the 1920s set the stage for the egalitarian policies that followed a decade later:

> when the 1929 crash hit, nativism was largely at bay and workers living in this country were presumed to be here to stay. This in itself was enough to engender more of a sense of unity among working

Figure 3   Immigration and unionization trends, selected countries, 1960–2012[2]

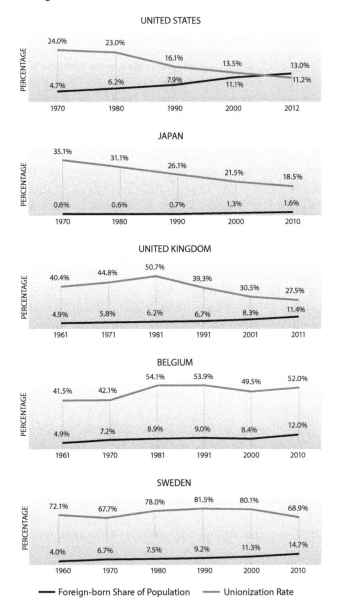

Source: see note 2.

people than before. By effectively neutralizing one of the most common reasons why a sense of unity or shared economic destiny had fallen apart in the past, the mitigation of the nativist impulse helped shape an era of greater equality.

When immigration resurfaced slowly in the generation after the 1965 immigration reforms, so did neo-Know Nothings and the militant nativism of an earlier age, returning "the" working class to historical patterns of internecine hostilities and political divisions reminiscent of the pre-New Deal era ... For most of American history, battle lines have been drawn around the social reality and policy issues of immigration – except during the period of the New Deal order. (Cowie 2016: 20–1)

Cowie's claim that the decline of nativism laid essential groundwork for the growth of mass production unionism in the 1930s and 1940s draws on the work of other labor historians, including Lizabeth Cohen's (1990) authoritative study of the CIO's success in building a "culture of unity" among first- and second-generation European immigrant workers, mentioned in chapter 2. For Cohen, the CIO's success was predicated partly on the homogenizing effects of the mass media and popular culture that developed in the 1920s but also on unionists' deliberate efforts to challenge ethnic and racial divisions among workers. Cowie's account of this crucial era of U.S. labor history has a more deterministic valence, however, suggesting that nativism declined because of immigration restriction, not as a result of the CIO's strategic initiatives.

Briggs's contention that "the percentage of the labor force that is unionized is inversely related to immigration trends" (Briggs 2001: 3) is even more deterministic, drawing on the abstract logic of neoclassical economics. Although he discusses only the U.S. case, if his argument is accurate, it should also apply to other advanced capitalist countries. Unionization levels did indeed fall sharply in most wealthy nations starting in the late 1970s, and the decline was often preceded by increased immigration. Yet, as the data in figure 3 show, many countries fail to conform to the pattern Briggs predicts. Japan is perhaps the most striking example: its unionization rate fell precipitously, from 35 percent in 1970 to 19 percent in 2010, yet that decline was not associated with immigration growth. On the contrary, between 1970 and 1990, when de-unionization was especially rapid, the foreign-born share of Japan's population hardly changed at all. As late as 2010 it stood at only 1.6 percent – more than double the 1990 figure (reflecting a slight relaxation of immigration restrictions in the face of an acute labor shortage and an aging population), but still minuscule by any standard.

The United Kingdom also deviates from the pattern Briggs posits. There, the period when immigration expanded most rapidly *followed* union decline. As figure 3 shows, the foreign-born share of the U.K. population rose modestly starting in the 1960s, from 4.9 percent in 1961 to 8.3 percent forty years later. It increased faster in the early twenty-first century, reaching 11.4 percent in 2011. But by then the drama of British labor's collapse was already a *fait accompli*: unionization had plummeted from its peak of 50.7 percent in 1980 to only 30.5 percent in 2000. After that the decline continued, but far more slowly: in 2010 the unionization rate was 27.5 percent.

Finally, the experience of Northern Europe also calls Briggs's argument into question. There the neoliberal turn came relatively late, and unionization levels fell less and later than in other wealthy countries – but with no apparent relationship to immigration trends, as illustrated by the two examples at the bottom of figure 3. In Belgium, the foreign-born share of the population climbed steadily starting in the 1960s, yet unionization *rose* in the 1960s and 1970s and then stabilized, with only minor erosion after 1990. Similarly, in Sweden, where the foreign-born share of the population nearly doubled between 1970 and 2000, unionization initially increased and then plateaued over that thirty-year period. The foreign-born share of the Swedish population continued to rise over the following decade, even as unionization declined sharply. That seems more consistent with Briggs's claim, yet Sweden's unionization rate was higher in 2010 than it had been in 1970.

Each of these countries has its own distinct and complex history in regard to both immigration policy and fluctuations in unionization levels. But the crucial point is that the non-U.S. data in figure 3 falsify Briggs's contention that rising immigration has an inexorable and negative effect on labor movement strength, and that unions can flourish only when immigration is restricted.[3] On the contrary, these data suggest that the relationship between immigration trends and unionization rates is not predetermined by the "laws" of supply and demand but, instead, is shaped by an array of contingencies that vary over time and cross-nationally.

Returning to the case of the United States, even if immigration restriction did play some role, however minor, in facilitating the labor upsurge of the 1930s, it does not necessarily follow (once the determinism of Briggs and Cowie is abandoned) that the resumption of immigration after 1965 was a significant driver of de-unionization or of the broader unraveling of the New Deal order. The rest of this chapter argues that, on the contrary, the late twentieth-century surge of low-wage immigration was a *consequence* of the labor market transformations that unfolded in the neoliberal era, not their *cause*. Employers would eventually come to appreciate the advantages of hiring foreign-born workers, but that consideration did not influence the neoliberal strategies they developed in the late 1970s, when deindustrialization, de-unionization and deregulation radically restructured the labor market.

Faced with rising international competition, along with inflation and economic stagnation at home, American manufacturing firms in the late 1970s and 1980s rapidly shifted production offshore to sites where labor was cheaper, generating a massive wave of U.S. plant closures. In other sectors, such as construction and services, jobs remained in the country but were systematically degraded by employer efforts to weaken or eliminate unions and reduce labor costs. Organized labor was anathema in the neoliberal era, insofar as it obstructed the workings of the "free" market. As David Harvey (2005: 75) puts it, unions "had to be disciplined if not destroyed in the name of the supposedly sacrosanct individual liberty of the isolated laborer."

Deregulation, another hallmark of neoliberalism, also contributed to job degradation in many industries, dismantling previous legal constraints that had taken "wages out of competition." In some of the affected sectors, such as trucking, as documented below, deregulation directly undermined union power. More generally, this era was marked by radically reduced state intervention in the economy, reversing the logic of the New Deal with a turn to laissez-faire policies. That reversal was accompanied by widespread corporate efforts to externalize market risks, spawning new layers of subcontracting as well as the proliferation of "independent contractors" performing tasks formerly carried out by wage and salary workers (Weil 2014).

Starting in the 1970s, then, a broad swath of jobs that had previously offered high wages, employment security, health insurance, and pension benefits – largely as a result of unionization – were either outsourced to other countries or transformed into non-union, low-wage, precarious jobs with limited or no benefits (Standing 2011; Kalleberg 2011). Sweatshop labor, which had nearly vanished in the New Deal era, now reappeared along with employment practices of questionable legality: all-cash wage payments, lack of overtime compensation, and violations of minimum wage laws (Bernhardt et al. 2009). At the same time, the burgeoning ranks of independent contractors were excluded entirely from coverage by labor and employment laws.

This radical labor market restructuring disproportionately affected non-college-educated U.S.-born workers. As the anti-union offensive of the 1980s, along with deregulation and subcontracting, relentlessly drove wages and conditions downward, those workers increasingly abandoned the jobs affected. Employers then turned to immigrants, many of them unauthorized, to fill the resulting vacancies. This was the process through which foreign-born workers entered the bottom of the job queue, in the degraded jobs that their U.S.-born counterparts had rejected. In short, the reversal of fortune suffered by non-college-educated American workers in this period was the product of labor market restructuring. Their exodus from newly degraded jobs stimulated growing immigration – not the other way around. Nevertheless, in a textbook case of "blaming the victim," many of these workers were led to believe that their own plight was the result of labor market competition from immigrants – a conviction fueled by the immigrant threat narrative discussed in the Introduction.

Labor market restructuring was already well underway before the influx of low-wage immigration took off. Although the 1924 national immigration quotas had been eliminated by the Hart–Celler Act of 1965, fifteen years later only 6 percent of the civilian labor force was foreign-born. That figure would nearly triple by 2017, when it reached 17 percent (Migration Policy Institute 2018). Similarly, the unauthorized share of the labor force was relatively modest at the outset of the neoliberal era: as late as 1995 it was only 2.7 percent. But it doubled over the following decade, peaking at 5.4 percent in 2006, on the eve of the Great Recession (Passel and Cohn 2018). In this way, as labor market restructuring generated growing employer demand for low-wage labor, both legal and unauthorized immigration surged upward.

Although neoliberalism brought reduced state intervention in the economy as a whole, the laissez-faire approach did not extend to immigration policy. As Mae Ngai points out, the "immigration debate was never over whether to restrict, but by how much and according to what criteria" (2004: 248). Although it did remove the national quotas enacted in 1924, the Hart–Celler Act also included a new provision limiting total annual immigration from the western hemisphere (which had until then been unrestricted) to 120,000. That cap went into effect in 1968, and eight years later Congress imposed new quotas of 20,000 for each western hemisphere country, with especially dramatic effects on Mexico. The net result, Ngai argues, was to "recast Mexican migration as 'illegal'" (ibid.: 261). Indeed, after 1965, unauthorized migration from Mexico surged, as did deportations. This marked the onset of what Douglas Massey, Jorge Durand and Nolan J. Malone call the "undocumented migrant era," when the *bracero* program was replaced by new legal arrangements that "produced a stable, well-defined population of international migrants who were young ... [and] largely undocumented ... who easily entered the United States and found employment." Under this regime, employers "got a steady supply of workers for jobs that natives were loath to take" (Massey et al. 2002: 70–1).

As had been the case under the *bracero* program, after 1965 the enforcement regime of the Immigration and Naturalization Service

(INS) operated so as to minimize any interference with business (Calavita [1992] 2010; Brownell 2009).[4] But as unauthorized migration crept steadily upward, political concern mounted, eventually leading to the passage of the 1986 Immigration and Control Act (IRCA). That legislation aimed to resolve the problem definitively by granting legal status to about 3 million undocumented immigrants while simultaneously increasing border enforcement to restrict future flow. Additional legislative measures to reinforce the U.S.–Mexican border were passed in the 1990s. However, as Massey and his colleagues have shown, "a perverse consequence of draconian border enforcement is that it does not deter would-be [unauthorized] migrants from trying to enter the country so much as it discourages those who are already here from returning home" (Massey et al. 2002: 128–9; see also Minian 2018).

Indeed, defying the intentions of IRCA and subsequent legislation to stem the tide of unauthorized immigration, the flow continued to grow in the 1990s and 2000s, until it was brought to a sudden stop by the 2008 financial crash. After 1986, the previous pattern of circular migration from Mexico and Central America was transformed into permanent settlement, which in turn led growing numbers of family members to join male migrants in *el Norte*. IRCA's employer sanctions also proved woefully ineffective. As Peter Brownell has documented, employers rapidly "captured" the INS, which consistently devoted the bulk of its resources to securing the border rather than to workplace enforcement (Brownell 2009: ch. 5). Similarly, Massey and his colleagues conclude that, while it may have functioned as a useful form of symbolic politics, on the ground, IRCA "had little detectable effect, either in deterring undocumented migrants or in raising the probability of their apprehension" (Massey et al. 2002: 140). Thus the influx of unauthorized immigrants continued in direct response to the explosive growth in employer demand for low-wage labor – demand that was generated by the processes of economic restructuring that steadily degraded the "good jobs" that had been widely available to non-college-educated U.S.-born workers up until the neoliberal turn of the 1970s.

Capital Mobility and Deindustrialization

One of the key forces reducing the availability of such jobs was deindustrialization. In capitalist economies it is not only labor but also capital that regularly moves from place to place, both within and across national borders. Some industries – construction and hospitality, for example – are place-bound, unable to operate outside of the local communities they serve. But manufacturing (and some service industries as well) can and often does relocate in pursuit of new consumer markets, to escape from unions and/ or government regulation, or in search of cheaper, more tractable labor. Indeed, soon after World War II a wave of factory closures swept the Northeastern and Midwestern "Rustbelt" as firms moved their operations to the "Sunbelt" (the South and Southwest), where wages were relatively low and unions were weak or nonexistent. In the 1970s and 1980s, when new technologies reduced transportation and communication costs, jobs increasingly left the nation entirely (Bluestone and Harrison 1982). Thus, as workers migrated to the United States from Mexico and other parts of the global South, capital was heading in precisely the opposite direction.

No one seriously suggests that rising immigration *caused* deindustrialization. But when employers abandoned industrial communities, workers often relocated as well, and sometimes immigrants arrived to replace them. The historic textile city of Lawrence, Massachusetts, exemplifies this phenomenon, as Llana Barber (2017) has documented. Shortly after World War II, the city's textile firms shifted the bulk of their production to the South, and by 1953 Lawrence had lost 18,000 textile jobs, lifting its unemployment rate to 20 percent. In response, many of the city's residents (99 percent of whom were white) moved out, mostly to nearby suburbs where affordable housing was increasingly available. Lawrence's population declined by 12 percent in the 1950s alone (ibid.: 27, 43–4). "At the same time that the city was undergoing disastrous disinvestment," Barber notes, "Puerto Rican, Dominican and Cuban immigrants began to arrive in Lawrence in the 1950s and 1960s" (ibid.: 3).

Some of the newcomers opened small businesses, helping to revitalize the local economy; others found low-wage jobs in the few factories that remained open. As Barber recounts, when Lawrence "lost its white ethnics to the suburbs, manufacturers scrambled to replace them with a new wave of migrants" (Barber 2017: 76). Some employers went so far as to offer bonuses to workers who recruited family members and friends into factory jobs. The influx of immigrants took place *after* the textile industry had devastated the city, yet many white residents "believed, mistakenly, that Lawrence was in a state of crisis because Latinos had *brought* poverty, blight and other 'urban problems' to the small city" (ibid.: 4). This prefigured the immigrant threat narrative that would become ubiquitous across the nation in later decades.

The textile firms that abandoned Lawrence and other parts of New England in the 1950s and 1960s were "runaway shops" that moved from the Rustbelt to the Sunbelt. But, starting in the 1970s, more and more capital mobility was international in scope. In those years plant closures spread rapidly across the United States – no longer confined to the Rustbelt – as firms facing declining profit rates and growing global competition turned to a "spatial fix" (Silver 2003). They unceremoniously abandoned the industrial communities that had flourished in the New Deal years, when unionization had provided millions of blue-collar workers with "middle-class" incomes. For example, American tire manufacturers closed twenty-four U.S. factories (eleven of them in the Sunbelt) between 1975 and 1981 alone while investing in new factories in Brazil, Turkey, and Spain. In the steel industry, similarly, U.S. companies closed dozens of domestic plants while investing extensively overseas (Bluestone and Harrison 1982: 37, 145–7).

One of the steel towns most affected by this process of disinvestment was Youngstown, Ohio, where unemployment climbed to nearly 25 percent as plant closures eliminated 50,000 jobs in steel and steel-related industries between 1977 and 1983 alone (Gest 2016: 79). Unionization fell sharply, and most of the blue-collar jobs that remained in the city were poorly paid and unstable. Like their counterparts in Lawrence decades earlier, many of

Youngstown's white working-class families "fled to the city's suburbs or left the region altogether to pursue work elsewhere," as Justin Gest has documented (2016: 82). Youngstown's population fell from 140,000 in 1970 to 96,000 twenty years later. Whites were overrepresented among those who departed: they formed 74 percent of the population in 1970 but only 59 percent in 1990; the rest were mostly African Americans (ibid.: 81, 139).

Unlike Lawrence, Youngstown did not attract a significant immigrant population; less than 3 percent of its residents were foreign born as late as 2013–17.[5] Nevertheless, many of the non-college-educated whites who remained in the city were "frustrated by the government's leniency about undocumented immigrants, who they believe are likely to work below established wages, driving them down for others." This frustration led many of them to support Donald Trump's 2016 presidential campaign (Gest 2016: 196). Even Trump did not suggest that foreign-born workers were to blame for the plant closures that devasted Rustbelt cities such as Youngstown, yet U.S.-born white workers affected by deindustrialization often embraced nativism anyway. This response had an eerie historical precedent in the pre-New Deal era. "Anger at displacement, blamed on 'aliens,' sometimes rested on actual experience but more often on imagination and fear stoked by demagoguery," Linda Gordon points out in her study of the Ku Klux Klan in the 1920s. "We know this because the Klan flourished in areas with few 'aliens'" (2017: 183). In contemporary Europe, similarly, Poland and Hungary, with the continent's lowest levels of immigration, are the nations most intolerant of immigrants (Kaushal 2019: 7, 10).

Management's Anti-Union Offensive

The most important driver of labor degradation in the neoliberal era was a concerted, multi-pronged managerial effort to reduce the power and influence of organized labor. The U.S. unionization rate had suffered slow but steady erosion since its peak in the mid-1950s, but in the late 1970s it went into free fall, dropping from 24 percent of all wage and salary workers in 1977 to 17 percent a decade later (see figure 2). In the private sector the decline was even sharper, as the unionization rate fell from 22 percent in 1977 to 13 percent in 1987. Although manufacturing was especially vulnerable because of the ever-present threat of outsourcing, place-bound sectors such as construction also experienced rapid de-unionization. The erosion continued in later decades, and by the century's end unionization rates had fallen to levels not seen since the early 1930s. By 2018, only 10.5 percent of all U.S. wage and salary workers, and only 6.4 percent of those in the private sector, were union members (Hirsch and Macpherson 2019).

De-unionization was not a spontaneous implosion but the result of a deliberate corporate offensive. In industries where they were strong, unions had managed to "take wages out of competition" during the New Deal era: industrywide collective bargaining agreements meant that all covered employers had similar labor costs, providing stability for both workers and firms alike. Under these conditions, competition among firms was based on the quality of goods or services and productivity, not squeezing labor. But in the neoliberal era the market fundamentalist credo that unions interfered with the "free" workings of the labor market, combined with increased global competition in tradeable industries, led to a full-scale corporate assault on organized labor. Employers devoted vast financial and human resources to weakening or eliminating unions where they were already entrenched, while systematically resisting any new organizing efforts that surfaced and implementing policies carefully designed to pre-empt future union drives. Those efforts took off in the 1970s (even earlier in some industries), but they became especially visible and pervasive after 1981. That was the year President Ronald Reagan summarily fired thousands of striking air traffic controllers, a draconian move with no precedent in the postwar period and one that employers read as a green light for their own escalating anti-union efforts.

Across the private sector, de-unionization brought stagnation or decline in workers' real wages, along with cutbacks in health insurance and other benefits, the widespread elimination of defined-benefit pensions, reduced job security, and deterioration in working conditions. Even workers who remained in the union fold experienced some of these effects: whereas, in the 1950s and 1960s, many non-union employers had matched union wages, benefits, and working conditions to discourage labor organizing, in the neoliberal era that dynamic was upended, as non-union competition drove down compensation and labor standards among unionized firms. At the same time, workers' ability to defend themselves was crippled as large-scale strikes – previously the most effective expression of union power and leverage – became conspicuous by their absence after 1980, when employers began routinely hiring "permanent replacements" for striking workers (Milkman 2013).

The most common response of workers impacted by de-unionization was to abandon their newly degraded jobs and search for alternative employment. As suggested in the epigraph to this chapter, once workers were effectively deprived of union representation and the accompanying ability to voice their concerns without fear of being fired, exit often was the most salient option.[6] Some were fortunate enough to find more desirable positions elsewhere, especially in the early phases of labor market restructuring, although that became increasingly difficult as the availability of good jobs for the non-college-educated continued to narrow. In Youngstown, for example, by the early twenty-first century most of the working-class jobs available were poorly paid "flexible positions that have replaced benefit-earning, longer-term roles and can be easily shed during declines in sales or in response to unexpected rises in overhead costs" (Gest 2016: 91).

In many industries employers began to recruit immigrants to fill the vacancies left by U.S.-born workers who abandoned de-unionized, degraded jobs for greener pastures. Some employers were initially wary of making this transition, but their doubts soon dissipated, and instead they came to regard immigrants as highly desirable, even ideal workers. Yet few of the management actors who orchestrated the efforts to weaken unions anticipated that their efforts would lead to a shift from U.S.-born to foreign-born labor. Their goal was simply to reduce labor costs and restore unilateral control over workplace decision-making. Indeed, immigrants are almost never mentioned in the vast scholarly literature on union decline in the neoliberal era. As sociologists Roger Waldinger and Claudia Der-Martirosian (2000: 52) note, there are "two distinct literatures" on immigration and unionization, each of which is "only peripherally aware of the other's existence."

To expose the interconnections between de-unionization and immigrant recruitment, the rest of this section explores the transformation of three industries: residential construction, building services, and meatpacking. They vary in regard to the timing of union decline as well as in the mechanisms of the transition to immigrant labor, but all three share the same basic trajectory. In each case, corporate-led attacks on unionism sparked an exodus of the U.S.-born from degraded jobs, followed by an influx of low-wage immigrant workers. It is noteworthy that outsourcing work to other countries was not a driver of union decline in any of these cases.

Residential construction

As Marc Linder has documented, business groups representing the interests of construction employers were among the first to aggressively attack trade unions, starting in the Vietnam War years. Leading the charge was the Business Roundtable, founded in 1968 to "move toward an organized counterattack on soaring [union] wage demands and declining productivity" in construction (Linder 2000: 182). Another major player was a trade association founded in the South in the 1950s, Associated Builders and Contractors (ABC), whose mission was to promote the non-union sector of the industry. In the early 1970s, ABC expanded its efforts to the national level (ibid.: 171). As a result of the efforts of such organizations, the unionization rate in construction was nearly halved between 1970 and 1990, falling from 42 to 22 percent. Although disaggregated data are not available, by all accounts the residential homebuilding sector was especially hard hit (Allen 1994: 426).

The key mechanism driving the de-unionization process in construction, an industry that had always relied on layers of subcontracting, was "double-breasting" – whereby the same corporate entities established twin union and non-union subsidiaries. The building trades unions challenged the legality of this practice, but they lost that battle in 1973 when a crucial National Labor Relations Board decision deemed it legitimate (Palladino 2005: 176). Always a cyclically sensitive industry, construction slowed dramatically during the recessions of the mid-1970s and early 1980s; during the subsequent recovery periods, non-union contractors gained ground by systematically underbidding their unionized counterparts. "The prices dropped out from underneath the union contractors," an employer recalled, "so they were unable to compete. Some double-breasted and went nonunion, but most of them went out of business" (Milkman 2006: 93). This process was concentrated in the residential sector of the industry.

In most regions of the country, the building trades unions' efforts to organize the growing ranks of non-union contractors were few and far between. Los Angeles, a city that anti-union construction employer groups such as ABC had targeted as an early proving ground for their campaigns, is a revealing example. Both residential and commercial construction in Los Angeles had been unionized wall-to-wall in the 1960s, but by 1987 the union share of the industry had declined to 53 percent. The losses were concentrated on the residential side, while in commercial construction the unions maintained a strong presence.[7] Thanks to a building boom in southern California during the 1980s, union jobs were plentiful in the commercial sector, and the building trades did little to resist the erosion of their power in residential construction. "That's all we cared about," a union official recalled. "Residential is a lost industry, we'll just concentrate on commercial" (Milkman 2006: 94). As a result, residential construction wages and working conditions spiraled downward. "Once the union was actually broken out of the business," a contractor declared, "these guys were taking a screwing, it was as simple as that" (ibid.: 94).

Similar processes unfolded across the country. In 1950 unions represented about half the residential construction workforce nationwide; but by the early 1970s that figure had plummeted to an estimated 20 percent (Rabourn 2008: 12). The building trades unions did little to counter this development. "With the memberships of many construction locals nearly fully employed on large public or commercial projects, few unionists were interested in residential work," a union researcher explained, adding that "The unions at the time generally were not oriented to organizing new workers" (ibid.: 14). Similarly, Linder (2000: 180) concluded, "Residential construction was not a primary battleground between unions and anti-union employers, but rather was abandoned to nonunion employers by default."

In 1977–8, 90.6 percent of unionized construction workers were white males, and that figure was nearly as high (89 percent) in 1989 (Allen 1994: 415). Despite the collapse of unionism in residential construction, initially the racial and ethnic (and gender) composition of the workforce remained stable. In 1980, when building trades unionism had already suffered major erosion, only 6 percent of the nation's construction workers (union and non-union combined) were Latinx; by 2000 that number had more than doubled, to 15 percent, about 70 percent of whom were foreign-born (Rabourn 2008: 15). But the influx of immigrants was geographically uneven. Los Angeles – which was growing rapidly and had a vast foreign-born working class – was on the leading edge: there Latinx workers, most of them immigrants, already made up over a third of the blue-collar construction labor force in 1990 (Milkman and Wong 2000: 178). Over time this transformation was widely replicated across the country, as U.S.-born workers abandoned the expanding low-wage, non-union segments of the industry, and employers increasingly recruited Latinx immigrants to replace them.

Once immigrants entered the local labor market, their numbers rapidly expanded, as immigrant kinship and social networks became active sources of recruitment. "It was like an atomic explosion," one L.A. construction contractor recalled. "One guy would get in and he'd bring two or three relatives, make a crew, and then one or two guys would split off that crew and make two new crews, and before you knew it, you had this huge number of people" (Milkman 2006: 110). But these networks were typically exploited by labor market intermediaries, known in this industry as labor brokers (among other terms), mostly bilingual Latinx middlemen with previous work experience in the industry to whom construction contractors increasingly turned over the tasks of hiring and training workers. These were functions that unions often had fulfilled previously, through hiring halls and apprenticeship programs. Thus the brokers moved into the vacuum created by union decline and created a system strikingly similar to that long established in California agriculture (see chapter 2). Paid a lump sum by employers to complete a particular set of tasks, the brokers recruited workers, arranged their housing and transportation (taking payroll deductions from already meager wages), and supervised the work itself.

Initially, some employers were skeptical about making the shift from hiring U.S.-born workers to taking on immigrants, but before long they were persuaded that the result had been an upgrade in the quality of labor. "The good old days of the Anglo-Saxon worker, there were good sides to it and there were bad sides to it," a contractor explained. "Communication was good. Work ethic was bad ... You really got the bottom of the work status in the white Anglos. Where in the Hispanic, you're getting mainstream, you're getting more of the family-oriented. For them, it was a good job. It was a much better job than picking strawberries. So you got a better class of worker" (Milkman 2006: 112).

Construction employers benefited from these arrangements in myriad ways: they were freed not only from the challenges of hiring and supervision but also from union work rules and grievance procedures. In the residential sector of the industry, where labor can account for as much as half of all production costs, the resulting savings sharply increased profits, and even the risk of cost overruns was now absorbed by the labor brokers. As one employer explained, "If you just put it out as so much money and let them [the brokers] worry about getting it done, you've already locked in your margin" (Milkman 2006: 96). The labor brokers were also responsible for compliance with immigration and employment laws and regulations, so that the contractors who used their services could simply look the other way if abuses attracted the attention of enforcement agencies or the wider public.

Workers themselves suffered pay and working conditions dramatically inferior to those that had existed when the residential sector was highly unionized, along with systematic violations of basic wage and employment laws. "Stories of workers being abused or shorted money are not uncommon," one researcher observed, adding that "Safety issues are often neglected as well" (Rabourn 2008: 17). As an L.A. union staffer recalled, many of the brokers took full advantage of the immigrants they recruited:

> They were controlling pools of thirty and forty people, living off these guys. They would give them twenty, thirty bucks a day. They could get away with this because in Mexico you're lucky if you were making $30 a week ... Some of [the brokers] had a big house and he had them live with him and he'd charge them rent. So he's whacking 'em twice. He charges 'em gas to go to work and he charges 'em for living with him. (Milkman 2006: 96)

A report from Nebraska similarly found that labor brokers "cheated construction workers out of overtime pay, improperly deducted money from their paychecks, and overcharged them on rent for apartments supplied by the brokers ... workers couldn't complain about injuries, improper paycheck deductions, or work conditions because they feared being fired" (Rabourn 2008: 17).

Building services

Whereas in construction the de-unionization process began in the 1960s, in the building services industry, which employs janitors to clean large commercial buildings and workers who perform related tasks, it took off in the late 1970s and the early 1980s. Even at the peak of union strength, compensation levels had never been as high for janitorial work as in construction, in part because the former requires less skill. Not coincidentally, while historically the construction trades were predominantly white and male, African Americans and Latinx workers had a longstanding presence among unionized janitors, as did women. Despite these differences, however, the two industries had one key structural feature in common: pervasive subcontracting. Indeed, the key mechanism driving union decline in building services, as in construction, was double-breasting.

By the 1950s, janitors in large commercial office buildings had been organized by the Service Employees International Union (SEIU) in major cities across the country. The first major wave of anti-union efforts in this industry followed the mid-1970s recession, when building owners were under growing pressure to cut costs and when hostility to organized labor was burgeoning in corporate circles. The SEIU-represented share of the industry in major U.S. metropolitan areas declined from 62 percent in 1977 to 52 percent in 1981 (Mines and Avina 1992: 429), although once again the national data obscure extensive geographical variation.

The 1980s was a period of consolidation among firms in the building services industry, with a flurry of mergers and acquisitions. The largest unionized companies were multinational corporations, in some cases headquartered outside the United States. But the anti-union offensive was led by U.S.-based executives who spun off new non-union janitorial firms from those unionized entities. As one contemporary analyst pointed out, many of the new non-union firms "seemed to have been formed with the knowledge, if not the outright assistance, of the management in certain unionized firms" (Mines and Avina 1992: 437). In short, the de-unionization of building services relied on the same double-breasting tactic that had so effectively undercut unions in the residential construction industry (Fisk et al. 2000: 201–5).

Large enough, and with leadership experienced enough, to persuade the owners of large commercial buildings that they could deliver high-quality professional services, the new non-union companies capitalized on the fact that building cleaning contracts typically had thirty-day cancellation clauses. This meant that, once a building switched to a non-union contractor, the union's only recourse was to organize that firm, which demanded extensive effort and expense. Moreover, even in the unlikely event that such organizing succeeded, the building owners could simply switch contractors once again. Once it took off in a given labor market, therefore, de-unionization became a downward spiral. To remain solvent in the face of growing non-union competition, the union firms put pressure on the SEIU to grant them wage and benefit concessions. As a result, janitorial pay and conditions deteriorated across the board (although they were significantly worse in the non-union sector).

The best-documented case of janitorial de-unionization is in Los Angeles, which was also the most popular destination of low-wage immigrants from Mexico and Central America in this period. As in construction, the growth of non-union building services was facilitated by the building boom experienced by the city in the 1980s. Its janitorial employment doubled between 1980 and 1990, and the Latinx immigrant share rose from 28 to 61 percent (Fisk et al. 2000: 202). Immigrants particularly dominated the non-union sector, but they also became a growing presence in the SEIU-represented part of the industry. The African-American share of the L.A. janitorial workforce declined from 31 percent in 1980 to 12 percent in 1990, while the white share fell from 24 to 11 percent over that decade. Yet because of the expansion of janitorial work during the 1980s, the absolute level of African-American employment held steady (ibid.), suggesting that forcible displacement was rare.[8]

The extent to which U.S.-born workers voluntarily abandoned the L.A. building services industry as de-unionization progressed cannot be determined from the available data. But, as janitorial pay and working conditions declined, many U.S.-born workers left for better opportunities. The city was growing rapidly at the time, and alternative employment options abounded. For African Americans in particular, who historically had made up a large share of the city's janitorial workforce, job opportunities were improving in this period as a result of the efforts of the civil rights movement. Indeed, data from other U.S. cities show that an influx of immigrants into the janitorial workforce occurred even where building services unionization remained intact. For example, in New York, where the SEIU did not experience significant membership erosion in this period and wages and benefits did not deteriorate, by 1990, 57 percent of all janitors were foreign-born, only slightly less than the 64 percent level in Los Angeles at that time (Milkman 2006: 106). Similarly, in Silicon Valley, where the non-union share of the industry increased only marginally in the 1980s and where Mexican, Filipino, and Portuguese workers had a longstanding presence among janitors, the immigrant share of the workforce rose in union and non-union firms alike as building service employment grew with the 1980s "tech" boom (Mines and Avina 1992: 441–4).

In the non-union sector, where wages were lower and working conditions far worse than in the part of the industry that remained unionized, Latinx immigrants, including many who were undocumented, became the dominant janitorial workforce in the 1980s in cities across the nation. Paralleling the rise of labor brokers in construction, bilingual "crew leaders" emerged as labor market intermediaries in non-union building services firms. As Richard Mines and Jeffrey Avina (1992: 432) reported in their study of California janitors in this period, management delegated "a great deal of decision-making power to Hispanic crew leaders, who typically recruit, hire, fire and pay workers. These foremen are aware of different networks of potential workers." As in construction, this arrangement opened the door to unscrupulous and illegal labor practices in non-union janitorial work, as the *Los Angeles Times* reported in mid-2000:

> He says he earns far less than the minimum wage, and just laughs when asked about overtime pay for his 56-hour weeks. Strong chemicals make his nose bleed, burn his fingers and eat the soles of his cheap sneakers ... Typically paid in cash or personal checks, with no deductions for Social Security, Medicare, or federal and state income tax, they [non-union janitors] are part of a thriving underground economy ... [None of the workers] could name the company for whom they worked. They knew only the subcontractor, who showed up twice a month to pay them in personal checks .... They told of weeks they went unpaid, of arbitrary schedule changes. (Cleeland 2000)

In non-union building services, as in residential construction, then, the pay and conditions of immigrant workers rapidly came to resemble those long entrenched in agriculture. Meatpacking, an industry where work was consolidated in large plants, is different in that respect, although it too underwent a "shift from the use of well-paid, unionized workers to a low-wage workforce composed almost entirely of immigrant labor from Mexico" (Champlin and Hake 2006: 49).

Meatpacking

As in construction and building services, managerial opposition to unionism was the primary driver of change in meatpacking, although, in contrast to those place-bound industries, capital mobility was part of the corporate toolkit as well. Beef and pork processing was not outsourced to other countries (although some poultry processing was).[9] But, in the 1970s and 1980s, many packinghouses did relocate from urban to rural areas within the United States "to reduce transportation costs and associated risks to livestock ... and not coincidentally to decrease the likelihood of union organizing" (Kandel and Parrado 2005: 452).

An influential ethnographic study of early twenty-first-century meatpacking argues that "the extent to which Latino/a immigrants 'displace' or 'replace' native-born whites and African Americans ... is difficult to untangle" (Ribas 2016: 60–1). A historical approach, however, goes a long way toward clarifying that question in regard to this industry. As Jackie Gabriel summarizes, "workers' bargaining power, as well as wages and working conditions, in the meatpacking industry declined *prior to* the rapid incorporation of Latino immigrants" (Gabriel 2006: 338, emphasis added). Similarly, Faranak Miraftab's study of a meatpacking plant in rural Illinois, where the workforce had once been entirely white and U.S-born, concludes, "It was the lowering of wages and the increasing harshness of labor conditions that turned the industry to ethnic and minority labor rather than the other way around" (Miraftab 2016: 53). Indeed, as detailed below, native-born workers abandoned the industry only *after* jobs had been degraded.[10] However, the architects of the meatpacking industry's restructuring, which took off in the 1960s and 1970s, were employers who aimed primarily to cut costs and weaken or eliminate unionism. At this point they do not appear to have envisioned the shift from a U.S.-born to a foreign-born workforce. In meatpacking, the shift to immigrant labor was triggered by labor shortages, largely unanticipated, in the rural communities where new plants were located.

Meatpacking had been notorious in the early twentieth century (when its labor force was also overwhelmingly foreign-born) for low pay, poor working conditions, and multiple occupational hazards, famously described in Upton Sinclair's 1904 novel *The Jungle*. But, in the 1930s and 1940s, unionization transformed the industry (Cohen 1990), successfully taking wages out of competition and dramatically improving conditions. By the 1960s unions represented 95 percent of U.S. meatpacking workers outside the South, and in 1969 wages in the industry were 115 percent of the national manufacturing average (Craypo 1994: 69–71; Stanley 1992: 109). Union contracts provided workers with health insurance, pensions, job security, grievance procedures, and a shop steward system that effectively limited managerial authority on the packinghouse floor. In this era "meatpacking was a high-wage industry which provided workers with middle class incomes. It was not uncommon for workers who had entered the plants as young adults to retire many years later with good retirement pensions" (Stanley 1992: 113).

However, in the 1960s a group of "new breed" meatpacking firms began to radically disrupt these arrangements. Leading the charge was Iowa Beef Packers (IBP), founded in 1960 by a pair of industry insiders – meat salesmen formerly employed by Swift & Co., one of the "Big Four" unionized firms that dominated the industry at the time (Brueggemann and Brown 2003: 332; Bjerklie 1996: 10). Over the next four decades, IBP grew into a corporate behemoth. By 1976 it was the single largest and most profitable U.S. beef packer (Craypo 1994: 66); a decade later it ranked as the world's largest hog slaughterer (Bjerklie 1996: 10). In 2001, IBP was acquired by poultry giant Tyson Foods, creating the world's largest "protein processing" company (Barboza and Sorkin 2001).

IBP's first major innovation was "boxed beef," introduced in the 1960s and adopted industrywide by the late 1970s. This transfer of boning and cutting operations from skilled supermarket-based butchers into the packinghouses, where the tasks involved were automated and subdivided, dramatically reduced beef processing costs. IBP also took the lead in the industry's geographical restructuring. Historically, most packinghouses had been located in urban centers where consumers and rail lines were concentrated, but in the 1970s IBP and the other new-breed firms began to situate their plants near sources of livestock instead. This innovation capitalized on the growing consolidation of cattle raising during the 1960s: by 1973 more than two-thirds of "final feeding" took place on large commercial feedlots, whereas a decade earlier most of it had occurred on small farms scattered across the country (Lauck 1998: 138). Relocating packinghouses near the feedlots not only cut transportation costs but also took advantage of the low wages and limited union presence in rural communities. Like boxed beef, this change was soon adopted industrywide. Between 1963 and 1984, the share of U.S. meatpacking workers in rural areas doubled from 25 to 50 percent (Horowitz 2002: 33).

"The biggest advantage enjoyed by the emerging firms involved labor costs," notes economic historian Jon Lauck, adding that "the meatpackers that established operations in the rural grain belt ... benefited from state right-to-work laws" (Lauck 1998: 153).[11] At first, however, the new breed companies were not impregnable to unionization: by the mid-1960s three of IBP's Iowa plants were organized, and after a bitter strike in 1969 workers also won union representation in the company's flagship plant in Dakota City, Nebraska. Even in its organized plants, however, IBP was able to negotiate wages lower than at other unionized packinghouses. It also expanded the use of conveyor belts ("disassembly lines"), speeding up the pace of work. Chain speeds were increased by up to 80 percent in some of the company's packinghouses. "Management truly ran the plants," an IBP official stated bluntly. In contrast to other unionized packinghouses, he added, "no restrictive agreements prevented the company from introducing productivity improvements" (ibid.: 155).

From the outset, organized labor was anathema for IBP. In the 1970s it closed or sold all of its unionized plants in Iowa while building new non-union facilities in Texas and Kansas. After a six-month lockout in 1973 in Dakota City, the union was forced to accept concessions that widened the wage gap between IBP and the industry's other unionized firms. Nine years later the company broke a strike at that plant, extracting an additional 12 percent wage cut (Craypo 1994: 73–4; Horowitz 2002). IBP's intransigent anti-unionism, like its other innovations, soon spread across the industry. "Old and new packers alike had to imitate IBP's anti-union model once its competitive efficiency was evident," notes labor economist Charles Craypo (1994: 88). Indeed, starting in the 1970s, all of the Big Four meatpacking companies demanded labor concessions. Other pressures on the industry were salient in this period as well. Consumer demand for beef was declining, creating significant excess capacity (Lauck 1998: 142). Meatpacking employment declined by nearly a third between 1960 and 1984, and over 400 beef and pork slaughterhouses were closed between 1972 and 1987 (Craypo 1994: 65, 75).

In response to these developments, in 1979 the Amalgamated Meat Cutters (which had absorbed the more militant United Packinghouse Workers union in 1968) merged with the Retail Clerks Union, which represented supermarket workers, to form the United Food and Commercial Workers (UFCW), creating the largest union in the AFL-CIO at the time. Two years later, facing unrelenting employer demands for concessions, coupled with threats of plant closures, the UFCW began what it called a "controlled retreat" in meatpacking, agreeing to an industrywide wage freeze. From 1979 to 1990, real wages in the industry fell 30 percent, and by 1990 its wages were 20 percent below the U.S. manufacturing average (Horowitz 2002: 35; Stanley 1992: 109).

The failed 1985–6 strike at Hormel's plant in Austin, Minnesota, marked another turning point in the union's downward spiral. Hormel's labor costs once had been the industry's highest (Lauck

1998: 156), but in 1978 the company extracted extensive concessions from the Austin workforce, and six years later it cut wages there by 23 percent. When workers went on strike in 1985, Hormel hired replacement workers and kept the plant open. Austin's Local P-9 and the UFCW's national leadership were bitterly divided on strike strategy; after a year the dispute was settled largely on the employer's terms (Craypo 1994: 86; Rachleff 1993).

With far less drama, dozens of other unionized packinghouses closed in the 1980s. Some later reopened on a non-union basis, but meanwhile the industry's center of gravity had shifted decisively to the rural right-to-work states. In 1992, UFCW contracts still covered about two-thirds of all beef-packing workers, but the union's once formidable power had been eviscerated. By then only six of IBP's nine plants were unionized; even more significantly, wages in union plants industrywide were a mere 2.4 percent higher than those in non-union plants (Craypo 1994: 79–80). Reduced pay and benefits were accompanied by a rapid speedup in the pace of work and a spike in occupational injuries (Horowitz 2002: 35–6). By 1990, meatpacking was the most dangerous industry for workers in America (Craypo 1994: 77–8; Human Rights Watch 2004).

Once the union was effectively defanged and jobs in the industry thereby degraded, the composition of the workforce began to change, as the U.S.-born workers who had historically formed the overwhelming majority of the meatpacking labor force increasingly abandoned it. Some groups, for example African Americans in Chicago, a central node of the industry in the Big Four era, may have been displaced as production moved to rural locations, although in this period their job opportunities were expanding as a result of the civil rights movement. But more often, as meatpacking jobs became increasingly undesirable, U.S.-born workers voluntarily exited (or declined to enter) the industry.

The most dramatic upheaval in the meatpacking labor force took place not in the cities but instead in the sparsely populated rural communities to which the industry increasingly migrated in the 1970s and 1980s. A unionized pork-packing plant in Storm Lake, Iowa, that closed down in 1981 and then reopened as a non-union IBP operation the following year – with wages cut to half the former rate – illustrates the basic dynamic. By 1996, the Storm Lake facility would grow into the world's second-largest pork-processing plant (Grey 1996: 14). In 1982, the town, devastated by the plant closing the previous year, "welcomed IBP as its savior," a journalist noted. "To the wage-starved community, [it] sounded like an investment by Fort Knox" (Bjerklie 1996: 12). IBP initially hired from the local population – overwhelmingly white and native-born – but that soon proved unsustainable. While, under the previous owner, the Storm Lake plant had a stable workforce and "extremely low" turnover (ibid.), with the degradation of pay and conditions that the new managerial regime introduced, turnover spiked upward. The resulting labor shortage led IBP to start recruiting Latinxs from Texas and southern California, as well as Asian refugees (Grey 1997: 249).

> IBP filled its labor rolls with others from the region. Soon, however, a growing work force and high turnover and injury rates forced the plant to look elsewhere. In many cases, new workers arrived from out of state. Most of the new workers were minorities, immigrants, or refugees. By 1992, IBP employed 1200 workers [at Storm Lake], one-third of whom were immigrants or refugees from Laos or Mexico. (Grey 1995: 257–8)

This plant's shift to foreign-born labor was accelerated further by IBP's deep anti-union animus. It hired only thirty workers from among a few hundred who had worked at Storm Lake under the previous owner and who applied for IBP jobs when the plant reopened. In part, this high rejection rate reflected "high wage expectations," but reportedly the main reason was that most workers with union experience were deliberately excluded. One such worker whom IBP did hire was abruptly fired after he launched a union organizing effort inside the plant (Grey 1995: 256–7). But, even if all of the rejected applicants from this group had been hired, the local labor supply would soon have been exhausted as a result of the plant's skyrocketing turnover rate. Indeed, in non-union meatpacking in this period, annual turnover was typically as much as 100 percent, and even higher in newly established plants (Grey 1999: 17; 1997: 256). IBP's packinghouse in Lexington, Nebraska, which opened in 1990, had an annual turnover rate of 250 percent in its first 21 months of operation.

As at Storm Lake, IBP's other plants hired U.S.-born workers at first. "The company has for years dispatched recruiting teams to poor communities throughout the United States," Eric Schlosser reported in his bestselling book *Fast Food Nation*. "It has recruited homeless people living at shelters in New York, New Jersey, California, North Carolina and Rhode Island. It has hired buses to import these workers from thousands of miles away" (Schlosser 2001: 162). However, such efforts proved inadequate to address the company's ever-expanding need for labor. At IBP's Lexington plant, as at Storm Lake a decade earlier, "During start-up [late 1990] 81% of those hired were non-Hispanic, but by the end of the study period [mid-1992], that figure had fallen to 37%." By 1997, Latinx workers made up three-quarters of the plant's workforce, and smaller numbers of Asian refugees were employed there as well (Gouveia and Stull 1997: 6, 8).

In Lexington, IBP initially focused its labor recruitment efforts on the region surrounding the plant and the wider Great Plains area. At first this approach was adequate: "print and electronic advertisements in packing towns, and pockets of high unemployment continued to bring in a steady flow of applicants" (Gouveia and Stull 1997: 9). As a company official told a researcher, local women were also a key recruitment target. IBP "projected that 60 percent of the processing workers would be women, mostly single mothers or farm wives" (ibid.: 8). With that in mind, the plant even set up an on-site day-care center. Yet the female share of the plant's workforce fell from 29 percent at the outset to 20 percent a year later as a result of the soaring turnover among U.S.-born workers (ibid.: 9). Soon the plant began to recruit workers further afield. "Company officials say they want to fill labor needs locally, but given plant size, the limited labor pool in and around Lexington, and high turnover, IBP rapidly runs through the local supply of willing workers," even with bonuses offered to workers for recruiting new hires. "The majority of jobs in the meatpacking industry are unattractive to native-born workers," the researchers concluded (ibid.).

Other case studies offer similar assessments, such as Faranak Miraftab's ethnographic study of a Cargill pork-processing plant in Beardstown, Illinois, that had formerly been operated by Oscar Meyer, which closed it after a prolonged labor dispute. In 1987, Cargill bought the plant and reopened it on a non-union basis with much lower wages. "Some of the senior workers were able to change their line of work to better paying jobs ... some left town. By the late 1980s, following wage cuts, the company faced a labor shortage: workers in the area were not willing to take the lower-paying jobs ... in the early 1990s, the plant management turned to recruitment among immigrants" (Miraftab 2016: 7).

U.S.-born workers shunned non-union meatpacking jobs in the South as well, as a study based on interviews with human resource managers in meat-processing and other low-wage manufacturing industries in North Carolina found. "These low wage, high stress manufacturing firms simply could not compete for native workers with the low wage service sector firms," the researchers reported, adding that, in fast-food jobs, "wages were comparable but the work was air-conditioned" (Leiter et al. 2001). Similarly, demographers William Kandel and Emilio A. Parrado (2005: 467) concluded in their study of meatpacking that "Immigrants are not substitutes for native workers. Instead they appear to be taking unstable, unpleasant and often low-paying jobs in declining sectors of the economy that better-educated native residents find unattractive."

The transition from U.S.-born to immigrant labor unfolded across the U.S. meatpacking industry in the 1980s and 1990s, although its timing and magnitude varied widely. At one IBP plant the Latinx share of the workforce grew from 8 to 22 percent between 1984 and 1992, while at another it rose from 27 to 63 percent over that period (Gouveia and Stull 1997: 8). A 1988 survey of fifteen plants at the nation's three largest meatpacking firms (including IBP) found that the foreign-born share of the workforce ranged from 3 to 60 percent. In Iowa and Minnesota, this survey found, the industry's workforce was still predominantly white and native-born, while in Nebraska, Kansas, Colorado, and Texas the majority of workers were Mexican immigrants and Asian refugees (Stanley 1992: 110). But the overall trend was unmistakable:

> Plant closures and relocations, lower wages, and increased injury rates have led to the decline of the "traditional" labor force even as increased turnover rates have resulted in a higher absolute demand for labor. This demand has been met by Asian refugees, Mexican immigrants, and native-born white and Mexican-American migrants, many of them actively recruited by the meatpacking firms. While their employment in the industry has coincided with the deterioration of wages and working conditions, *this has been more the result of that deterioration, rather than its cause.* (Ibid.: 113)

Meatpacking shop-floor managers were uneasy at first about the change from a U.S.-born to an immigrant workforce.[12] A study conducted at a pork-processing plant in Iowa at the point when more than a third of the hourly workforce was still U.S.-born is revealing in this regard. Almost all the supervisors and managers at the facility were male "Anglos" who had started out as hourly workers and worked their way up within the company ranks. They openly acknowledged to the researchers that they were "uncomfortable" with "the industry's growing reliance on immigrants, particularly Latinos." Indeed, this study found that many immigrant workers at the plant quit their jobs because of conflict with supervisors (Grey 1999: 24–5). At another packinghouse studied in the early 1990s, when about half the workforce was foreign-born, immigrant workers similarly "complained of poor relations with management ... lack of recognition and respect ... and poor communication (including, but not limited to, language barriers)" (Gouveia and Stull 1997: 20).

But management attitudes toward immigrants changed over time, and by the early twentieth century most managers had developed a decisive preference for immigrants over U.S.-born workers. López-Sanders's ethnographic study of a South Carolina meatpacking plant – one of many that opened in the South in the 1990s and early 2000s in a new phase of the industry's expansion

– documents a deliberate effort to replace African-American workers with Latinx immigrants. "When employers talked about Hispanics they always referred to them as 'hard workers,' 'reliable' and 'dependable,'" López-Sanders reports, adding that "Native born workers complained and developed 'an attitude' ... about the increased demands placed on them. Immigrant workers, on the other hand, expressed no complaints" (López-Sanders 2009: 14, 17, 24; see also Johnson-Webb 2002; Waldinger and Lichter 2003). At this plant the Latinx presence grew in a single year from only two people to over a third of the workforce.

Meatpacking employers' immigrant recruitment efforts initially targeted those who had already settled in the United States. About half of the Latinx workers at the Lexington IBP plant in 1992 came from California or elsewhere in the Southwest, where many had been employed as farm workers (Gouveia and Stull 1997: 16). And at a unionized IBP plant in Perry, Iowa, where anthropologist Deborah Fink worked in the mid-1990s, the bulk of the Latinx immigrant workers had been recruited from East Los Angeles (Fink 1998: 145). Many employers also encouraged immigrant workers themselves to recruit their friends and family members. "The company pays us a bounty of two hundred dollars for a worker we recommend who stays at least three months," a foreign-born meatpacking worker in Omaha, Nebraska, told a researcher in 2003 (Human Rights Watch 2004: 108; see also Fink 1998: 149). Soon immigrant workers were also being recruited directly from their home countries. Schlosser reported in 2001 that IBP "maintains a labor office in Mexico City, runs ads on Mexican radio stations offering jobs in the United States, and operates a bus service from rural Mexico to the heartland of America (Schlosser 2001: 162). Another study found that meatpacking employers "regularly contact their regional consulates to inquire about recruiting Mexican nationals" (Johnson-Webb 2002: 411).

Managers also engaged "supervisory staff and various types of intermediaries and other agents that provide specialized services to would-be migrants and new immigrants for fees or sinecures paid for by the immigrants and/or their employers" (Krissman 2005: 13). For example, IBP hired a trilingual agent (she spoke English,

Low German and Spanish) to help recruit Mennonite workers from Chihuahua, Mexico, to the plant in Storm Lake. "Not only did this agent provide access to potential workers, but she processed their immigration applications (for a fee), thereby ensuring her role as gatekeeper to IBP jobs" (Grey 1996: 17). That plant also hired as a personnel representative a Laotian refugee who had resided in the area for years and become a naturalized citizen. "Not only was he instrumental in early direct recruitment of refugees, but he also had the power to decide which refugees would be hired ... and [he was] key to their continued employment" (ibid.: 15). Similarly, at a Nebraska beef-processing plant, as a worker explained in a 2003 interview, the personnel manager "is a Mexican. He knows who is undocumented and who isn't, and he holds that over us. He says, 'I know how you got here' and 'I know you don't have papers but I'm going to take care of you.' That just makes people afraid of crossing him" (Human Rights Watch 2004: 111).

In meatpacking, such intermediaries had less power and autonomy than the labor brokers in construction or the crew leaders in janitorial work described earlier: workers received company paychecks and their work was not directly supervised by labor recruiters. Yet intermediaries often did influence (or, in some cases, control) hiring and firing. Most were handsomely compensated for their efforts – not only by employers but also by the immigrants they recruited. As Fred Krissman argues, they also served to obscure the centrality of employers to the immigrant recruitment and hiring process:

> Many employers have claimed not to know how they obtain their own workers, even though they readily admit that access to an ample supply of low cost labor is critical to the continued viability of their labor-intensive operations ... Layers of supervisory personnel and/or the use of labor contractor firms help employers maintain plausible deniability vis-à-vis ... health, safety, labor, and/or immigration violations in their workplaces, and generally helps them evade criminal penalties for the illegal activities that they foster. (Krissman 2005: 31)

Despite meatpacking's notoriously dangerous and dirty working conditions, for many immigrants it was a big step up from employment in agriculture. "To farm workers who've labored outdoors, ten hours a day, for the nation's lowest wages, meatpacking jobs often seemed too good to be true," Schlosser declares, noting that "cutting meat in a Colorado or Nebraska slaughterhouse can pay almost twice" as much as picking strawberries in California (Schlosser 2001: 162). "The workers say these are the good jobs, the ones that pay *mucho dinero* ... the ones that command workers respect in their communities," reports Vanesa Ribas (2016: xv). Deborah Fink, similarly, notes that "IBP meant good money" to her Latinx co-workers. "Many believed they were doing well ... They knew that their attraction to IBP was their willingness to do jobs under conditions that Yankees would not accept" (Fink 1998: 150).

In the early twenty-first century, the meatpacking firms expanded beyond the Midwestern right-to-work states where the industry had become concentrated in the 1980s. They opened new plants in the deep South (where poultry processing had long been centered), which had even lower unionization rates and wages to match. In this region, many meatpacking employers recruited African-American workers to work in the plants alongside recent immigrants, and relations between the two groups were often fraught. Yet one ethnographer who conducted participant observation in a North Carolina pork-processing plant found that, despite the fact that many Latinx workers viewed the African Americans in the plant negatively, the African-American workers themselves did "not talk or behave as if they are especially threatened by economic, political or cultural competition from Latinos/migrants" (Ribas 2016: 24).[13]

In any case, immigrants had become the dominant workforce in meatpacking by the early twenty-first century. It is impossible to determine precisely the extent of unauthorized employment in the industry, but estimates range from 20 to 50 percent (Champlin and Hake 2006: 63). Employers consistently professed ignorance of this reality, especially after 1986, when IRCA made hiring undocumented immigrants illegal. But there is substantial evidence that, as López-Sanders (2009: 14) argues, "foreign-born Hispanics were preferred [by employers] to native-born Hispanics, and Hispanics with a tenuous legal status were the most favored of all."

On the other hand, in the mid-2000s meatpacking plants became a frequent target of workplace raids by U.S. Immigration and Customs Enforcement (ICE) – not because they employed a higher proportion of unauthorized immigrants than workplaces in other low-wage industries, but simply because these workers were so conveniently concentrated in large plants, in contrast to far-flung construction sites, office buildings, or agricultural fields. On December 12, 2006, in the largest workplace immigration raid in U.S. history, "Operation Wagon Train," ICE agents swept through six Swift & Company meatpacking plants simultaneously (in six different states) and detained over 1,300 workers for immigration violations, most of whom were later deported (Preston 2006a, 2006b). A year and a half later, the industry was in the headlines again when ICE raided a kosher meatpacking plant in Postville, Iowa, and arrested hundreds of workers (Saulny 2008). Workplace raids were rare in the Obama years, but the Trump administration has revived them, with meatpacking and poultry prominently included (Elk 2018; Jordan 2018, 2019).

In residential construction, building services, and meatpacking alike, employers' deliberate efforts to weaken or eliminate unions drove down wages and benefits, degraded working conditions, and eliminated job security. Whenever they could, U.S.-born workers responded by abandoning the jobs affected. To fill the vacancies, employers then recruited immigrants, both authorized and undocumented, with the help of labor market intermediaries, reproducing labor practices long established in agriculture. Violations of minimum wage laws and other abuses became increasingly widespread, especially among unauthorized immigrants, again recalling conditions that had long prevailed in agriculture.

Deregulation and Subcontracting

In some industries, labor degradation was not the direct result of an employer anti-union offensive but instead was driven by deregulation, which indirectly spurred union decline. A case in point is the trucking industry. The Motor Carrier Act of 1980 eliminated both price regulation and rules restricting entry to the industry that had been in place since the New Deal era (Belzer 2000: 57–67).[14] Immediately after its passage, unionization declined sharply, leading to a precipitous fall in earnings and benefits. The legislation also led to a shift away from standard forms of employment and greater use of owner-operators and "independent contractors."

Supporters of trucking deregulation, many of whom explicitly targeted unionism as an obstacle to market efficiency, included the National Association of Manufacturers and the major international shipping companies. Most trucking firms, as well as the Teamsters union, which represented a large part of the industry's workforce at the time, opposed deregulation (Moore 1986: 17–18; Belzer 2000: 58). But, in a period when the volume of imports was rapidly expanding, the powerful shipping firms and their retail customers were eager to reduce the cost of moving containers inland from the nation's ports, and their interests ultimately prevailed.

In 1979, when the Motor Carrier Act became law, 60 percent of the nation's truck drivers were union members; twenty years later that figure had plummeted to only 25 percent, with the bulk of the decline taking place in the early 1980s (Rose 1987: 1162; Perry 1986: 110). Drivers' wages went into free fall, health and pension benefits evaporated, and working conditions deteriorated rapidly, as the industry devolved into what Michael Belzer (2000) aptly calls "sweatshops on wheels." Even among truckers who remained unionized, concession bargaining in the early 1980s led to deep erosion of compensation and benefits. In addition, many unionized firms began double-breasting, setting up non-union subsidiaries that recruited drivers as independent contractors instead of employees. As barriers to entry fell, small firms proliferated and cutthroat competition flourished, putting still more downward pressure on truckers' earnings. As Belzer (2000: 7) summarizes, "low wages, long hours, and unsafe and unsanitary working conditions" like those in the pre-New Deal era "have returned to trucking."

Short-haul trucking from the nation's ports experienced the largest upheaval, especially on the West Coast, whereas in long-distance trucking the union maintained a precarious foothold. Ground shipping prices fell, but this was not a result of market efficiency, as advocates of deregulation had promised: instead an estimated 80 percent of the savings came directly from reductions in truckers' earnings (Belzer 2000: 45). At the ports, far from illustrating the virtues of unfettered market competition, the industry exemplified exactly the opposite: as the number of small firms proliferated, and as more and more port truckers became independent contractors paid by the truckload instead of by the hour, chronic delays at shipping terminals became a conspicuous example of market failure.

More generally, in the new deregulated environment, as small firms and owner-operators replaced the large, unionized trucking companies that previously had dominated the industry, market risks were increasingly transferred to workers. Drivers (U.S.- and foreign-born alike) were often genuinely attracted by the idea of "being my own boss" and thus embraced the status of independent contractor: "There is the promise that through hard work and putting in extra hours, they might be able to make some money and move up and become a real independent business owner" (Bonacich and Wilson 2008: 215–16). But the downside was that they were forced to absorb all the costs of owning and maintaining the trucks, and they were newly vulnerable to unpredictable fluctuations in fuel prices, fines for overweight loads, traffic bottle-necks, and other factors beyond their control. Drivers no longer covered by union contracts also lost health insurance and pension coverage, sick pay, and paid vacations. Nationwide, truck drivers' real earnings fell by 21 percent between 1973 and 1995, nearly twice the average decline for blue-collar workers in that period (Belman and Monaco 2001: 502).

As an industry insider explained, in the post-deregulation era trucking became a highly stratified occupation:

> At the top are full-time employees of major trucking companies that pay well and provide extensive benefits. Many of these jobs are still unionized …

Owner-operators are farther down the pyramid, and tiers exist within this segment. From best to worst they are contract logistics, domestic and international. Within these strata, owner-operators have varying levels of market freedom to seek higher compensation and better working conditions. At the bottom of the pyramid are owner-operators hauling international containers ... After expenses, many of them make about $6 an hour, less than what many fast food jobs pay. (Prince 2005: 13)

The industry still includes many true owner-operators, especially in its long-haul segment, but whether port truckers fit the legal definition of "independent contractors" is hotly disputed. A 2006 survey of port truckers in Houston found that 90 percent "belong to a trucking company," their nominal status as independent contractors notwithstanding (Harrison et al. 2007: 33). In other jurisdictions, numerous court cases have argued that port truckers are misclassified as independent contractors and that they should instead be treated as employees, with all the legal protections that status confers (Jaffee and Bensman 2016; Smith et al. 2014). At the ports, the trucking companies typically make all the arrangements for drivers to purchase or lease trucks, providing access to financing and insurance as well. The drivers are then required to pay all the associated costs, while the companies no longer have any obligation to pay workers' compensation, unemployment insurance, or other payroll taxes. Moreover, since as "independent contractors" these drivers are considered self-employed, they are not covered by minimum wage or overtime laws or other basic employment protections. Most drivers work for one and only one firm, which assigns them to pick up specific loads.

These truckers often earn less than the legal minimum wage, and in some cases their expenses actually exceed their revenues (Murphy 2017; Viscelli 2016: 145). As independent contractors, they are paid by the load, not by the hour (as they were before 1980) and receive no compensation while waiting to receive their cargo at the ports – waits that can consume many hours (Harrison et al. 2007: 35; Prince 2005: 13; Milkman 2006: 178–9). Truck lease agreements often include draconian penalties for missing a payment or for any absences from work (Murphy 2017). Moreover, many such agreements stipulate that a contractor who does not complete the full term of the lease is nevertheless responsible for all future payments, an arrangement that "traps drivers in a form of debt peonage," as Steve Viscelli (2016: 148) puts it.

As deregulation transformed port trucking from a well-paid, unionized job into a poorly paid, highly precarious one, many U.S.-born drivers abandoned that segment of the industry; some shifted into long-haul trucking and others into new lines of work. As the *Journal of Commerce*, a logistics trade publication, reported in 2005:

> As long as trucking paid as well as flipping burgers, the "chrome and cowboy" aspects of the job were reason to be driving.
>
> However, today fast-food jobs look increasingly attractive to many former truck drivers, especially in high-cost areas such as New York–New Jersey and California. An owner-operator earning $20,000 to $25,000 a year is likely to be working 60 to 70 hours a week for it. ...
>
> Qualified drivers are migrating to better-paying trucking jobs in truckload, construction and other sectors. (Prince 2005: 13–14)

As Bonacich and Wilson (2008: 212) summarize, starting in the 1980s, port trucking "gradually ... shifted to an immigrant occupation, as mostly white native-born drivers left the industry and Latino immigrants entered." As in residential construction, documenting this transition is difficult because the available data do not disaggregate the various segments of the industry. Nationally, according to U.S. Census data, the foreign-born proportion of truck drivers grew from 3 percent in 1970 to 9 percent in 2000. In the five-county Los Angeles metropolitan area, home to the nation's largest ports and also to a vast foreign-born population, that proportion grew from 8 to 41 percent over the same period (Milkman 2006: 108, 200). Although comprehensive data are not available for port truckers specifically, surveys and a variety of qualitative sources show that, by the late twentieth century, the vast majority of those working at the Los Angeles and Long Beach ports were foreign-born (Milkman 2006). Bonacich and Wilson found that the Latinx proportion of port truckers there doubled between 1984 and 1986 alone, and that by the early twenty-first century it was 92 percent Latinx (2008: 213, 215).

Data are even more fragmentary for other port cities. A 2006 survey found that the majority of port truckers in Seattle were immigrants (Port Jobs 2006). That same year, in a survey of Houston port truckers (which did not ask about place of birth), 37 percent of respondents completed the questionnaire in Spanish (Harrison et al. 2007: 33). Another study found that the majority of New Jersey's port truckers are Latinx (Jaffee and Rowley 2009). In contrast to most other industries that employ primarily foreign-born workers, however, unauthorized immigrants are few and far between among port truckers, who must obtain commercial driver's licenses and who may be subject to security checks by federal officials. In Los Angeles and Long Beach, a 2004 survey found that 57 percent of port truckers were U.S. citizens, although only 11 percent were U.S.-born (Bonacich and Wilson 2008: 215).

Deregulation was the key driver of union decline and labor degradation in this industry, but the conversion of truckers' hourly jobs into independent contractor positions, and the accompanying transfer of market risk to drivers, is equally significant. Independent contracting proliferated in a variety of other industries starting in the 1970s. Some of them, for example taxi driving, remained highly regulated – yet with similarly deleterious effects on wages and working conditions. (The platform-based ride companies such as Uber and Lyft that emerged more recently are relatively unregulated, but the classification of their drivers as independent contractors is a continuing topic of contention.) The proliferation of independent contractors is one aspect of a far larger phenomenon that David Weil (2014) terms "the fissured workplace," the product of efforts by large firms to focus on their "core" business and to outsource functions such as payroll processing, graphic design, office cleaning, and food service. This form of subcontracting-based cost-cutting typically reduces compensation for workers and renders their employment more precarious. Indeed, its proliferation has transformed the jobs of millions of U.S.-born workers as well as those of immigrants such as the port truckers.

Conclusion

Despite all the drawbacks of independent contracting, the appeal of the entrepreneurial aspect of trucking elevated it to the top of the job queue for low-wage male immigrant workers relative to the other occupations considered in this chapter. Meatpacking came next in the pecking order: despite its intensity and extreme occupational hazards, at least it was part of the formal economy, so that workers received company payroll checks and unions, albeit with far less power than in the past, had an ongoing presence. Non-union residential construction and janitorial jobs were less desirable, largely because in these industries employers' extensive reliance on labor brokers replicated some of the most exploitative features of agricultural labor – even if the work was far less physically taxing. Indeed, agriculture itself remained at the very bottom of the job queue for immigrant workers.

In the neoliberal era that began in the mid-1970s, the effects of deindustrialization, de-unionization and deregulation combined to rapidly erode the improvements in pay, benefits, and working conditions that non-college-educated workers had achieved in the New Deal era. Many unionized manufacturing jobs left the United States entirely. In place-bound industries such as construction, building services, and meatpacking, employers' efforts to weaken or eliminate unions led to the rapid degradation of many formerly high-wage jobs. In other cases, such as trucking, deregulation produced similar results. In response, U.S.-born workers increasingly abandoned the industries affected. The most fortunate among them moved into commercial construction or long-distance trucking, or similar sectors where high pay, extensive benefits, and union protections remained largely intact. Meanwhile, employers recruited immigrants to fill the vacancies that proliferated in the newly degraded jobs that U.S.-born workers disdained.

Male workers predominate in all the industries discussed in this chapter, although both building services and meatpacking included women in substantial numbers. In contrast, chapter 4 focuses on female-dominated sectors such as domestic work and nail salons and on the gender-mixed restaurant industry. In such "personal service" industries, the shift from U.S.-born to immigrant labor was predicated not on job degradation but instead on the spectacular growth of economic inequality in the neoliberal period. Although union decline was prominent among the forces leading to widening inequality, its effect was indirect; indeed, unionization was weak or nonexistent in the industries discussed in chapter 4 (with the partial exception of restaurants, where unions took root in a few U.S. cities in the early twentieth century). Instead the dynamic driving employment in personal services was the growing income gap between the haves and the have-nots.

4

Growing Inequality and Immigrant Employment in Paid Domestic Labor and Service Industry Jobs

The rich are rich because they can afford to buy other people's time. They can hire other people to make their beds, tend their gardens, and drive their cars. These are not privileges that become more widely available as people become more affluent. If all workers' wages rise at the same rate, the highly paid professional will have to spend a constant percentage of his [*sic*] income to get a maid, a gardener, or a taxi.

Christopher Jencks et al. (1972)

Inequality in income and wealth grew explosively in the United States starting in the late 1970s, alongside (and largely as a result of) the processes of deindustrialization, de-unionization, and deregulation discussed in chapter 3. The fortunes of the legendary "1 percent" rose most dramatically, while those in the top 20 percent of the income distribution also enjoyed substantial gains. For the rest of the population, however, real incomes stagnated or even declined (Piketty and Saez 2014; Reeves 2017). De-unionization alone accounted for one-fifth to one-third of the growth in income inequality between 1973 and 2007 and contributed to erosion of the New Deal era's egalitarian norms as well (Western and Rosenfeld 2011). In a direct reversal of the "Great Compression" from the 1940s to the 1960s, when U.S. income inequality sank to a record low (Goldin and Margo 1992), over the following four decades it soared to a new high (Piketty and Saez 2014: 839). Inequality in wealth also increased sharply in these years, ushering in what some commentators have dubbed the "New Gilded Age" (Krugman 2002).

Growing economic inequality stimulated increased demand for paid domestic workers and for a variety of other services catering to the needs and desires of affluent individuals and families. At the same time, the aging of the population and rising labor force participation among mothers of young children generated growing demand for in-home eldercare and child-care workers, respectively. Employment also expanded for housecleaners and in occupations such as food preparation and serving, as well as for manicurists and others providing "beauty services." Many of these fields had previously relied on U.S.-born low-wage women workers, typically African Americans and other women of color, but in the late twentieth century immigrants from the global South increasingly dominated these low-wage service-sector jobs.

In contrast to residential construction, building services, meatpacking, and trucking, domestic and service workers never had been extensively unionized; indeed, these poorly paid, low-status female-dominated occupations had long been at or near the bottom of the job queue. Nor were such jobs further degraded by the labor market restructuring that took off in the 1970s. Instead the African-American and other women of color historically concentrated in these fields abandoned them once the civil rights movement opened up better employment opportunities in the formal sector of the labor market, from which these workers had previously been excluded.

Demand for domestic and service workers thus expanded just as the labor supply historically associated with these types of work was being depleted. In response to the resulting labor shortages, more and more female immigrants (and a few male immigrants) were drawn into these sectors. Their entry was facilitated by changes in U.S. immigration law, starting with the 1986 Immigration Reform and Control Act (IRCA). As noted in chapter 4, the tightening of border enforcement under IRCA and subsequent laws had the unintended consequence of transforming the composition and character of migration. As the costs of repeated border crossings soared, many male migrants who had previously oscillated back and forth from Mexico now opted to stay in the United States permanently, and their wives and other family members often followed (Massey et al. 2002). That was one source of increased female immigration to the United States; another was that growing numbers of women from Latin America and elsewhere in the global South immigrated independently of their families in this period – partly in response to surging demand for labor in domestic work and other service jobs.

The Impact of Rising Inequality on Domestic and Personal Service Work

"The demands placed on the top-level professional and managerial workforce in global cities are such that the usual modes of handling household tasks and lifestyle are inadequate," noted Saskia Sassen at the turn of the twenty-first century. "As a consequence we are seeing the return of the co-called 'serving classes' ... made up largely of immigrant men and women" (Sassen 2001: 322). Demand for household services has indeed expanded since the late 1970s, and, crucially, the growing polarization of income and wealth in the same period made those services increasingly affordable for the affluent. The critical driver was not the *absolute* amount of income or wealth available to potential service consumers but, rather, the growing gap between rich and poor. Latent demand for assistance with domestic tasks is always present (especially in households with young children); it becomes effective demand only when "help" is easily affordable. With growing economic inequality, income disparities widened and the *relative* cost of domestic help (and various other personal services) fell.

Until recently, the sociological literature on paid domestic work largely ignored this dynamic, focusing instead on the qualitative aspects of interaction between domestic workers and their employers. But over the years a few commentators have recognized the relationship between inequality and the extent of employment in domestic labor, including Christopher Jencks and his colleagues, as quoted in the epigraph to this chapter, writing in 1972. Decades earlier, Nobel laureate George S. Stigler similarly observed that "The wealth of a nation has no obvious effect upon the number of servants," adding that "the *equality* of the distribution of income, rather than the amount, may be a factor of considerable importance. A society with relatively many families at both ends of the income scale would provide both a large supply of servants and a large demand" (Stigler 1946: 6). My colleagues and I tested this proposition empirically in an analysis of 1990 census data and demonstrated that income inequality was a significant predictor of the share of female workers employed in domestic labor in the 100 largest U.S. metropolitan areas (Milkman et al. 1998).

Merita Jokela's (2015) cross-national study of seventy-four countries yielded similar results. Daniel Schneider and Orestes Hastings (2017) have further documented the effects of inequality on the capacity of U.S. households to "outsource" an array of housework-related tasks, analyzing data on time use and household expenditures. They show that highly educated, high-income women do less housework and outsource more household services than less privileged women, and that this class gradient increases with income inequality. Elizabeth Currid-Halkett calculated that, in 2014, the top 1 percent in the U.S. income distribution spent about twenty times more on child care than the middle class (which she defines as the sixtieth to ninetieth percentile) and the top 10 percent spent about five times more. Spending on other types of domestic work is similarly top heavy, especially in urban settings. "The top income groups have the option to have someone else mop their floors, mow their lawn, and water their plants, while the data suggest that lower income groups do these chores themselves," observes Currid-Halkett (2017: 64–6, 168).

As many commentators have noted, the rising workforce participation of married women and mothers has contributed substantially to the growth in demand for domestic labor in recent decades. But a striking manifestation of growing inequality in the twenty-first century is that many wealthy American households in which wives are *not* employed outside the home also purchase domestic services, as Rachel Sherman documented in her study of affluent New York City families. "All the households in which one partner did not work for pay employed housecleaners, and interviewees seemed to take for granted that they would not do this kind of work themselves," she notes. Some of the stay-at-home mothers Sherman interviewed were "conflicted" about engaging the services of "personal assistants, personal chefs or night nannies," but most did so nevertheless (Sherman 2017: 85–6). Not surprisingly, hiring such workers is even more common in households where both partners are employed in demanding jobs. The aging of the population is another driver of the growing demand; indeed, by 2012, direct-care aides for the elderly and disabled made up about half of all in-home workers, and labor market projections suggest that their ranks will continue to grow (Schierholz 2013: 4, 22).

Widening Inequality among Women

Employment opportunities for highly educated upper-middle-class women expanded dramatically starting in the 1970s. As these women entered elite professional and managerial occupations from which they had previously been excluded, their earnings rose rapidly. The extent of occupational segregation by gender declined starting in the 1960s, and women's average annual earnings increased from 60 percent of men's in 1970 to 77 percent in 2010 (Blau et al. 2013; Hegewisch et al. 2014). But few working-class women (especially those of color) shared in these gains, which were skewed toward the most privileged, highly educated women. Gender segregation declined sharply in professional and managerial jobs but hardly budged in lower-level occupations; most non-college-educated women were still stuck in traditionally sex-stereotyped "pink-collar" jobs where pay and status remained low (England 2010; Dwyer 2013).

Thus, even as the gender gap in pay declined, income inequality *among* women expanded. Between 1979 and 2017, the real (controlling for inflation) hourly earnings of white women at the ninetieth percentile of the U.S. income distribution increased by 69 percent, while the real hourly earnings of African-American and Latina women at the tenth percentile *fell* by 3 percent and 8 percent, respectively. Inequality among women over that period grew faster than that among men: real hourly earnings for white men at the ninetieth percentile rose by 44 percent, while those of African-American men and Latinos at the tenth percentile fell by 6 and 9 percent, respectively (Donovan and Bradley 2018: 8–9). Further complicating the picture, however, was the fact that, although in absolute terms highly educated women in elite occupations advanced economically far more than other women, the gender gap in earnings inequality was smaller for the most privileged women – simply because the earnings of men in elite jobs rose more rapidly than those for any other group. In contrast, the real earnings of non-college-educated men fell sharply in this period, another factor contributing to the narrowing of the gender gap in pay (McCall 2008: 309).

Endogamous marriage and "assortative mating" – technical terms for the longstanding tendency for people to choose partners and spouses from class (and racial) backgrounds similar to their own – further magnified the growth in inequality among women in this period. Apart from their own earnings, highly educated women in elite occupations sharing a household with a male spouse or partner employed at a similarly high occupational level benefit from the soaring incomes of those men (as well as from their wealth). Class endogamy among U.S. married couples is not new but has intensified since the 1970s. The affluent also have lower separation and divorce rates than their less privileged counterparts (Burtless 1999; McCall 2008; Damaske 2011), and single parenthood is far less prevalent among the rich: in 2015, in the top fifth of the income distribution only 9 percent of households were headed by single parents, compared to 40 percent in the bottom two-fifths (Reeves 2017: 28). For all these reasons, since the 1970s, class disparities among women have become greater than ever before. This set the stage for the expansion of paid domestic work, reversing the trend of the previous three-quarters of a century.

Domestic labor itself is a microcosm of the growing class inequality among women. As Judith Rollins (1985) observed long ago, one highly unusual feature of this type of work is that both the employer and the employee are typically female (see also Katzman 1978: 153). Rollins's work is part of a larger scholarly literature documenting the ways in which racial and ethnic inequalities shape the asymmetrical interactions between domestics and their employers, especially in the United States, where the legacy of slavery casts a long shadow over the occupation. Although by the turn of the twenty-first century domestic work had become the prototypical entry-level job for female immigrants, especially the undocumented, for a century after the end of the Civil War in 1865 it was dominated by African Americans, particularly in the South. Even today, although some types of domestic work pay better than other female-dominated occupations (many of which are similarly unregulated and precarious), it remains at the bottom of the job queue. As one commentator summarizes, "Domestic service was typically a job of last resort, taken because of economic need and because other jobs were unavailable" (Kornrich 2012: 205). It has long been highly stigmatized and characterized by many undesirable features, as Rollins observes:

> While any employer–employee relationship is by definition unequal, the mistress–servant relationship – with its centuries of conventions of behavior, its historical association with slavery throughout the world, its unusual retention of feudal characteristics, and the tradition of the servant being not only of a lower class but also female, rural, and of a despised ethnic group – provides an extreme and "pure" example of a relationship of domination in close quarters. (Rollins 1985: 8–9)

Paid Domestic Labor in Historical Perspective

In the late nineteenth-century United States, paid domestic labor was by far the largest female occupation. In absolute terms it reached a peak in 1940, when nearly 2 million women worked in private households, but that year domestic workers accounted for only 18 percent of the female labor force, down from 50 percent in 1870 (Milkman et al. 1998: 491; Katzman 1978: 53). The number of domestic workers per family was consistently higher in urban than in rural areas, but with marked regional variations. Southern cities had the highest ratio of domestics per family and Western cities the lowest. In 1880, for example, there were 564 domestics per family in Atlanta, 239 in Boston, and 136 in San Francisco (Katzman 1978: 61).

The population groups performing domestic work also varied over time and space. In the late nineteenth century, European immigrants, especially the Irish, dominated the occupation in the cities of the Northeast, while African Americans did so in the South, Mexican Americans in the Southwest, and Japanese Americans in Hawaii and parts of California (Glenn 1992: 8–10). Before abolition, although the vast majority of enslaved women in the South worked in the fields, many others were "house slaves." In 1860 over two-thirds of free black women (and 4 percent of free black men) worked as domestic servants, as did half of all employed white women (many of them U.S.-born), mostly in the North (Branch 2011: 49).

White U.S.-born women were the first to exit the occupation. They were replaced in the nation's Northern cities starting in the late nineteenth century by Irish and German immigrants, although, in smaller towns outside the South, U.S.-born women remained the majority of servants well into the twentieth century (Katzman 1978: 65). But foreign-born white women increasingly abandoned domestic service too as they gained access to factory jobs and, later, to sales and clerical work. "Sometimes women were willing to accept lower wages [in other types of work] simply to avoid service," notes historian David Katzman, for domestic work had "the lowest status of any widespread occupation in American society" (Katzman 1978: 241–2). By 1930 only 11 percent of all white women were domestic servants. In the first half of the twentieth century the field became increasingly dominated by African-American women, whose labor force participation rates were higher than those of their white counterparts and who were excluded from most other types of work, even in the Northern and Midwestern cities to which so many descendants of former slaves had migrated (Katzman 1978: 79; Glenn 1992: 11; Branch 2011: 55–7). By 1950, the proportion of African-American women workers who were domestic servants was ten times that of white women (Branch 2011: 59).

Over time, however, women of color increasingly found work outside of private homes, doing "the heavy, dirty 'back-room' chores of cooking and serving food in restaurants and cafeterias, cleaning rooms in hotels and office buildings, and caring for the elderly and ill in hospitals and nursing homes, including cleaning rooms, making beds, changing bedpans and preparing food" (Glenn 1992: 20, 22). Although the tasks involved were often similar, most preferred these "public jobs" to domestic service. Some women of color also gained access to factory jobs, especially during the labor shortages created by World War II (Branch 2011: ch. 4). Others were employed as professionals or in small businesses within their own communities. Yet, apart from these exceptions, job opportunities for African Americans and other women of color remained highly restricted, and domestic service was often their only employment option.

That finally changed with the passage of the 1964 Civil Rights Act and the wider effects of the civil rights movement, which opened the doors for women of color to clerical and sales jobs and to other occupations from which they previously had been excluded. By 1980 only 5 percent of all employed African-American women were in domestic work, down from 39 percent in 1960 (Branch 2011: 132–4). Occupational segregation between black and white women declined precipitously in this period (King 1992: 33), with a dramatic effect on earnings: in 1960, African-American women's average hourly earnings were about 65 percent of white women's; by 1980 that figure was 99 percent. However, men's earnings, especially those of white men, remained far higher; job segregation by gender remained largely intact and, even as racial barriers fell, most African-American women remained confined to traditional female occupations (Branch 2011: 134). Economists Francine Blau and Andrea Beller found that, from 1960 to 1980, African-American women with twenty or more years of work experience "had the largest increases in relative earnings of any gender-experience group over the period," noting that "their large gains were tied to a reduction in their concentration in private

household employment" (Blau and Beller 1992: 285). Progress
stalled after 1980, however, when the political climate shifted
abruptly and economic growth faltered.

As African-American women definitively abandoned domestic
service, the size of the occupation declined sharply. By 1980, the
U.S. Census found only 1.4 percent of all employed women in
"private household service," down from 17.7 percent in 1940
(Milkman et al. 1998: 491). Indeed, the field shrank so much
that sociologists began writing obituaries for it. In 1973, just
before inequality (and immigration) began to skyrocket, Lewis
Coser declared that the role of domestic servants was "obsolete in
modern society." He noticed the influx of West Indian immigrants
into the occupation following the exodus of African Americans,
but nevertheless predicted its imminent demise. "The status [of
domestic work] is now so stigmatized that it can hardly attract
potential recruits among ordinary citizens and must increasingly
turn to a pool of otherwise 'undesirable' foreigners," he wrote.
"When conditions have reached such an impasse, the status and
role become obsolescent" (Coser 1973: 39; see also Chaplin 1978).

This prophecy proved premature, however. Although the size of
the occupation has not rebounded to the high levels of a century
ago, it has expanded substantially in recent years. Between 2004
and 2010 alone, one study found, the number of housecleaners,
nannies and caregivers working in private households and paid
directly by their employers increased by 10 percent, and that
figure does not include the growing number of domestic workers
employed through agencies or cleaning companies (Burnham
and Theodore 2012: 10). A more comprehensive analysis of
government data on "in-home workers," including agency-based
direct-care aides, nannies, and housecleaners, estimated that, in
2012, there were 2 million in-home workers in the United States,
90 percent of them female. These fields accounted for 3 percent of
the nation's employed women – double the 1980 level. (This does
not include housecleaners and others employed by companies such
as "Merry Maids" and dispatched to work in private homes or
workers hired through platforms such as Taskrabbit or care.com,
for which no reliable data are available; it does include child-care

workers who work in their own homes.)[1] Even this estimate is conservative, since it does not adjust for the fact that neither unauthorized immigrants nor workers paid "under the table," many of whom are employed in this sector, are fully captured by official statistics.

Domestic work has become an immigrant-dominated occupation in the past half-century. No industry group (including agriculture) has a higher percentage of foreign-born workers than "private household labor" (DeSilver 2017). In 2012, 62 percent of all U.S. "maids and housekeeping cleaners" were foreign-born (Schierholz 2013). The immigrant share of the industry group is even higher in some urban labor markets. For example, in New York City, 81 percent of domestic workers (housecleaners, nannies, and home-care aides) were foreign-born in 2016, while the nationwide figure that year was 34 percent (Milkman 2018: 10). In addition, this field is a major source of employment for female immigrants: in 2012, 7 percent of all foreign-born women, and 11 percent of those with a high-school degree or less, were in-home workers (Schierholz 2013).

Pay and Conditions in Domestic Work

The average pay of domestic workers is notoriously low, and few have access to employer-provided health insurance or pension benefits. Working conditions vary, but the informal, isolated character of in-home employment opens the door to exploitation and abuse, and, as many studies document, domestic workers often feel deeply disrespected by their employers (Rollins 1985; Hondagneu-Sotelo 2001; Milkman 2018). In-home workers' median hourly pay in 2012 was about 25 percent below that of demographically similar workers in other occupations; they are disproportionately likely to live in poverty (Schierholz 2013: 2–3, 19). That year, only 12 percent of in-home workers had employer-provided health insurance, and only 7 percent had employer-provided pension plans. (Nearly all of those with these benefits were agency-based home-care workers.) These data, however, conceal the high level of stratification among domestic workers. In a 2011–12 survey of over 2,000 nannies, house-cleaners, and caregivers in fourteen U.S. metropolitan areas, the median hourly wage was $10, but 8 percent of respondents earned over $18 per hour. This survey also found that Latinx respondents had lower average earnings than other racial/ethnic groups, and immigrants earned less than the U.S.-born. Undocumented immigrants, who accounted for about a third of the respondents, reported the very lowest pay rates (Burnham and Theodore 2012).[2]

Since 1974, most domestic workers have been covered by the minimum wage and overtime pay provisions of the federal Fair Labor Standards Act, and in 2015 that law's overtime provisions were extended to include most live-in workers. Domestic workers have additional rights in many states, eight of which have enacted Domestic Workers Bill of Rights legislation in recent years. But enforcement of these laws is notoriously poor, especially in the context of private homes. In a 2008 survey of low-wage workers in Chicago, Los Angeles, and New York, my colleagues and I found that 42 percent of all private household workers and 66 percent of child-care workers had been paid less than the legal minimum wage during the previous work week; among those who had worked enough hours to be eligible for overtime premium pay, fully 89 percent had not received it in the previous work week. Violation rates were higher for women than men and highest of all among unauthorized female immigrants (Bernhardt et al. 2009: 30–4, 43). Compounding these problems, many domestic workers are unaware of their legal rights, and those who are aware often fear retaliation and therefore fail to complain about violations, especially if they are unauthorized immigrants.

Live-in housekeepers and nannies typically earn less than those who live independently. Although "live-ins" save on rent and related costs, such positions are consistently at the bottom of the job queue and are disproportionately filled by recent and/or unauthorized immigrants. Pierette Hondagneu-Sotelo found in her study of Latina domestics in Los Angeles that "Most women are repelled by live-in jobs. The lack of privacy, the mandated separation from family and friends, the round-the-clock hours … and especially the constant loneliness prompt most Latina immigrants to seek other job arrangements" (Hondagneu-Sotelo 2001: 36). Rhacel Parrenas's study of Filipina domestic workers documents similar complaints among live-in nannies. "I felt like I was in prison," one worker told her (Parrenas 2015: 128). Live-in eldercare providers, who had more autonomy and felt appreciated by their clients, were less dissatisfied, however.

In this context, it is often the case that, as Shellee Colen argues, "the ideology of family is used to manipulate the worker ... to encourage people who are *not* family members to perform tasks or to tolerate treatment that may be exploitative" (Colen 1986: 60). The underlying tension sometimes surfaces in what Hondagneu-Sotelo (2001: 114) calls "blowups" that expose the "otherwise invisible fissures" in the employment relationship and sometimes lead to abrupt firing (or quitting). Domestic workers are hardly unique in their lack of job security; most U.S. private-sector employees can be legally terminated without cause, but domestic workers' low pay and lack of benefits render them especially vulnerable in the event of sudden job loss.

Scholars have documented the historical processes through which African-American and Latina domestic workers, respectively, sought to professionalize their jobs, "taking active steps to ... eliminate the vestiges of servitude ... [and] establish a businesslike environment" (Romero 1992: 143). The shift from live-in to live-out day work was their signal achievement. Starting in the 1920s, "black workers ... sought to transform domestic service from a norm of full-time, resident service to a job with limited hours and clearly defined tasks" (Palmer 1989: 68; see also Katzman 1978: 90–1). Having multiple employers maximized scheduling flexibility; workers could limit their contact with employers and manage expectations about the specific tasks to be performed, and charging a flat rate for the job (rather than an hourly wage) improved their earnings (Romero 1992: 147–60). But, as Hondagneu-Sotelo notes (2001: 37): "Live-in work never completely disappeared ... [and] in the last decades of the twentieth century it revived with vigor, given new life by the needs of American families with working parents and ... by the needs of newly arrived Latina immigrants."

The intimate character of domestic work, especially for nannies and other caregivers (and most of all for "live-ins"), makes some affluent women uncomfortably aware of the stark inequality between themselves and their household employees. Rachel Sherman found that such employers routinely hid purchases from their nannies and housekeepers or removed price tags from newly acquired clothing, or even from expensive food items (Sherman 2017: 105–6). At the same time, many employers gloss over inequalities by framing their intimate relationships with domestic workers in familial terms, deploying what Judith Rollins (1985) calls "maternalism." The African-American housecleaners she interviewed in the early 1980s were rarely deceived by this, however. "All domestics concurred that employers appreciated some forms of deference and outward signs of subservience," she notes, adding that this expectation generated deep resentment among workers (Rollins 1985: 147, 156, 225–8). Indeed, that is why so many African-American women exited the occupation once other job opportunities began to open up in the 1970s.

Inequality and Growth in Low-Wage Restaurant Jobs

In recent decades, as economic inequalities widened, just as affluent families more easily could afford to employ in-home workers, they also had more disposable income to pay for restaurant meals and other household and personal services (Schneider and Hastings 2017). The resulting expansion of service industries drove rapid employment growth at the bottom of the labor market, as Rachel Dwyer's analysis of job polarization between 1983 and 2007 shows. "Jobs that support operations of daily life such as food service, domestic service, and housekeeping," she reports, comprised 40 percent of job growth in the bottom quintile of the workforce in that period; most of these jobs were held by women (Dwyer 2013: 398, 403). Among them were "back of the house" jobs in restaurants and other labor-intensive service industries, many of which (like domestic service) previously were held by African Americans.

In 1960, 21 percent of all employed African-American women were in service jobs outside private households, while about one-fourth of this group worked in "eating and drinking places" at that time (U.S. Women's Bureau 1964: 44, 46). But in later decades many African Americans abandoned both types of work, as better opportunities opened up in the wake of the civil rights movement. As Roger Waldinger and Michael Lichter point out, "The word *service* implies a *servant*." Even in the formal sector, "service work shares more than a little with the household servant of old, wrapped in a uniform, wearing tags that display only his or her first name, expected to address customers as *sir* or *madam*" (Waldinger and Lichter 2003: 39–40).

Thus, paralleling the dynamic in private household employment, labor demand in low-level service-sector jobs surged just as the labor supply began to shrink. That led employers to recruit immigrants to fill the gap, as Michael Piore testified to the U.S. Congress in 1975:

> The new immigration is a response to what employers perceive as a vacuum at the bottom of the labor market, a shortage, that began in the middle '60s, of workers to fill the menial, low-wage, unstable, dead end jobs in ... restaurants, hotels, laundries and hospitals. Faced with this shortage, employers began active recruitment abroad ... The labor shortage, of which this recruitment is a result, is attributed by employers to the growing reluctance of black workers to accept the kinds of low-wage jobs that blacks traditionally filled. (Piore 1975: 424–5)

The restaurant industry expanded particularly rapidly in this period. Between 1970 and 1985 alone, restaurant employment grew three and a half times as fast as total employment, (Bailey 1987: 10). Over those years, the restaurant sector's share of total U.S. nonagricultural employment grew from 4.5 to 8 percent (Ozimek 2017). By the 2010s, Americans were spending more money on dining out than in grocery stores; indeed, consumer spending in restaurants and bars rose much faster than in other retail sectors such as clothing or cars (Thompson 2017). The industry's growth partly reflected the rise of the fast-food sector, which between 1972 and 1989 swelled from 26 to 40 percent of all restaurant industry sales (Cobble and Merrill 1994: 466). Soon after, take-out food and home-delivered meals also gained market share.

High-end full-service restaurants have disproportionately thrived in recent decades, and indeed this is the sector of the industry where rising inequality has had the greatest impact. Fine dining caters to "rich city-dwellers" in places such as San Francisco, New York, and Los Angeles, "the playgrounds of wealthy, young, highly educated people who ... have plenty of disposable income," observes journalist Derek Thompson. Similarly, the chief economist of the National Restaurant Association points out that "Growth in the number of higher-income households is a positive sign for restaurants, as this demographic group represents the majority of spending in the industry" (Grindy 2016). In contrast, Thompson notes, mid-level "casual dining" has stagnated in recent years: "In an economy where typical middle-class jobs are disappearing, the middle is hollowing out in the restaurant industry as well," partly replaced by take-out and delivery (Thompson 2017).

Although 20 to 25 percent of restaurant workers were unionized in the 1950s, by 1970 that figure had plummeted to 8 percent and by 1990 to less than 2 percent (Cobble and Merrill 1994: 449, 451). Organized labor had already nearly disappeared from this industry before its growth took off in the 1970s; unlike the cases discussed in chapter 3, here de-unionization was not a significant driver of rising immigrant employment. But the absence of unionism does help to account for the industry's notoriously poor pay and benefits. In 2017, the median wage of the 10.5 million workers employed in "restaurants and other eating places" was $10.25 per hour, including tips (U.S. Bureau of Labor Statistics 2017). Almost half of all U.S. workers earning less than the legal minimum wage were restaurant workers. Hours in this industry are often irregular, aggravating the problem of low earnings, and opportunities for career advancement are minimal (Batt et al. 2014). In 2014, only 14 percent of restaurant workers had access to employer-provided health insurance and only 8 percent to pensions, compared to 49 percent and 42 percent, respectively, for workers in other industries (Schierholz 2014: 21).

African Americans shared in the restaurant industry's expansion. From 1983 to 1991, overall restaurant employment grew by 8 percent, while African-American employment in the industry increased by 50 percent. However, Latinx restaurant employment (in which immigrants predominated) grew more than twice as fast, by 123 percent (Cobble and Merrill 1994: 454). In this period, African Americans (especially teenagers) were concentrated disproportionately in the fast-food sector of the industry, where initially immigrants were rarely employed, although that later changed (Schlosser 2001: 70–1). In contrast, immigrant-owned restaurants, another rapidly growing part of the industry, disproportionately employed foreign-born workers, including many from Asia.

Latinx immigrants were increasingly hired in "back of the house" jobs (line cooks, prep cooks, bussers, and dishwashers) in full-service restaurants (Bailey 1987: 32), the segment of the industry that historically had employed African Americans. Although systematic data are sparse, a 1967 study of restaurants within the hotel industry in twelve U.S. cities found that 56 percent of dishwashers, 44 percent of "bus help," 38 percent of "kitchen help," and 32 percent of cooks were African American (Koziara and Koziara 1968). As late as 2000, "cook" was among the top six occupations for both female and male African Americans, although Latinx immigrants (mostly males) already were beginning to replace them (Reskin and Padavic 2002: 69; Waldinger and Lichter 2003: 249–50).

By 2014, 22 percent of all U.S. restaurant workers were foreign-born (and the figure was much higher in areas with large immigrant populations). They were concentrated at the bottom of the industry: 38 percent of dishwashers and 37 percent of cooks were foreign-born (Schierholz 2014: 14). The Pew Research Center estimated that, in 2014, 12 percent of all U.S. restaurant workers were lawful immigrants, while another 10 percent were unauthorized. The unauthorized share was highest in "back of the house" occupations: among dishwashers (19 percent) and "food cooking machine operators" (20 percent), for example (Passel and

Cohn 2016: 30–1). Server jobs were entirely different; for those, employers hired U.S.-born workers and others with English proficiency (often including actors and students).

Restaurants have high turnover rates (among both firms and workers), and, as noted earlier, the industry has grown spectacularly in recent decades, leading to chronic labor shortages. As a result, most commentators agree, the declining presence of African Americans in the industry reflects not displacement but, rather, the fact that U.S.-born workers (of all races) have increasingly shunned low-wage "back of the house" restaurant jobs. "Relatively few African American workers are even *trying* to compete with immigrants" in such jobs, Waldinger and Lichter conclude in their study of the low-wage labor market in Los Angeles. "I can't remember the last time a black man came looking for a job," a veteran Los Angeles restaurant owner told them. And a coffee shop owner declared, "Black men – even American white men – they say, 'I'm not going to wash dishes.' Or, 'I went to high school and I deserve better'" (Waldinger and Lichter 2003: 20, 177, 214).

As in the industries profiled in chapter 3, once employers made the transition to hiring immigrants for jobs in the back of the house, they rapidly came to prefer them over the U.S.-born. "If we had a good native labor force we'd use it, but we don't," explained a full-service restaurant owner in San Diego. "These Mexican guys take these jobs seriously. Their work ethic is incredible" (Morales 1992: 148–9). "I've gone through six dishwashers," a Milwaukee restaurant owner recalled. "The first five were U.S. citizens, and they were problematic – they'd complain, they'd arrive late, they didn't want to do the work. The sixth guy is an immigrant – he has stuck around and is doing a great job" (McElmurry 2017: 8–9). Similarly, as a North Carolina chain restaurant manager gushed, "The Latino workforce … these guys know how to work" (Lester 2019: 23).

Immigrants in the Nail Salon Industry

Alongside the restaurant industry, in which paid workers have increasingly replaced the unpaid labor previously performed by women in the home, a variety of other service fields proliferated during and after the 1970s. Some occupations, such as fitness instructors or "life coaches," required workers with English proficiency and/or specialized training, while others relied on low-wage immigrant labor, as in the case of manicurists, whose employment grew spectacularly starting in the 1980s. Many of the new services catered primarily to the affluent, as shown earlier for the cases of domestic labor and high-end restaurants, while others were affordable to a far wider population, such as fast-food restaurants and nail salons.

In contrast to earlier eras, when professional manicures were a luxury good, and indeed a symbol of class status, in this period they became available at modest cost and gained popularity across a wide swath of income groups. As journalist Virginal Postrel notes:

> Human beings of all incomes and levels of technology crave beauty and diversion. As people get richer, they can afford to spend more on such luxuries. By historical standards, Americans are extremely rich. It's not surprising, then, to find smart entrepreneurs creating economic value by catering to our happiness as well as to our physical needs. To find them, however, you have to look. Try the Yellow Pages, under "manicures." (Postrel 1998)

The beauty industry grew slowly in the late nineteenth and early twentieth century, but it took off in the 1920s. During that decade, the U.S. Census Bureau found, the number of women barbers, hairdressers, and manicurists (occupations that were not yet enumerated separately) more than tripled, reaching a total of 113,000 in 1930 (Erickson 1935: 2). Further growth was slowed by depression and war, but, by 1950, 190,000 women were employed in these fields (Pidgeon and Mitchell 1956: 2). Visiting a beauty salon for a haircut had become routine for most American women by the 1960s, but professional manicures were still a luxury service. Working-class women simply could not afford them, and, even for the middle class, "nail care remained a do-it-yourself beauty practice" (Willett 2005: 64). For men whose work did not involve manual labor, professionally manicured nails were a visible marker of class in the mid-twentieth century, but starting in the 1960s this aspect of male grooming began to disappear (Willett 2005).

Before World War II, and in some regions for much longer, women's "beauty shops," which offered not only haircutting and hairdressing services but also manicures, were racially segregated. A study of the industry in the 1930s found a few African-American women working in white establishments, but most were employed in "Negro shops." At the time, although "all-around operators" often offered manicure services, full-time manicurists had the lowest earnings in the beauty industry. Theirs was an entry-level job that required relatively little training and in which licensing standards were lower or, in some jurisdictions, nonexistent (Erickson 1935). Manicurists were also employed in men's barbershops in this period, often as "the only female in the shop and hired in part for ... looks and ability to flirt with men" (Willett 2005: 63).

In both women's beauty salons and men's barbershops, then, manicurists had been at the bottom of the job queue, with low pay and status. Their clients, in contrast, were typically wealthy. But, in the 1980s, the consumer base for this service was democratized, as stand-alone nail salons suddenly began to proliferate, offering affordable manicures (and pedicures) that quickly gained popularity across the class spectrum. Traditional beauty salons continued to offer manicures, but at a premium price, serving a more affluent clientele. Most of the new stand-alone nail salons were owned by Korean and Vietnamese immigrant entrepreneurs (the Korean operators were concentrated in New York City while Vietnamese dominated the industry on the West Coast and elsewhere). They employed low-wage immigrant women, often including members of the owner's family, at rock-bottom wages. They further lowered costs by exploiting newer technologies such as electric-powered nail files and acrylics to shorten the time required for a manicure (Kang 2010: 38–40). These low-end nail salons are a classic "ethnic niche," dominated by Asian immigrants (Eckstein and Nguyen 2011). Whereas in the other industries profiled in this book most low-wage immigrant workers are Latinx, in nail salons Asian women predominate. Many earn less than the legal minimum wage and suffer poor working conditions and extremely long hours (Nir 2015), belying the stereotype of Asian immigrants as well-paid, highly educated professionals.

In 2018, according to the U.S. Bureau of Labor Statistics (2018), 110,170 manicurists and pedicurists were employed nationwide, but other data suggest that the actual figure is at least double that number. The previous year *Nails* magazine (2018) found over 439,000 licensed "nail techs" in the United States, about half of whom were "actively practicing." Even this may be an under-count, however, since enforcement of licensing requirements is often lax. The *New York Times* reported that many manicurists work without licenses, and that "licenses are frequently fabricated, bought and sold" (Nir 2015). Moreover, many nail salon workers are undocumented immigrants who may elude government enumerators (Kang 2010: 85–7; Nir 2015). California alone had 66,800 licensed manicurists in 2002, although the active proportion is unknown (Federman et al. 2006: 303).

By all accounts the nail salon workforce is predominantly female and Asian, but it also includes some Latinx immigrants, as well as U.S.-born African-American and white women (Eckstein and Nguyen 2011: 648; Nir 2015). Over half of the respondents to an on-line survey conducted in 2017 by *Nails* magazine (2018) were Vietnamese, and more than a third were white, but salon owners were probably overrepresented in this group. In California in 2002, 59 percent of licensed manicurists were Vietnamese immigrants (Federman et al. 2006: 303). In New York City salons, Korean workers are reportedly the best-paid workers (favored by the Korean owners who dominate the local industry), followed by Chinese immigrants, with Latinx workers at the bottom (Nir 2015).

The U.S. Bureau of Labor Statistics (2018) reported that the median hourly wage for manicurists and pedicurists was $11.70 in 2018, but other accounts suggest that the pay is often far lower. A 2015 *New York Times* investigation that included interviews with over 100 nail salon workers found that "a vast majority of workers are paid below minimum wage" and that "sometimes they are not even paid" at all. The same investigation found that "Asian-language newspapers are rife with classified ads listing manicurist jobs paying so little the daily wage can at first appear to be a typo," citing examples with starting wages of $10 a day. Manicurists "spend their days holding hands with women of unimaginable affluence, at salons on Madison Avenue and in Greenwich, Connecticut," the *Times* reported, but "away from the manicure tables they crash in flophouses packed with bunk beds, or in fetid apartments shared by as many as a dozen strangers" (Nir 2015).

Although women in all walks of life patronize nail salons, the industry remains stratified along class lines. As Milann Kang has documented in detail, workers in upscale "nail spas" patronized by white middle- and upper-class women are expected to offer "intense emotional and physical attention" and "pampering" (Kang 2010: 145). These establishments have high-end equipment and offer a variety of services, not only manicures and pedicures; the manicurists are trained to behave deferentially to customers and go to great lengths to help them feel relaxed. By contrast, in the low-end salons "a nail job ... was closer to a stint on a factory assembly line," and clients expected far less emotional attention or deference from workers (ibid.: 182–3). "I could make a lot more money if I spoke great English and catered to rich white people who ... are paying higher prices for talking services," a manicurist in northern California explained to a researcher. She preferred clients who were working-class women of color who "care more about the quality of the work done on their nails than the quality of service" (Hoang 2015: 122).

Conclusion

The rapid growth of employment in domestic work and other low-wage service fields since the 1970s reflected the explosive expansion of economic inequality, which increased the ability of affluent individuals and households to pay for the services of housecleaners, nannies, and other in-home workers, as well as restaurant meals and a variety of other personal services. The surge in demand for low-wage labor in this sector coincided with an exodus from it of African Americans, for whom better job opportunities opened up in the 1970s as a result of the civil rights movement. Their abandonment of low-wage service jobs was not driven by de-unionization or work degradation, in contrast to the dynamic that led U.S.-born workers to exit the industries analyzed in chapter 3. But the end result was the same: foreign-born workers came to dominate occupations that previously had been filled by the U.S.-born.

Another distinctive feature of low-wage service-sector work involves gender: immigrant *women* dominate the workforce in domestic work and other in-home employment as well as in low-wage service industries such as nail salons. To be sure, some male immigrants also work in the service sector, for example as *carwasheros* and gardeners, and many restaurants employ both male and female immigrants at the "back of the house." In contrast, the industries discussed in chapter 3 are largely male-dominated: construction and trucking employ very few women; meatpacking and building services are more mixed but also have a predominantly male workforce. In general, the service sector, where the shift to immigrant employment was driven by rising inequality, employs primarily women, while men are the bulk of the workforce in the cases where labor degradation and de-unionization spurred the change.

In both cases, the influx of foreign-born workers led to a transformation of the labor queue as employers came to view immigrants as both more industrious and less likely to complain about job conditions or to engage in collective action to win improvements. Employers' assumptions about immigrants and the African-American workers who previously had performed many of the same service-sector jobs diverged starkly. "Happiest with subordinates who quietly accept subordination – a readiness more necessary at the bottom of the labor market, where the demand for subordination is great and rewards are few," Waldinger and Lichter declare, "employers gave black workers bad marks" (Waldinger and Lichter 2003: 175). In contrast, immigrants were typically presumed to be more pliable, deferential workers – all the more so if they were undocumented, and thus plagued by "a palpable sense of deportability," as Nicholas De Genova terms it. He argues that "the category 'illegal alien' is a profoundly useful and profitable one that effectively serves to create and sustain a legally vulnerable – and hence, relatively tractable and thus 'cheap' – reserve of labor" (De Genova 2002: 439).

And yet, as the next chapter demonstrates in some detail, many low-wage immigrant workers defied the nearly ubiquitous expectation (among employers and external observers alike) that they would be tractable and perpetually remain in the category of "cheap labor." Instead, in the late twentieth and early twenty-first century, they began to join labor unions and other types of worker organizations and to build an immigrant rights movement that fought to expand their rights and improve their economic status. The same desire to improve their livelihoods that spurred these workers to migrate to the U.S. in the first place also motivated them to pursue collective action to advance themselves economically, whenever opportunities to do so presented themselves. Although the Trump administration's anti-immigrant policies have recently blocked most such opportunities and thrown efforts to organize or advocate for immigrants onto the defensive, before 2017 such efforts were widespread and often successful, to the surprise of friends and foes alike. That is the subject of chapter 5.

5

Immigrant Labor Organizing and Advocacy in the Neoliberal Era

American labor has always been a movement in which immigrants, often in the most thankless and dangerous jobs, have played leading roles – often stopping the race to the bottom that employers entered them in. The young immigrant women who worked in the clothing and garment industries of New York and other cities in the early 20th century ... paved the way for the reforms that led in time to the New Deal, minimum-wage laws, the eight-hour day, and the weekend. In more recent times, from the grape strikes of the 1960s to the Justice for Janitors movement of the past quarter-century, immigrant workers have made significant gains by organizing into unions ... The same drive and fortitude that led these immigrant workers to risk everything for a better life for the family by coming here led them on a path to ... organizing.

Hector Figueroa and Cristina Jiménez Moreta (2018)

Union organizing has become increasingly difficult for U.S.- and foreign-born workers alike since the late 1970s, when the nation's employers launched a broad offensive against organized labor (see chapter 3). Nevertheless, confounding the expectations of most observers, in recent decades unions and other worker organizations have successfully recruited substantial numbers of low-wage immigrants into their ranks in the late twentieth and early twenty-first century, including many undocumented workers. By 2018, over 2 million foreign-born workers were members of U.S. unions (Hirsch and Macpherson 2019: 29), upending the conventional wisdom that low-wage immigrant workers are reluctant to become involved in labor organizing. On the contrary, as it turned out, the same powerful motivation to advance economically that led so many foreign-born workers to migrate to the United States has also propelled some of them into collective action in the workplace.

Alongside traditional unions, two additional forms of immigrant labor organizing emerged in this period. One was comprised of the "worker centers" that proliferated across the nation, starting in the early 1990s. These "alt-labor" groups rarely engage in traditional collective bargaining, but they organize low-wage workers (most of them foreign-born) at the grassroots level and advocate on their behalf for such public policies as enhanced rights for domestic workers and stronger penalties for wage theft. The third form of immigrant labor organizing is the immigrant rights movement itself. Although typically framed in terms of human rights and civil rights, economic issues are also central to the movement's agenda. The vast majority of unauthorized immigrants in the U.S. are low-wage workers (or family members dependent on such workers) whose lack of legal status traps them at the bottom of the labor market. Insofar as the goal of the immigrant rights movement is to remove that formidable barrier to economic advancement, it functions as a type of labor movement.

These three strands of immigrant worker organizing developed independently of one another, but over time they have increasingly converged, borrowing strategies and tactics from one another and also collaborating on specific campaigns. All three were shaped by the political and economic transformations that unfolded starting in the late 1970s, which, as discussed in chapter 3, restored many features of the pre-New Deal era. By the turn of the twenty-first century, indeed, unionization rates had fallen to single-digit levels not seen since the 1920s and far below the peak levels of the mid-1950s. New Deal-era regulations that had "taken wages out of competition" in many industries also were rolled back, giving rise to sweatshop conditions much like those early twentieth-century labor reformers had fought to eliminate. In keeping with this historical devolution, the collective action repertoire of immigrant labor organizing in the late twentieth and early twenty-first century recuperates tactics and strategies used in the pre-New Deal trade union and labor reform movements.

Before exploring the dynamics of the three strands of the immigrant labor movement in more detail, the next section of this chapter deconstructs the myth – once widely believed by employers and unionists alike – that immigrants, and especially the undocumented, are "unorganizable." The following sections turn to analyze labor unions, worker centers, and the immigrant rights movement and their contributions to immigrant organizing. Parallels to pre-New Deal labor activism are a key theme in the discussion of unions and worker centers, but there is no such historical precedent for the contemporary immigrant rights movement. As noted in chapter 2, the existence of a large unauthorized foreign-born population deprived of basic civil rights had no counterpart in the early twentieth century, when Europeans – who dominated that era's immigrant influx – could enter the United States with relative ease and rapidly become naturalized citizens. To be sure, that was not the case for Chinese and other Asian immigrants, but their numbers were relatively modest at the time, and their struggles for legal status took place primarily in the courts (see Ngai 2004), not through a public-facing social movement.

The Myth of Immigrant "Unorganizability"

As the ranks of low-wage immigrant workers multiplied in the 1970s and 1980s, most employers presumed that they would be unlikely candidates for recruitment into unions or other types of labor organizations. Similarly, most union leaders assumed that foreign-born workers were "unorganizable," especially if they were undocumented. After all, many immigrants were (or imagined themselves to be) sojourners, entering the United States for a short period as "target earners" to help support their families at home. If they would not remain in the country long enough to reap the benefits of labor organizing, why would they assume the risks involved? In addition, while their wages and working conditions may have seemed problematic by "American" standards, immigrants were presumed to be using a different yardstick, based on their work experiences in their countries of origin – so that, from their perspective, the jobs might not look so bad. Moreover, employers and unionists alike presumed that fear of apprehension and deportation would lead immigrants, particularly the undocumented, to avoid the high-risk, publicly visible activity of labor organizing.

For all these reasons, not only employers and union leaders, but also most academic and journalistic commentators, believed that immigrants were more tractable workers than their U.S.-born counterparts and had little or no appetite for organizing or activism, especially if it involved potential confrontation with state authorities. In his pioneering 1993 book, however, Hector Delgado challenged this view. Pointing out that "the unorganizability of undocumented workers because of their legal status [had] become a 'pseudofact'" (Delgado 1993: 10, citing Merton 1959), he presented a detailed case study undermining that claim.

Delgado's research focused on a successful 1980s union organizing drive among immigrant workers, mostly undocumented, employed at a mattress factory in Los Angeles. In this case, he reported, "Workers reported giving little thought to their citizenship status and the possibility of an INS [Immigration and Naturalization Service] raid of the plant," adding that one "said that he had a better chance of 'getting hit by a car' – and he didn't worry about that either." Workers stated "that if deported they would have simply returned (in some cases, 'after a short vacation')." One declared, "They're not going to kill you! The worst thing they can do is send me home and I'll come back!" (Delgado 1993: 61, 63). A decade later, a Salvadoran janitors' union organizer I interviewed echoed this statement almost verbatim. "There [El Salvador], if you were for a union, they killed you," she said. "Here, you lose a job for $4.25 an hour [the California minimum wage at the time]" (Milkman 2006: 128).

Over time, as they witnessed extensive evidence to the contrary on the ground, labor organizers abandoned the assumption that foreign-born workers would be unresponsive to their efforts. "It's not true that immigrants are hard to organize," a San Francisco hotel union staffer insisted. "They are more supportive of unions than native workers" (Wells 2000: 120). A Justice for Janitors activist was even more emphatic: "We Latino workers are a bomb waiting to explode!" (Waldinger et al. 1998: 117). By the twentieth century's end the conventional wisdom had been upended, and unionists had come to believe instead that immigrant workers were more "organizable" than their U.S.-born counterparts. This led the AFL-CIO to abandon its longstanding support for "employer sanctions" (legal penalties for hiring unauthorized workers, enacted under IRCA in 1986). In early 2000 the Federation reversed its stance and officially endorsed comprehensive immigration reform and a path to legalization for the undocumented (Bacon 2001). By that time, after a string of organizing successes, immigrant workers had become a rare beacon of hope for the otherwise beleaguered U.S. labor movement.

The revisionist view also appeared in journalistic reports on union organizing drives and in academic studies of this period. For example, a 1999 *New York Times* article about a strike at a meatpacking plant where the workforce was 90 percent foreign-born highlighted "the receptivity that many immigrants feel toward union activity and their growing confidence that ... the potential benefits of pressing for better wages and working conditions outweigh any risks" (Verhovek 1999; see also Waltz 2018). Historian Leon Fink's study of Guatemalan immigrant workers' successful organizing at a North Carolina poultry plant made a similar assessment. Fink elaborated, "For workers steeped in a paternalistic relationship to authority – as is classically the case in the Latin American countryside – the cold expediency of U.S. industrial relations invited alternative if not outright oppositional forms of loyalty" (Fink 2003: 180).

Survey data regarding immigrants' attitudes toward labor organizing are fragmentary, but those that are available provide further support for the view that, on the average, foreign-born workers are more receptive to unionism than their U.S.-born counterparts. The data show that both Latinx and Asian workers (regardless of nativity) are more pro-union than whites (although

African Americans are even more likely to express receptivity to unionism). The 1994 Worker Representation and Participation Survey (WRPS), for example, found that 51 percent of Latinx respondents (regardless of nativity) who were not union members said that they would vote for a union if a representation election were held in their workplaces, compared to 35 percent of non-Latinx respondents. Similarly, 49 percent of non-union Asian-American respondents said they would vote for a union, compared to 35 percent of non-Asian Americans. Non-union African Americans had an even stronger showing, with 64 percent stating they would vote for a union, compared to 32 percent of non-African Americans (Milkman 2006: 128).

Despite ramped-up border enforcement and rising xenophobia in the years since these surveys were conducted, these attitudes do not appear to have changed. A 2017 survey asking exactly the same question as the one in the WRPS found that non-union Latinx and Asian respondents were more than twice as likely as whites to say they would vote for a union (Kochan et al. 2019: 21–2). Neither the 1994 nor the 2017 survey disaggregated U.S.-born from foreign-born workers; but a statewide survey of California workers in 2001–2 did so, once again asking the identical question about whether non-union respondents would vote for a union. In that survey, 66 percent of non-citizen respondents said they would vote for a union, compared to 54 percent of foreign-born citizens and 42 percent of the U.S.-born (Weir 2002: 121).

Along with their receptive attitudes to unionism, several other factors help explain why immigrant workers are often easier to organize than their U.S.-born counterparts. First, working-class immigrants have stronger social networks than all but the poorest U.S.-born workers, networks that often become embedded in the workplace. Secondly, collective action is more compatible with the lived experiences and worldviews of immigrants (especially Latinx immigrants) than with the famously individualistic orientation of the U.S.-born. Thirdly, immigrants' shared experience of stigmatization (regardless of their legal status) after settling in the United States fosters labor solidarity, especially in the many employment settings where they comprise the vast bulk of the workforce. Separately and in combination, these three factors facilitate collective action and tend to outweigh the considerations once presumed to render immigrant workers docile and "unorganizable."

Networks

Working-class immigrants depend far more heavily on kinship and community-based social networks than their U.S.-born counterparts, in part because they have so few alternative resources on which to draw. Newly arrived immigrants routinely turn to family members and others from their hometowns to find housing, employment, child care, and other forms of assistance with daily life. Since many employers fill job vacancies via referral hiring, immigrant social networks are routinely reproduced inside the workplace. Employers themselves sometimes recognize that this can foster labor solidarity. As one told a researcher, "Too many families at one location creates problems. If you do something to my brother then we're all gonna walk off, that type of situation." Another stated baldly, "Families lead to unionization" (Waldinger and Lichter 2003: 119).

Studies of immigrant labor organizing often highlight the facilitating role of social networks. "Networks played an important role ... as workers recruited friends and family members [into the union drive]," notes Delgado (1993: 27) in regard to the L.A. organizing campaign he documented. Similarly, an analysis of a protracted strike in a frozen-food factory in California's Central Valley in the 1980s attributes the fact that not a single worker crossed the picket line to the power of networks: "The frozen-food workers all lived and worked in the same community, went to the same churches, played and watched soccer games in the same parks. Large numbers of strikers were actually related to each other, members of the same extended families ... they already had close relations and were used to a level of cooperation practically forgotten in metropolitan Anglo culture" (Bardacke 1988: 171). By all accounts, immigrant social networks also contributed to the success of the 1992 southern California drywallers' strike. Most of the leaders and many of the workers involved were from the same part of the Mexican state of Guanajuato. "That was the key, right there," one organizer recalled. "Having that big group from one area." Another activist explained how networks were deliberately mobilized to help secure support for the strike:

> In a lot of cases there were three or four workers to one, talking about what was really happening, and how those folks staying on the job were really hurting them, hurting their families, and their families' future. That if they didn't do this [strike] and do it now, and join us as part of that battle, that they would ruin their future ... It was done with not just one or two people, but by a group of people, and usually by people that the other person knew – in some cases, extended family. (Milkman 2006: 135–6)

Immigrant networks are hardly a new phenomenon: newcomers with limited economic or cultural capital, past and present, have always drawn on social ties to other migrants for daily survival. But what was striking about the late twentieth century was that these networks galvanized classic forms of workplace mobilization that by then had widely come to be seen as anachronistic – mobilization that emerged not despite but because of globalization.

Immigrant worldviews

One possible explanation for immigrants' relatively favorable attitudes toward union organizing is their previous experience of workplace collective action in their countries of origin. Indeed, Latinx immigrants, especially those from Central America, as well as some Asian immigrants, most notably Koreans and Filipinos, often are more familiar with traditions of labor militancy than most U.S.-born workers are. One example is the 2008 Republic Windows campaign in Chicago, which was led by immigrant workers from Mexico and Central America. Deploying a tactic widely used in Latin American labor protests (and also commonplace in the 1930s in the United States, but not since) the workers occupied their factory for nearly a week to protest the firm's secret decision to close it down (Dangl 2009; Brooks 2008).

Rank-and-file immigrant workers who become labor activists in the United States often turn out to have had previous experience in unions or progressive social movements in their native lands, although no systematic data exist on the prevalence of this phenomenon. For example, the leader of a 1990 wildcat strike at an L.A. wheel factory, who later became the plant's local union president, had left Mexico after being blacklisted by employers for his labor organizing activity there (Zabin 2000: 153–4). Similarly, Salvadoran and Guatemalan immigrants who had been active in left-wing or union activity at home were prominent rank-and-file leaders of the L.A. Justice for Janitors campaign in the 1980s and 1990s (Milkman 2006: 159). Rachel Sherman and Kim Voss have documented other cases in which veterans of social movements in the Philippines and Mexico became union organizers after emigrating to the United States (Sherman and Voss 2000: 104). This pattern is hardly new: as noted in chapter 2, in the early twentieth century, many immigrant union leaders from Southern and Eastern Europe were veterans of socialist and labor movements in their home countries.

Both reinforcing and reinforced by this transnational dynamic, foreign-born workers with no previous history of activism also seem more supportive of unionization efforts than their U.S.-born counterparts. Again systematic evidence is lacking, but many commentators have noted that today's working-class immigrants typically understand their fate as linked to that of their community, whereas U.S.-born workers more often believe that their fate is determined by their individual attributes or achievements. A Justice for Janitors organizer recalled in regard to the rank-and-file Latinx immigrants she recruited, "If you ask, 'Que piensa de la union?' [What do you think of the union?], they answer, 'La union hace la fuerza' [Union is power]." This worldview may originate in pre-migration experiences, but it is reinforced by the hostility that foreign-born workers encounter in the United States.

Stigmatization

Even after residing for long periods of time in *el Norte*, immigrants regularly face stigmatization and racism, reinforcing the conviction that their individual fate is linked to that of their communities. That may explain why the lived experience of being under siege in a hostile environment, rather than generating fear or passivity, often helps to galvanize solidarity and collective action. As David Gutiérrez (1998: 324–5) argues, as a result of "simultaneously demonizing and criminalizing Latinos as foreign, nonintegrated 'Others' while continuing to ensure that their labor can be exploited at maximum efficiency, American policymakers and employers have unwittingly helped to create a vast new subnational social space that has virtually guaranteed the emergence of alternative – and potentially deeply subversive – diasporic social identities, cultural frames of reference, and modes of political discourse."

The stigmatization of immigrant workers not only reinforces their collectivist worldview but also intensifies their dependence on kin and community-based social networks; all these factors combine to create favorable conditions for organizing. If labor organizers offer a helping hand, immigrants often respond enthusiastically. Finally, as noted earlier, although participation in unionization drives and other types of labor activism often does involve risk of job loss and employer retaliation, such hazards are modest relative to those entailed in crossing the border without authorization. That helps explain why fear of apprehension and deportation rarely seems to have deterred immigrants from participating in labor organizing efforts.

Immigrants and Union Organizing

In 2018, only 6.4 percent of U.S. private-sector workers were union members, down from 24.2 percent in 1973 (Hirsch and Macpherson 2019). Public-sector unionization rates remained much higher (33.9 percent in 2018) in the absence of the intense employer anti-union animus that pervades the private sector – although concerted efforts to undermine public-sector collective bargaining laws have gained growing traction in recent years (Lafer 2017). The precipitous drop in private-sector unionization has made obituaries for organized labor a perennial theme in both academic and public debate. "If they were an animal or plant, private-sector unions would fall on the endangered species list of the U.S. Fish and Wildlife Service," opined economist Richard B. Freeman (2002) two decades ago. More recently, David Rolf of the Service Employees International Union (SEIU) declared, "The economic and political environment that once supported unions has largely disappeared ... Within our lifetimes, many of America's existing unions will likely perish or recede into irrelevance" (Rolf 2013).

Indeed, since the late 1970s, union representation drives have faced daunting challenges even in settings where workers seem eager to organize, with increasing resistance from employers – who typically engage professional anti-union "labor consultants" at the first hint of interest among workers. Many unions have retreated entirely from organizing the vast unorganized workforce, devoting their resources instead to providing services for existing members, defending past gains, lobbying, and supporting union-friendly political candidates. Moreover, the few unions that have remained active in organizing efforts in the difficult years since the 1970s increasingly avoid the National Labor Relations Board (NLRB) system, which has become "ossified" (Estlund 2002) and is routinely manipulated by anti-union employers and their labor consultants (Bronfenbrenner 2009).

Despite the formidable obstacles to success, a number of unions did undertake serious immigrant organizing efforts in the 1980s and 1990s and generated some high-profile successes that stood out on the otherwise bleak late twentieth-century labor landscape. The best-known example is the SEIU's Justice for Janitors (JFJ) campaign. Although it began in Denver and would eventually spread to other cities across the nation, its most celebrated victory was its breakthrough in 1990 in Los Angeles, where the union won recognition after a dramatic strike and the brutal beating by police of janitors participating in a street protest (Milkman 2006; Fairchild 2018; Waldinger et al. 1998). The L.A. campaign brought 8,000 immigrants, many of them undocumented, into the union fold and eventually led to improvements in their pay, working conditions, and job security.

JFJ became the iconic case of the new immigrant unionism (it was even the subject of a major motion picture, Ken Loach's critically acclaimed *Bread and Roses*, released in 2000) and did much to help liquidate the myth of immigrant "unorganizability." It was complemented by a series of less widely publicized successful immigrant unionization drives in sectors such as construction, manufacturing, and hospitality. Among the largest was the strike in 1992 of 2,300 drywall workers in six California counties, from the Mexican border to just north of Los Angeles, as a result of which the Carpenters union won recognition from the drywall employers. Southern California, with its vast concentration of Latinx immigrant workers, was the epicenter of the 1990s wave of immigrant union organizing (for reasons detailed in Milkman 2006), but over time similar efforts emerged across the nation (Fink 2003; Milkman 2006; Ness 2005; Roca-Servat 2010; Waltz 2018; Wells 2000).

One striking feature of this wave of immigrant union drives is that almost all of them involved former affiliates of the American Federation of Labor (AFL), a union federation founded in the nineteenth century, which merged in 1955 with the Congress of Industrial Organizations (CIO) to form the AFL-CIO. Because the AFL unions were established long before the passage of the 1935 National Labor Relations Act (NLRA), their strategic repertoire took shape entirely outside of that law's framework. Starting in the late 1970s, as the New Deal order collapsed, that historical legacy became a comparative advantage. In sharp contrast, the former CIO unions were established alongside the NLRA, so that most of their tactics and strategies were tailored to it. That was often an advantage in the 1930s and 1940s, but it became a handicap as the NLRA became increasingly dysfunctional and as the manufacturing sector – the CIO's base – was undermined by deindustrialization and outsourcing in the 1970s and 1980s.

For those reasons it turned out that the labor unions best equipped to survive the seismic shifts in the political economy in that period were those shaped by the experience of pre-New Deal conditions – conditions that in many cases have now been restored. This historical perspective helps explain why former AFL affiliates

– including the SEIU, the Carpenters (which led the 1992 drywall strike mentioned above), and the Hotel and Restaurant Employees union (now part of UNITE HERE) – launched so many of the immigrant unionizing drives that emerged in the 1980s and 1990s. These AFL unions, as Dorothy Sue Cobble (1991) has argued, had a historically rooted occupational focus that was especially suited to the "post-industrial" age, with its fragmented industries and increasingly unstable workplaces – in contrast to the industrial unionism of the former CIO affiliates which had flourished in oligopolistic sectors. In addition, the former AFL unions' historical experience included union drives whose goal was to take wages out of competition in unregulated labor markets, a strategy that was not part of the CIO's strategic repertoire. The former AFL affiliates also had experience with tactics designed to extract recognition from employers outside the NLRA framework – tactics that dated back to the pre-1935 era.

For all these reasons, several key former AFL unions managed to survive and even grow in the late twentieth century (in part through immigrant organizing), while the former CIO unions were often mired in defensive struggles, as they faced massive plant closings and outsourcing. Indeed a key advantage for the building trades unions, most importantly the Carpenters and Laborers, whose members are relatively unskilled, as well as for service-sector unions such as SEIU and UNITE HERE, was that none of their members' jobs were moving overseas. On the contrary, their jurisdictions (hospitality, building services, and construction) expanded just as the former CIO's manufacturing base was rapidly shrinking.

The JFJ campaign illustrates the non-NLRA organizing approach used in many recent immigrant unionization drives and, at the same time, exemplifies the successful revival of tactics from the historical playbook of the former AFL-affiliated unions. JFJ organizers developed a "comprehensive campaign" strategy to maximize pressure on all the janitorial employers in each local labor market. They targeted not only the janitorial firms but also the building owners who contracted for their services – since the latter had most of the decision-making power. This focus on pressuring multiple employers across the local labor market for union recognition presents a sharp contrast to traditional NLRA-oriented organizing (typical of former CIO affiliates), which concentrates instead on persuading workers to vote for the union in a representation election at a single workplace, firm, or "bargaining unit." The latter approach is simply not feasible in the janitorial industry: most office cleaning contracts include thirty-day cancellation clauses, so, if the union wins an NLRB election, the building owner can simply switch to a new, non-union contractor and thus nullify the result.

The legacy of AFL unionism, which historically had relied heavily on "top-down" organizing directed at employers, was one key resource for the JFJ campaign. Another was of more recent vintage, namely the strategic repertoire developed by the United Farm Workers (UFW) in the 1960s and early 1970s (see chapter 2). For example, UFW organizers systematically built alliances with elected officials, students, and faith leaders, as well as the wider public; JFJ did the same. The UFW also had a history of creating public spectacles to call attention to the plight of low-wage workers. Similarly, JFJ staged a variety of media stunts to shine a bright light on the low pay and poor working conditions of hardworking immigrant janitors, while "naming and shaming" the building owners and tenants. The UFW's "bottom-up" organizing among low-wage immigrant farm workers, leveraging their pre-existing social networks, also influenced the JFJ campaign. These parallels to the UFW's strategic repertoire were not accidental: as Randy Shaw (2008) has documented, key JFJ organizers had once worked for the UFW (as had many organizers at UNITE HERE).

Such campaigns as JFJ demonstrated that, when labor unions actively sought to recruit low-wage foreign-born workers, including the undocumented, not only did those workers welcome them, but also the inevitable resistance from employers often could be overcome through organizing strategies that drew on both the top-down AFL tradition and the bottom-up UFW one (Milkman 2006). These campaigns ultimately won higher wages and benefits as well as improved working conditions and more job security for immigrant workers. Yet such efforts required significant funding and staffing, and even when those resources were available the campaigns were not always successful. In short, while the JFJ organizing and similar efforts did provide proof of concept, demonstrating the potential for unionizing the burgeoning foreign-born workforce on a larger scale, that potential was never fully realized. At the time of writing the vast majority of immigrant workers are outside the union orbit, toiling long hours for minimal pay, often with poor working conditions. The traditional union movement refuses to die, but its share of the labor force has been whittled down to a level comparable to that of the 1920s.

The 2 million immigrant workers who were union members in 2018 in most cases had entered the ranks of organized labor not through a new unionization drive but, instead, by being hired into a job that was already covered by a union contract. For U.S.-born workers and immigrants alike, a relatively small proportion of current union membership is the product of recent organizing. Under the winner-take-all U.S. industrial relations system, indeed, individual workers rarely have the opportunity to make independent decisions about union affiliation (exceptions include those employed under an "open shop" collective bargaining contract that makes union membership optional, as well as those who have the opportunity to vote in an NLRB election as a result of new organizing). Whether or not an individual is a union member is typically determined simply by where she or he happens to be employed, and whether or not at some point in the past that workplace was organized by a union. Once established, unionization tends to persist over time, unless establishments close or relocate or workers reject the union in an NLRB "decertification" election.

Like women and racial minorities, immigrants are not evenly distributed through the workforce but instead are concentrated in particular occupations and industries (see chapter 1). As a result, their representation in the ranks of union members is determined by the extent that those occupations and industries were unionized at some point in the past. That is why the relatively strong pro-union sentiments among immigrants (noted above) are not reflected in their actual unionization rate. Instead, the single largest factor that yields different rates of unionization for immigrants than for U.S-born workers is the fact that relatively few foreign-born workers are employed in the highly unionized public sector.

The gap between the unionization rates of foreign-born and U.S.-born workers has been fairly stable over time, even as both have steadily declined. In 1996, 14.8 percent of U.S.-born workers and 12.1 percent of foreign-born workers were union members (Grieco 2004); by 2008, those figures had dropped, to 12.8 percent and 10.3 percent, respectively; and in 2018, they stood at 10.9 percent and 8.5 percent (Hirsch and Macpherson 2019: 29, 111). There are also significant variations in unionization rates *among* foreign-born workers. In the private sector, both naturalized citizens and immigrants who arrived in the United States before 1990 have higher unionization rates than U.S.-born workers, while non-citizens and recent immigrants have far lower ones (the unionization rate for non-citizens is half that for immigrants who have naturalized, for example). Unionization rates also vary by nationality: they are far higher for immigrants born in the Caribbean and the Philippines or in parts of Eastern Europe and Africa than for U.S.-born workers (Milkman and Luce 2019; Kim and Kim 1997). Such variations reflect the distribution of nationality groups across industries, occupations, and regions, as well as their distinctive naturalization rates and the timing of their arrival into the United States.

Yet, for immigrants and U.S.-born workers alike, traditional unions have less and less room for maneuver, as new organizing efforts face unrelenting employer intransigence, legal developments continue to erode union rights, and labor law reform remains blocked. In sharp contrast to the period immediately after John Sweeney's election to the AFL-CIO presidency in 1995 on a "New Voice" platform that put organizing the unorganized at the top of organized labor's agenda, in the 2010s it has descended in importance. Less than a tenth of the federation's 2018–19 budget was earmarked for organizing, about a third of the level a decade earlier, while 35 percent was dedicated to funding political activity (Nolan 2019).

On the other hand, some unions have begun to experiment with alternative strategies for union revival, including efforts to establish European-style sectoral collective bargaining agreements on a tripartite basis (involving unions, employers, and the state), as well as state and local legislative campaigns to improve minimum wages and labor standards (Andrias 2016; Jacobs 2018; McCartin 2018). In recent years, unions have reached out to other social movements, among them the meteoric 2011 Occupy Wall Street movement. But none of these efforts involve significant numbers of immigrants. Moreover, most union leaders have been conspicuously absent from recent efforts to challenge the recent wave of deportations and other anti-immigrant policies under the Trump administration.

Worker Centers

Arguably there is no form of protection from employer abuse better than traditional unionism, with all its limitations. Although many immigrant workers are not aware of it, the fact that they are foreign-born, or even unauthorized, does not exclude them from the legal right to unionize guaranteed by the NLRA. There is one exception, established by the 2002 Supreme Court decision in *Hoffman Plastic Compounds, Inc. v. NLRB*, which ruled that unauthorized immigrants illegally fired for organizing activities are not entitled to back pay or to reinstatement (the remedies the NLRA stipulates for such violations). Back pay and reinstatement awards are rare events, however, so this exception has affected relatively few workers. *Hoffman* did spark fears that the longstanding firewall between labor law and immigration law might be further eroded, but that has not occurred.

Yet the NLRA and its nominal guarantee of collective bargaining rights excludes vast swaths of immigrant workers. Agricultural workers and domestic workers were carved out of the law from the outset. More recently they have been joined by the disproportionately foreign-born day laborers and taxi and truck drivers who are excluded because they are classified as independent contractors

(Griffith 2015), since the NLRA covers only employees. In the face of this challenge, an "alt-labor" movement dedicated to organizing and advocating for low-wage workers, especially immigrants, has burgeoned. It is comprised primarily of worker centers, which are not labor unions but freestanding organizations that operate entirely outside the strictures of the NLRA.

In 2018, there were 226 worker centers operating in the United States, up from only five in 1985 and 137 in 2005 (Fine et al. 2018: 10; Fine 2006: 10). Some of the centers focus on a particular ethnic identity or nationality; others have a geographic or neighborhood orientation; still others target specific occupations or industries where unions are weak or entirely absent (often, but not always, because the jobs are excluded from NLRA coverage).

From the outset, some worker centers were directly incubated or funded by traditional unions, but more often labor leaders viewed these alternative organizational forms with skepticism, if not outright hostility. For their part, worker center leaders often looked askance at traditional unions, which they considered anachronistic and ill-equipped to meet the needs of the growing ranks of precarious workers. Whereas most unions are led by men who have worked their way up through the ranks (and thus tend to be middle-aged or older) and have extensive resources at their disposal, worker centers are more often headed by women, many of them relatively young (Milkman and Terriquez 2012), and most operate on shoestring budgets. As Janice Fine notes, what might have been a "marriage made in heaven" between unions and worker centers was instead "more of a mismatch" (Fine 2007: 336):

> Worker centers are non-bureaucratic, grassroots organizations with small budgets, loose membership structures, improvisational cultures and strategies that are funded by foundation grants ... the inverse of prototypical American unions ... Unions are often alienated by worker centers' non-connection to industry and employer, broad and blunt internal organizational structures, loose membership bases, and reactive organizational ways of operating. Ideologically, some unions are annoyed by some centers' anti-capitalist rhetoric and

are perplexed by their tendency to focus on the distant horizon as opposed to shorter-term political, policy, and industry organizing goals. (Ibid.: 341)

Worker centers indeed deviate sharply from the traditional union model, both structurally and culturally. The centers are hybrid organizations with multiple functions. They organize at the grass-roots level and mount campaigns against workplace injustice, exposing employer abuses to the public through media outreach, in many cases making direct appeals to consumers. The centers offer legal services to workers paid below the minimum wage or subjected to other workplace violations and engage in policy and legislative advocacy to improve labor law enforcement (Fine 2006). They also routinely provide basic information – in written form and/or through educational workshops – to low-wage immigrant workers about their rights under U.S. labor and immigration law, assistance that is urgently needed and highly prized by recipients.

Many centers soon find that the demand for direct legal and social services is overwhelming relative to their modest staff and financial resources, which has led many of them to set limits on this aspect of their work. They tend to view service provision as a detour from long-term institutional change – treating the symptoms rather than the root causes of low-wage workers' problems. This concern has led many worker centers to emphasize grassroots organizing and education, as well as leadership development. They lack the resources to mount large-scale popular mobilizations themselves but regularly encourage participation in mobilizations organized by other groups. Similarly, although the centers rarely attempt to establish collective bargaining relationships with employers themselves, some refer interested workers to established unions.

Many worker centers have filed back-pay claims and have pursued complaints about minimum wage and other workplace violations with government regulatory agencies; some have also initiated successful class action lawsuits over such issues, winning millions of dollars in settlements (Brady 2014). But most choose to focus their efforts on research, media outreach, and public campaigns to extract concessions directly from employers and to win improved state protections for precarious workers. Framing their campaigns as struggles for social and economic justice, the centers construct compelling narratives that include the voices of low-wage workers themselves, skillfully drawing public and media attention to their plight. They also conduct strategic research to identify vulnerabilities in the power structure and pressure lawmakers to win regulatory reforms and improved social protection.

In cases where the workers they represent are excluded from NLRA coverage, worker centers can launch consumer boycotts without violating the prohibition on "secondary" boycotts (efforts to influence one firm by putting pressure on another one, for example picketing a store that sells a boycotted product) under the 1947 Taft–Hartley amendments to the NLRA. For example, the boycott against Taco Bell by the Coalition of Immokalee Workers (a worker center discussed further below), a pivotal feature of their campaign to win higher pay for tomato workers, benefited from the NLRA's exclusion of farm workers (Marquis 2017). Right-wing critics have argued that worker centers representing non-excluded groups of workers, such as the Restaurant Opportunities Center, are acting like unions and thus should be compelled to conform to the NLRA – in effect recognizing the advantages of operating outside its strictures (Marculewicz and Thomas 2012). On the other hand, some worker centers have creatively used the NLRA provision that protects workers' "concerted activity," even in the absence of a union, to win concessions from employers (Garrick 2014).

However, the term "organizing" has a different meaning in the worker center context than in the traditional union world. Some centers do actively recruit "members," but most of them find it difficult to forge long-term relationships with workers once their immediate need for services has been met. Low-wage immigrants typically have long hours, time-consuming commutes, and families to care for, leaving little time for engagement in center activities, particularly without the incentive of ongoing representation of the sort unions can provide. As a result, *many worker* center campaigns are staff-driven, although some rank-and-file workers do become actively engaged. When those involved are undocumented, as is often the case, their participation in such campaigns may draw them into a form of activism that Jennifer Gordon (2006: ch. 6) calls "noncitizen citizenship." Despite the fact that they lack voting and citizenship rights, the undocumented can and do testify at public hearings, make personal appeals to legislators, and engage in street protests. Indeed, the willingness of ordinary workers to tell their stories is a vital ingredient for many such efforts. Those stories – strategically disseminated via the mass media – are at the core of the symbolic politics that are the signature feature of worker center campaigns (Rosado Marzán 2017).

In this respect the centers closely resemble the transnational advocacy networks (TANs) that were the focus of Margaret Keck and Kathryn Sikkink's (1998) classic study. Like TANs, the centers are "nonstate actors ... [that] mobilize information strategically to help create new issues and categories and to persuade, pressure and gain leverage over much more powerful organizations and governments." Worker centers are locally rather than transnationally oriented (unless one considers immigration-related issues inherently transnational); but, apart from that, the parallels between their mode of operation and that of TANs are striking. Like TANs, worker centers are professionally led and staffed by advocates – typically young lawyers or individuals with other specialized training – who "introduce new ideas, provide information, and lobby for policy changes." Like their TAN-based counterparts, some worker center staff and activists circulate from one center to another: the "political entrepreneurs who become the core networkers for a new campaign have often gained experience in earlier ones" (Keck and Sikkink 1998: 1–2, 9, 14). Moreover, TANs and worker centers employ similar political strategies and tactics.

As noted earlier in regard to immigrant union activists, many worker center leaders are veterans of political and labor movements in their countries of origin. One example is the Coalition of Immokalee Workers, which spotlighted labor abuses in Florida's tomato fields and fought successfully to improve pay and working conditions in a high-profile consumer-directed campaign. As Susan Marquis's detailed history of the organization notes:

> What was to become the Coalition of Immokalee Workers had a critical asset from the beginning: recent immigrants from those nations where there was a long history of political organizing. The Haitians were particularly important. Fleeing the violence and retribution that followed the military's overthrow of Jean-Bertrand Aristide ... were political, not economic refugees, and many had been involved in political activism in Haiti ... At the same time, there was an increasing number of immigrants from Guatemala, El Salvador, and Chiapas ... [who] offered new tools for change ... [such as] the popular education ideas of Paolo Freire and variations of liberation theology. (Marquis 2017: 17)

Another example is Pablo Alvarado, who directs the National Day Laborer Organizing Network (NDLON). He emigrated to the United States in 1990 from El Salvador and was deeply influenced by his brother, who ran a literacy class for peasants in the village where they grew up based on Freire's ideas, a model that Alvarado later replicated in Los Angeles (Dreier and Maier 2016).

Worker centers in many respects recall the organizational forms that emerged among labor reformers in the late nineteenth and early twentieth century. The pioneering Working Women's Protective Union and the Boston Women's Educational and Industrial Union (Batlan 2015), and later settlement houses and labor reform groups such as the Women's Trade Union League, exposed sweatshops and employer abuses of immigrant workers, lobbied for protective legislation, provided educational and social services to immigrants, and assisted them in unionization efforts. Like today's worker centers, these groups typically relied on philanthropic support and were led by highly educated elites, in most cases female (Fine 2006: 34–5). When worker centers emerged in the 1990s, few were aware of these historical antecedents, but the parallels are not surprising when considered in relation to the restoration of pre-New Deal conditions in recent decades.

Worker center activists were more conscious of their reliance on tactics used by the United Farm Workers, such as reaching out to students and faith leaders for support (Marquis 2017: 35; Gordon 2005), tactics that union organizers also used in campaigns among immigrant workers, as noted earlier.

Despite the modest resources at their disposal, the worker centers have accomplished a great deal in recent years. Several have blossomed from local into national organizations, including the National Domestic Workers Association, the Restaurant Opportunities Center United, the National Taxi Workers Alliance, and NDLON. Yet the centers' advocacy-centered model has inherent limitations. As Steve Jenkins (2002) has observed, "unlike union campaigns where workers can potentially demand higher wages, vacation days, and health insurance," worker centers rarely if ever extend their efforts beyond seeking remedies for illegal employer practices. Indeed, even the most successful worker center campaigns typically win improvements in pay and conditions only for small groups of workers. As Shannon Gleeson has noted, "advocates are hampered by the shoestring budgets with which they operate, the limited remedies under the law, and the practical challenges posed by the behemoth bureaucracies that enforce the law and the quotidian struggles of low-wage workers' lives" (Gleeson 2016: 12). The alt-labor movement has been highly successful on the moral and discursive level, but on the ground it has made little progress in reversing the rapid growth of precarity at the bottom of the labor market.

Faced with these limitations, some worker centers recently have developed an interest in experimenting with traditional union models to expand the scale of their work and to build durable organizations that are financially independent (rather than continuing to rely on philanthropy). At the same time, traditional union leaders have been increasingly impressed by the achievements of the worker centers, about which they were initially deeply skeptical. In 2006 the AFL-CIO Executive Council passed a formal resolution calling on organized labor to build ties with worker centers in their communities (Narro and Fine 2018: 75).

A few unions have engaged in the highest form of flattery, adopting the worker centers' strategic and tactical playbook in their own efforts to organize low-wage immigrant workers. For example, in Los Angeles and later in New York City, the successful efforts in the 2000s to unionize *carwasheros* – immigrant car-wash workers, most of them undocumented – relied heavily on worker center-like tactics (Garea and Stern 2010; Jamieson 2013). A better-known example is the SEIU-funded "Fight for $15" campaign for fast-food workers, which was launched in New York in 2012 and rapidly spread nationwide, demanding minimum pay of $15 an hour and a union for all fast-food workers. Fast-food workers are ordinary employees and thus eligible for unionization under the NLRA, but, since most are employed by franchises with relatively modest profit margins, the SEIU's aim is an industrywide unionization strategy (as in its JFJ campaign decades earlier). Union recognition remains elusive, but the campaign did spark successful efforts to win legislation raising the minimum wage to $15 in multiple jurisdictions across the country (Andrias 2016).

Traditional unions and worker centers not only developed more synergies with one another over time but also drew closer to the broader immigrant rights movement in the twenty-first century. That movement had been quietly taking shape for decades, but in the spring of 2006 it exploded into public view with a wave of massive street protests across the nation. The provocation was the U.S. House of Representatives' passage in late 2005 of H.R. 4337, legislation that would have made unauthorized presence in the United States a felony rather than a civil violation. This move to criminalize undocumented immigration inspired one of the main slogans at the marches, "We Are Workers, Not Criminals," explicitly highlighting the centrality of labor issues to the immigrant rights movement. As noted above, building on the immigrant organizing of some of its affiliates in the 1990s, the AFL-CIO had officially endorsed immigrant rights in the year 2000; the worker centers had been close allies of the immigrant rights movement from their inception. The 2006 marches further consolidated these alliances among the three strands of immigrant labor activism.

The Immigrant Rights Movement

From the outset, the central goal of the immigrant rights movement was to eliminate or weaken the barriers to economic advancement for immigrants, especially the unauthorized – for whom the critical barrier is lack of legal status. In that sense the immigrant rights movement often functions as a *de facto* labor movement. Alongside traditional unions' efforts to organize immigrants and the worker centers, the immigrant rights movement expanded rapidly in the last decade of the twentieth century, soon after the passage of the Immigration Reform and Control Act (IRCA) in 1986. That law ramped up border enforcement and made it harder for employers to hire unauthorized immigrants, yet at the same time it granted some 3 million of them amnesty (Massey et al. 2002: 49).

Immigrant rights groups mobilized to help those eligible for the amnesty program navigate the application process. (Some unions and worker centers did so as well.) Ironically, as noted in chapter 3, although IRCA was intended to curtail unauthorized immigration, in practice it had the opposite effect. As enhanced border enforcement made circular migration more difficult, growing numbers of migrant workers settled permanently in the United States, and many of their family members later followed (Massey et al. 2002). In 1986, when IRCA became law, there were about 4 million unauthorized immigrants; twenty years later their numbers had swelled to an estimated 11 million (Passell 2006).

IRCA also institutionalized "employer sanctions" intended to penalize those who hired undocumented immigrants, a provision of the law that most unions supported at the time. This too had unanticipated consequences. Employers were rarely prosecuted under the new law, which merely required them to affirm that immigrants had presented documents authorizing them to live and work in the United States. Fraudulent documents soon became widely available, but employers had no incentive to challenge their authenticity. In the rare cases where invalid documents were discovered, the penalties were borne disproportionately by unauthorized workers themselves. They lost their jobs if they were apprehended by immigration agents and could also be detained and deported, while employers suffered few consequences (Brownell 2009).

In the post-IRCA years, unauthorized immigrant workers were also targeted by "no-match" letters (alerting employers that the names and social security numbers of their employees did not match), as well as periodic workplace raids. Employers resented such disruptions to their operations and the costs they impose, and a few have suffered criminal penalties. But in most cases they simply replaced the workers they lost with new recruits – an inconvenience, to be sure, but one widely regarded as a "cost of doing business." Adding insult to injury, that cost is often passed on to unauthorized workers themselves, whose wages deteriorated after IRCA became law (Phillips and Massey 1999).

IRCA was the political result of resurgent nativist alarm over undocumented immigration, yet it also stimulated the growth and consolidation of the immigrant rights movement (Zepeda-Millán 2017: 36; Nicholls 2019). That in turn set the stage for an ongoing movement–countermovement dynamic, in which anti-immigrant political backlash engendered increased immigrant rights mobilization, followed by renewed backlash (Bloemraad and Voss 2019). One example of this cycle emerged in 1994 in California, home to the nation's largest unauthorized immigrant population, when the state's voters passed Proposition 187, which would have denied most public services, including schooling, to undocumented immigrants. Although this measure eventually was struck down by the courts and thus never implemented, its passage sparked large street protests among immigrants across the state; in Los Angeles those demonstrations were the largest since the Vietnam War. Another unintended consequence of Proposition 187 was a wave of reactive naturalization among California's legal immigrants eligible for citizenship, with enduring political consequences. Because then Governor Pete Wilson had been a vocal supporter of the measure, along with the rest of the state's Republican establishment, most of the newly naturalized citizens who registered to vote – which immigrant rights groups and unions actively encouraged them to do – became loyal Democrats (Milkman 2011).

Two years later, a new federal law aiming to curb unauthorized immigration was signed into law by President Clinton. This was the Illegal Immigration Reform and Immigrant Responsibility Act (IIRIRA), which introduced restrictions on welfare benefits for *legal* immigrants, further increased border enforcement, and made it easier to deport immigrants, both legal and unauthorized, for relatively minor criminal offenses. Although IIRIRA was proposed by Republicans, it had synergies with Clinton's "welfare reform" and anti-crime initiatives (Lind 2016). The resulting hardships in immigrant communities spurred renewed growth in the immigrant rights movement.

The attacks of September 11, 2011, stymied the movement's progress, however, and put immigration reform into the deep freeze. Still the influx of unauthorized immigrants continued unabated; only in the aftermath of the financial crisis of 2007–8 would that change. Crossing the border became even more arduous as a result of the heightened security measures sparked by 9/11. Although the numbers of unauthorized immigrants continued to grow, they found it increasingly difficult to climb out of entry-level jobs at the bottom of the labor market, as so many of their predecessors had done, making the quest for a path to legalization all the more urgent.

These developments led immigrant rights groups – along with worker centers and labor unions with substantial numbers of foreign-born members – to ramp up their organizing efforts in the twenty-first century, with growing support from foundations as well as organized labor (Nicholls 2019). Street protests for immigrant rights became a regular May Day event, reviving a labor holiday widely observed in many immigrants' countries of origin but one that had become unfamiliar in the United States. Another significant effort in the aftermath of 9/11 was the 2003 Immigrant Worker Freedom Ride (IWFR), modeled on the civil rights movement's 1960s "Freedom Rides." The IWFR was organized by SEIU, UNITE HERE, and the AFL-CIO, along with a coalition of students, faith leaders, worker centers, and immigrant rights groups. Busloads of immigrant rights activists left from ten different cities, stopping for rallies along the way, and then converged in Washington, DC, and New York City. The IWFR in many respects prefigured the massive street marches three years later, although it received relatively limited publicity (Shaw 2008: 221–5).

In the political arena, meanwhile, conflict continued to escalate between immigrant rights advocates and supporters of immigration restriction. Even with tacit support from the business wing of the Republican Party, the Bush administration's repeated efforts to pass comprehensive immigration reform legislation foundered, intensifying the level of frustration in the immigrant rights community. The mounting tensions exploded when the U.S. House of Representatives passed H.R. 4437 in December 2005, as the embryonic immigrant rights movement responded with a series of organized mass protests.

The following spring, in Chicago, Los Angeles, and other cities and towns across the nation, millions of immigrants and their supporters took to the streets in huge outpourings that culminated on May 1, 2006. On a scale that surprised even the organizers themselves, thanks in part to the Spanish-language media's promotion of the marches, the vast but hitherto invisible Latinx immigrant community peacefully rallied all across the nation. By this time, more and more immigrant households included both individuals with legal status and others who were unauthorized, and the entire Latinx population was regularly subjected to the stigma attached to "illegal aliens," broadening the base of support. In Los Angeles, home to the largest marches, the protests drew "grandmothers, elderly *vaqueros* [cowboys], toddlers in strollers, people in wheelchairs … gardeners, nannies, construction workers, taco truck guys, contractors, business owners … no subsegment of the region's Latino population was left unrepresented" (Zepeda-Millán 2017: 89). The Catholic Church, unions, and worker centers supported the marches as well (Bloemraad et al. 2011).

H.R. 4437 never became law, and in that regard the 2006 protests were successful, but their larger purpose was unfulfilled. Soon after the marches, the Bush administration – by then apparently resigned to the failure of its earlier efforts to win immigration reform legislation – stepped up workplace raids and deportations. At the same time, many state and local governments passed laws targeting unauthorized immigrants (Gulasekaram and Ramakrishnan 2015: 6). This deepened the sense of economic threat in immigrant communities, sparking a new wave of reactive naturalization like the one that had followed Proposition 187, but this time on a national scale. During the fiscal year ending September 30, 2007, over 1.1 million immigrants filed applications for naturalization, up 55 percent over the preceding year. The coalition that organized the 2006 marches turned its energies to promoting naturalization and then voting registration among eligible immigrants.

Most of the new citizens generated by this effort were Latinx immigrants who would soon become loyal Democratic voters. In the 2008 presidential election, 67 percent of all Latinx voters, and 78 percent of Latinx immigrants, cast their ballots for Barack Obama, compared to 43 percent of whites (Milkman 2011: 211). According to post-election surveys, 15 percent of these Latinx voters had never before participated in an election. They fulfilled the promise of a slogan widely displayed in the 2006 protests: "Today We March, Tomorrow We Vote." Indeed, their votes proved crucial in battleground states such as Nevada, Colorado, New Mexico, and Florida. As a conservative commentator lamented, "The fear and the fury engendered in the broader Hispanic community has destroyed conservative prospects in the Southwest, weakened them in the West, and wiped them out in New England" (Nadler 2009).

During the Obama years the Democrats became increasingly aligned with the cause of immigrant rights, while the Republican Party offered a political home to the growing ranks of nativists – for many of whom the nation's first African-American president was anathema. This helped crystallize the era of political polarization (by no means limited to immigration policy) that endures to this day. That polarization in turn became an insurmountable obstacle to the Obama administration's efforts to advance comprehensive immigration reform, especially after the 2010 midterm elections, in which Republicans, with the help of the militantly anti-immigrant Tea Party, took control of the U.S. House of Representatives.

Although no mass demonstrations on the scale of those in 2006 have taken place since, the immigrant rights movement continued to develop during the Obama years. Its center of gravity shifted to the youthful "Dreamers," named for the proposed DREAM (Development, Relief and Education for Alien Minors) Act, first proposed in the U.S. Congress in August 2001 – just before the 9/11 attacks put immigration reform on hold. This legislation would have offered legal residency and a path to U.S. citizenship to unauthorized immigrants who had arrived in the United States as children if they had completed two years of college or of military service (among other conditions).

The DREAM Act was crafted by seasoned immigrant rights activists who hoped that the plight of unauthorized young people would generate public sympathy and help galvanize support for a path to citizenship for the larger undocumented population. The Dreamers were trained by the parent immigrant rights movement to articulate a narrative stressing that they had been brought to the United States as small children and had not themselves chosen to cross the border illegally (or overstay a visa). Growing up in the United States from an early age, the narrative continued, they were fully assimilated and spoke perfect English. Only as they approached adulthood, when they needed a Social Security number to apply to college or for a job, did they even learn of their lack of legal status.

This narrative, as Walter Nicholls (2013: 50–3) has noted, deliberately embraced such American national symbols as the flag and the Statue of Liberty, as well as values such as "hard work" and "fairness." Moreover, the chosen story-tellers were the "best and the brightest" – valedictorians, straight-A students, and other youth who were poised for upward mobility if only they could win legal status. They drew extensive and sympathetic attention from both ethnic and mainstream media, yet all the attempts to pass the DREAM Act (like broader immigration reform legislative proposals) failed in the U.S. Congress.

Although they initially accepted the mentorship of older immigrant rights activists, by 2008 the Dreamers – many of whom were now college graduates – began to break away from the "parent" movement to form their own autonomous organizations. They adopted a more radical ideology, rejecting any suggestion that they should apologize for their parents' having crossed the border without authorization, as the original narrative had implied, pointing out that their parents were simply seeking a better life for their families. Many Dreamers also "came out" publicly as undocumented in political meetings and on social media, embracing the language of intersectionality and developing a leadership cadre that was disproportionately female and LGBTQ-identified (Terriquez 2015). Yet, at the same time, they focused on specific legislative goals, like the larger immigrant rights movement. For both, the long-term aim was to win passage of the DREAM Act, along with comprehensive immigration reform, creating a path to legalization for undocumented immigrants. After 2010 it became obvious that congressional gridlock would block such efforts, and the Dreamers turned their efforts increasingly to campaigns for state-level legislation, with considerable success: by 2015 they had won laws granting undocumented students in-state college tuition laws in twenty states and access to financial aid in five states (National Conference of State Legislators 2015).

These efforts initially relied on conventional tactics such as lobbying elected officials, but after the 2010 elections the Dreamers increasingly turned to more direct action. For example, they occupied the Arizona office of U.S. Senator John McCain and launched a hunger strike in front of the office of California Senator Diane Feinstein (Zamorano et al. 2010). They regularly engaged in civil disobedience, deliberately courting arrest and deportation at immigrant detention centers along the border to protest the rising number of deportations under the Obama administration.

In early June 2012, a group of Dreamers staged a sit-in at one of Obama's campaign offices, demanding that he use his executive power on their behalf in the face of continuing congressional opposition to the DREAM Act. This led to the Deferred Action for Childhood Arrivals (DACA) program, established by a presidential Executive Order on June 15, 2012, which allows young undocumented immigrants to obtain work permits and protects them against deportation for a two-year renewable term. Although it did not provide a path to full legal status or citizenship, DACA was a key victory for the immigrant rights movement. Two years later, under ongoing pressure to act, Obama signed another Executive Order creating Deferred Action for Parents of Americans (DAPA), offering terms similar to DACA for unauthorized immigrants whose children are U.S. citizens or legal residents. But DAPA was successfully challenged in the courts and later nullified by the Trump administration.

All three components of the immigrant labor movement have been forced onto the defensive since Trump's unexpected election to the presidency and the ongoing barrage of xenophobic rhetoric and administrative initiatives targeting immigrants. Perhaps these developments will eventually spark further growth in the grassroots immigrant rights movement, as Proposition 187 and H.R. 4437 did in the past. But at the time of writing there is no sign of that. Instead, there is less cohesion among the three strands of the immigrant labor movement in the Trump era than before.

Most notably, unions have been conspicuously invisible among the progressive organizations directly challenging Trump's draconian immigration policies, although on the local level some unions with substantial foreign-born memberships (and many worker centers as well) have engaged in such rearguard efforts as training their members to prepare for deportations, workplace raids, or home visits from immigration authorities. Meanwhile, immigrant rights groups, with support from civil liberties groups and other progressives, as well as some worker centers, have devoted themselves to mounting legal challenges to the Trump administration's steady stream of initiatives targeting both legal and unauthorized immigrants. Indeed, since 2017 the struggle for immigrant rights has pivoted from the workplace and the streets to the courtroom, reflecting both rising fear within immigrant communities and the fact that the judicial system has proven to be the most effective check on the executive branch's unilateral efforts to reshape U.S. immigration policy. But another critical challenge for advocates of immigrant rights is to win the hearts and minds of the public, and especially of voters, with an alternative narrative to the one driving Trump's policies. That is the subject of the next chapter.

Conclusion

> No issue better illustrates the divide between America's working class and America's political class than illegal immigration. Wealthy politicians and donors push for open borders, while living their lives behind walls and gates and guards. Meanwhile, working-class Americans are left to pay the price for mass illegal immigration – reduced jobs, lower wages, overburdened schools and hospitals, increased crime, and a depleted social safety net.
>
> President Donald J. Trump, State of the Union address, 2019

This book's analysis of the impact of low-wage immigration on the U.S. labor market directly challenges the immigrant threat narrative that President Trump and his supporters relentlessly promote. Their claim that immigration has been a key driver of working-class emiseration may seem plausible at first glance, especially in regard to timing. Indeed, soon after the passage in 1965 of the Hart–Celler Act brought an end to four decades of highly restricted immigration, the economic status of white male non-college-educated workers, most of whom had prospered in the post-World War II years, began to spiral downward. These developments are indeed interconnected, but, as the previous chapters document, the line of causality is exactly the opposite of that suggested by the immigrant threat narrative. The reversal of fortune suffered by U.S.-born workers since the 1970s was caused not by immigration but by the devastating effects of deregulation, deindustrialization and de-unionization, along with rising inequality.

The primary driver of labor migration, past and present, is economic demand. While "push" factors in sending countries can spur emigration, it materializes on a large scale only in response to employers' search for new sources of labor (Piore 1979). The 2008 financial crisis illustrates this dynamic: as the U.S. economy imploded, and jobs in sectors such as construction and low-wage service industries evaporated, unauthorized labor migrants abruptly stopped crossing the border. Before the Great Recession, in contrast, immigration grew in direct response to rising employer demand for cheap and pliable labor. Refugee flows driven by threats to life in sending countries, which have grown worldwide in recent years, are another matter, beyond the scope of this book.

In manufacturing industries that once offered high-wage blue-collar employment to non-college-educated American workers, millions of jobs vanished over the past half-century. Some of those jobs were outsourced to other parts of the world; others were rendered obsolete by new technology. No one suggests that immigrants are to blame for these developments. However, in many place-bound industries, jobs did not disappear but instead were degraded by such business strategies as expanded subcontracting, deregulation, and efforts to weaken or eliminate labor unions. As those developments unfolded starting in the 1970s, many U.S.-born workers voted with their feet to reject the jobs affected, and employers then hired foreign-born newcomers to fill the resulting vacancies. In this way, both authorized and unauthorized immigrants entered the bottom tier of the labor market in a variety of "jobs Americans won't do."

Although this book focuses on low-wage labor, the phenomenon of job degradation spurring an exodus of U.S.-born workers and their subsequent replacement by immigrants is not limited to the blue-collar sector, as the *New York Times* reported recently:

> The latest wave of foreign workers sweeping into American jobs brought Donato Soberano from the Philippines to Arizona two years ago. He had to pay thousands of dollars to a job broker and lived for a time in an apartment with five other Filipino workers. The lure is the pay – 10 times more than what he made doing the same work back home ...
>
> Mr. Soberano is not a hospitality worker or a home health aide. He is in another line of work that increasingly pays too little to

attract enough Americans: Mr. Soberano is a public school teacher
… The school districts that recruit teachers like Mr. Soberano say
that they have few other options … they can't find enough American
educators willing to work for the pay that's offered. (Goldstein
2018)

This example parallels the dynamic in residential construction
and the other industries analyzed in chapter 3, albeit on a much
smaller scale.

Since the 1970s, demand for immigrant labor has also expanded
in domestic work and other low-wage service jobs formerly
dominated by African Americans. As chapter 4 showed, here the
key drivers of change were not employment restructuring and job
degradation but, instead, demographic changes and rising income
inequality. As maternal labor force participation rose, the nation's
increasingly affluent professional and managerial classes began to
devote a growing share of their incomes to purchasing services from
housecleaners and nannies, as well as services provided outside the
home such as restaurant meals. At the same time, the aging of the
population sparked increased demand for home health-care assistance and other types of eldercare. These developments occurred
at just the time when the civil rights movement won expanded
employment opportunities for African-American women, who
traditionally had been concentrated in domestic work and other
in-home occupations. But they began to shun those fields precisely
when labor demand in them surged, leading many households to
hire immigrants instead. Similarly, in the low-wage food-service
sector, starting in the 1970s, immigrants increasingly entered jobs
abandoned by U.S.-born workers of color who gained access to
better employment options. Other service industries also expanded
in this period, such as nail salons, sparking still further demand
for low-wage immigrant labor.

The immigrant threat narrative has served to distract attention
from these processes and thereby obscured the actual causes of
declining working-class living standards. Non-college-educated
American workers have every reason to be angry about rising
inequality and the growing scarcity of good jobs. The political

challenge for progressives is to redirect that anger to target the employers who deliberately outsourced or degraded formerly well-paid blue-collar jobs and the business interests promoting public policies that widen inequality. Only in this way can the immigrant threat narrative, which continues to fuel popular anxieties, be neutralized.

The Politics of Immigration in the Age of Populism

The immigrant threat narrative is more than a set of ideas. It has facilitated draconian anti-immigrant policy initiatives with vast ramifications both for the nation's foreign-born population and for American politics. Since taking power in 2017, the Trump administration has promulgated the Muslim travel ban, efforts to limit admissions of refugees and asylum-seekers, family separations at the border, workplace raids, and large-scale deportations. Superficially, there is continuity in regard to the last of these: not for nothing was Obama tagged with the moniker "deporter-in-chief." Yet most deportations in the Obama era involved newly arrived immigrants apprehended at the border and those with serious criminal records. The Trump administration, in contrast, has prioritized "internal removals" of the undocumented, regularly sweeping up those with no criminal records and others who have resided in the United States for many years. Under Trump, Immigration and Customs Enforcement (ICE) agents have also apprehended undocumented immigrants in courthouses and outside schools, locations avoided by previous administrations (Capps et al. 2018). ICE has also revived workplace raids, rare in the Obama years (U.S. Immigration and Customs Enforcement 2018). In addition, Trump has attempted to curb *legal* immigration, for example by seeking to end "temporary protected status" for Haitians, Central Americans, and others (Cohn et al. 2019). The president regularly boasts about these initiatives in his speeches and tweets, along with his beloved border wall.

As detentions and deportations have become increasingly arbitrary and unpredictable, fear and anxiety in immigrant communities have spiked to levels not seen for half a century (M. Greenberg 2018). That is one reason why the extent and scope of labor activism among immigrant workers has declined, especially relative to the 1990s and 2000s (see chapter 5). Nevertheless the unionization rate among foreign-born workers has not declined: it has actually increased slightly since Trump's election to the presidency, rising from 8.2 percent in 2016 to 8.5 percent in 2018, while over that same period unionization declined among the U.S.-born, from 11.2 to 10.9 percent (Dew 2018: 6; Rho and Brown 2019: 4). However, organized labor is no longer at the forefront of the struggle to defend immigrant rights, and a few unions – notably those representing ICE agents and border control officers – endorsed Trump in 2016 and ever since have been cheer-leaders for his "zero-tolerance" immigration policies. Meanwhile, other unions have provided support for immigrants threatened with deportation. In 2017 the AFL-CIO developed a "toolkit" to assist unionists threatened with workplace immigration raids, and several of its affiliates launched training efforts to educate members about how to respond to workplace raids or threats of deportation (Jamieson 2017). That is the mission of the Working Families United coalition, formed in 2017 by the Painters' union, the hotel workers' union, the United Food and Commercial Workers, and the Teamsters, as well as the Bricklayers and Ironworkers (Gies 2018). Worker centers and a few unions have also supported campaigns to maintain Temporary Protected Status and the 2012 Deferred Action for Childhood Arrivals program, in the face of Trump's efforts to end those programs (Johnson 2019).

The labor movement is uniquely well positioned to counter the immigrant threat narrative with the counternarrative this book offers. But it is hardly the only component of the progressive pro-immigrant coalition that has faltered in the wake of Trump's success (and that of right-wing populists in Europe) in galvanizing white working-class support by demonizing immigrants. In an interview published shortly after the 2018 midterm elections, for example, Hillary Clinton (who had advocated for liberal immigration policies during her presidential campaign two years earlier) declared, "If we don't deal with the migration issue it will continue to roil the body politic." David Frum (2019) echoed her warning in more hyperbolic language in an article in *The Atlantic* entitled "If Liberals Won't Enforce Borders, Fascists Will."

Other progressive commentators have ventured even further down this path. Recently liberal political analyst John Judis confessed his personal sympathy for Trump's nationalist agenda in his 2018 book, where he also endorsed the argument that low-wage immigration inevitably reduces the leverage of U.S.-born workers. "Enormous numbers of unskilled immigrants have competed for jobs with Americans who also lack higher education and have led to the downgrading of occupations that were once middle class," Judis asserts, adding, "without control of borders and immigration, it is very hard to imagine the United States becoming a more egalitarian society" (Judis 2018: 77, 146). In a similar vein, left-wing sociologist Wolfgang Streeck laments what he characterizes as left-wing "anti-statism dressed up as anti-nationalism" in Germany. "By fighting for deregulation of national borders to allow for open and open-ended immigration," he declares, "the Left abandons a central element of its historical pro-regulation agenda, which importantly involved restricting the supply of labor" (Streeck 2018: 6–7).

Even more pointedly, Andrea Nagle (2018) harkens back nostalgically to the days when U.S. trade unions embraced restrictive immigration policies, noting (accurately) that the main supporters of open borders have been free-market ideologues such as the Koch brothers, along with employers reliant on cheap labor. Historically, she notes, U.S. unions took the opposite view:

> They [unions] saw the deliberate importation of illegal, low-wage workers as weakening labor's bargaining power and as a form of exploitation. There is no getting around the fact that the power of unions relies by definition on their ability to restrict and withdraw the supply of labor, which becomes impossible if an entire workforce can be easily and cheaply replaced. Open borders and mass immigration are a victory for the bosses.

Conclusion

As noted in chapter 5, two decades ago the U.S. labor movement definitively abandoned the perspective promoted by Nagle, even if it has not yet stepped up to the challenge of frontally confronting Trump's immigration policies. Most other U.S. progressives do strongly oppose the restrictive policies advocated by Trump and his acolytes and vociferously support immigrant rights, although very few support "open borders" (exceptions include Manjoo 2019; Lee 2019). Judis, Nagle, and others who favor restriction, moreover, do not address the practical challenges involved. Late twentieth-century efforts to prevent migrants from crossing the nation's southern border without authorization were abysmally ineffective as long as demand for migrant labor remained in place (Cornelius and Salehyan 2007; Massey et al. 2002). In recent years, the number of unauthorized immigrants who acquired that status by overstaying their visas has exceeded that of those crossing the border illegally (Warren 2017). And the growing numbers of Central American women and children asylum-seekers present themselves openly to border control agents. Ramping up border enforcement would not stem either of those flows.

There are also compelling *economic* reasons for organized labor and other progressives to maintain their support of liberal immigration policies. Immigration surely does expand the labor supply, as Nagle emphasizes, but it also creates additional economic demand and, thus, more jobs. In addition, the relatively youthful immigrant workforce contributes to the sustainability of Social Security and Medicare, an increasingly urgent issue as the U.S. population ages. The consensus among experts, as discussed in the Introduction, is that immigration has minuscule negative impacts on U.S.-born workers, more than outweighed by its economic benefits.

But, as Eric Levitz (2018) points out, the case made by commentators such as Judis and Nagle as to why progressives should support restrictive immigration policies is "primarily an argument about *politics*, not economics," ultimately pivoting on the susceptibility of U.S.-born workers to right-wing populist appeals – especially the white swing voters in the Rustbelt states whose support for Trump helped make his 2016 electoral victory

167

possible. Indeed, Levitz argues that abandoning support for immigrant rights and embracing restrictive policies would be politically disastrous for the Democratic Party and the wider progressive community. Given the demographic trends that are moving the nation inexorably toward a "majority–minority" society, he points out, "the Democrats are going to be a visibly multiracial party in a browning America." He goes on to argue that, on both moral and pragmatic grounds, "there is no way for Democrats to avoid the liabilities of that position – they can only strive to capitalize on its benefits." Similarly, Ian Haney López makes a strong case that the only viable path forward for Democrats is to frontally challenge the racism and xenophobia of Trump and his allies. "The best response to divide-and-conquer is unite-and-build," he declares, adding that the challenge facing progressives is to "reframe racism as a weapon of the rich" (Haney López 2019: xxiii, 120).

Steve Phillips (2016) elaborates the practical implications of this position, urging Democrats to focus their resources on voter registration and electoral turnout efforts targeting the Latinx and African-American communities, whose numbers greatly exceed those of white working-class swing voters whose defections are so often lamented. The main factor underlying Republican electoral victories, Phillips maintains, is that so many voters of color stay home. Indeed, in 2016, a majority of Latinxs (52 percent) and a substantial share of African Americans (40 percent) did not vote (Haney López 2019: 92). When they do so, the vast majority of African Americans, and a growing majority of Latinx voters, support Democrats, so that "a multiracial progressive coalition can achieve an electoral majority with the *current* level of White working-class support" (Phillips 2016: 65, emphasis added). Signs of reduced tension between the African-American and Latinx communities, even before the 2016 election, are relevant in this regard. For example, the data in figure 1 (see p. 5) show that the proportion of blacks who view immigration as harmful to U.S.-born workers fell sharply between 2006 and 2016. There is also evidence of a similar shift in the workplace context, where union organizers have increasingly overcome employer efforts to drive a wedge between Latinx and African-American workers (Bacon 2008; Gordon and Lenhardt 2007; Waltz 2018).

The 2018 midterm elections offer further encouragement. Although a post-election survey found that those who voted for Republicans that year cited "open borders" as their primary concern, that electoral block was roundly defeated at the ballot box. A solid majority (54 percent) of voters in 2018 told pollsters that immigrants "strengthen our country." As Stanley B. Greenberg has pointed out, in that year's election campaign:

> Democrats embraced their diversity. They supported comprehensive immigration reform and the Dreamers, opposed Mr. Trump's border wall and opposed the separation of children from their families ... the Republicans lost badly in the House by running as an anti-immigrant party, while the Democrats made major gains as a self-confident multicultural party.

Progressive efforts to regain support from white working-class voters and campaigns to register and ensure turnout among Latinx and African Americans are not mutually exclusive. Insofar as Democrats do actively seek to attract white swing voters, however, they must explicitly counter the right-wing populist threat narrative that blames immigrants for the plight of U.S.-born workers. This book offers a counternarrative, documenting the ways in which employers have systematically reduced wages and undermined the labor movement from the late 1970s onward. Rather than joining Frum, Judis, Nagle, Streeck, and others on the anti-immigrant bandwagon, progressives aiming to gain the support of the white U.S.-born workers who supported Trump in 2016 should aim to shift the public conversation in this direction.

This counternarrative can also contribute to the effort to build a progressive form of populism – one that exposes the fallacies of right-wing xenophobic populist ideology while explicitly acknowledging the corruption of the existing political system and challenging the power of the elites who control that system. The challenge for progressive populists is to make the case that the interests of those elites are diametrically opposed *both* to those of the white working class *and* to those of people of color. It is equally critical to expose the ways in which right-wing populists (despite claims to the contrary) help to perpetuate elite power. Chantal Mouffe's account of the French workers who switched their allegiances from the National Front to the left-wing "La France Insoumise" in 2017 offers a promising example of how this might be done:

> Arguing with people who ... had been led to see immigrants as responsible for their deprivation, activists were able to make such voters alter their views. Their sentiment of being left behind and their desire for democratic recognition, previously expressed in xenophobic language, could be formulated in a different vocabulary and directed toward another adversary. (Mouffe 2018: 23)

This should also be possible in the United States, where voters' political allegiances are notoriously fluid. But centrist Democrats cannot credibly carry out this project; they are too deeply beholden to the very corporate interests whose anti-union efforts and campaigns for deregulation produced the emiseration of the white working class and the explosive growth of economic inequality. Indeed, that is precisely what inspired so many white working-class voters to embrace right-wing populism in the first place, and what has led many African Americans and Latinx citizens to refrain from voting at all. But progressives could construct a muscular left-wing populist alternative to the divide-and-conquer politics of right-wing populism, articulating the common interests of all working people in rejecting racism and xenophobia, while pressuring employers to upgrade jobs and demanding public policies that reduce inequality. The evidence-based counternarrative presented in these pages is a necessary, albeit insufficient, element for carrying out that project.

Notes

Introduction

1 Throughout this book I use the gender-neutral term Latinx (and the plural Latinxs) to refer to what many others call "Hispanic" or "Latino."

2 Not only has this narrative been explicitly disseminated for decades by conservative media outlets such as Fox News, but it has also been indirectly reinforced by immigration coverage in the mainstream media. As Abrajano and Hajnal show, between 1980 and 2011, the *New York Times* published four times as many stories with negative depictions of immigrants as with positive ones; over the same period, the share of *Times* stories that focused on Latinx immigrants, the central targets of the threat narrative, steadily increased (Abrajano and Hajnal 2015: 166).

3 Responses of "not much effect" and "don't know/refused" are not shown. Whites and blacks include only non-Hispanics; Hispanics can be of any race. These surveys of U.S. adults were conducted between June 20 and July 16, 2006 (n = 2003), and between May 25 and June 29, 2016 (n = 5006).

Chapter 1 Brown-Collar Jobs

1 These figures are for non-Hispanic whites, Asians, and blacks.

2 Agriculture is a special and more complex case, discussed in chapter 2.

Chapter 2 Immigration and Labor in Historical Perspective

1 H2-A visas are temporary guest worker visas. Created in 1952 as H-2 visas, they were initially few in number and co-existed with the *bracero* program; after its termination in 1964 H-2 use expanded. In 1986 the H-2 category was split into H2-A visas for agriculture and H2-B workers for other occupational fields. Agricultural employers facing a shortage of domestic

workers can apply to the U.S. government for a limited number of H-2 visas annually.

Chapter 3 The Eclipse of the New Deal

1 The term "neoliberal" refers to nineteenth-century economic liberalism, which opposed government interference with market forces – not the political liberalism associated with the Democratic Party. Harvey (2005: 2) defines it as "a theory of political economy that proposes that human well-being can best be advanced by liberating individual entrepreneurial freedoms and skills within an institutional framework characterized by strong private property rights, free markets, and free trade."

2 For the United States, the figure shown for unionization in 1970 is from 1973 (comparable data for 1970 are not available). For the United Kingdom, for all years, the unionization data lag a year behind those shown: the data given for 1961 are from 1960, for 1971 from 1970, etc. There is also a one-year lag in the unionization data shown for Belgium for 1960, 1980, and 1990. *Sources*: For the United States: www.migrationpolicy. org/programs/data-hub/us-immigration-trends#history and http://unionstats. com; foreign-born population in Japan: www.migrationpolicy.org/article/ its-population-ages-japan-quietly-turns-immigration; foreign-born population in the United Kingdom in 2011 and Belgium in 2000 and 2010: https://data. oecd.org/migration/foreign-born-population.htm; in the United Kingdom from 1961 to 2001: https://webarchive.nationalarchives.gov.uk/20100521053049/ http://www.statistics.gov.uk/downloads/theme_compendia/fom2005/08_ FOPM_ForeignBorn.pdf; for Belgium from 1961 to 1991: http://adapt.it/ adapt-indice-a-z/wp-content/uploads/2014/04/phalet_swyngedouw.pdf; for Sweden (all years): www.scb.se/en/finding-statistics/statistics-by-subject-area/ population/population-composition/population-statistics/pong/tables-and-graphs/yearly-statistics--the-whole-country/summary-of-population-statistics/; unionization data for Japan, the United Kingdom, Belgium, and Sweden are all from table 2 of http://ftp.iza.org/dp6792.pdf.

3 Briggs acknowledges that whether or not to allow extensive immigration is a policy choice, yet he argues that, once a country opts for it, the inevitable result is a larger labor supply and a weaker working class (Briggs 2001: 4–5).

4 The name of the INS was changed to Immigration and Customs Enforcement with the creation of the Department of Homeland Security in 2002.

5 In 2017, the U.S. Census Bureau reported that 49 percent of the city's population was white, 43 percent was black, and 11 percent was Hispanic (a group that includes multiple races; hence the total adds to more than 100 percent). See www.census.gov/quickfacts/fact/table/youngstowncityohio/ PST045217.

6 Freeman and Medoff (1984) rely here on Albert Hirschman's (1971) influential discussion of "exit" and "voice" – in this context, workers deprived of "voice" by de-unionization have no other option but "exit" to express their discontent.

7 The available unionization data do not separate the residential and commercial sectors of the industry, but extensive qualitative evidence indicates that de-unionization occurred first and most extensively in residential.

8 Mines and Avina (1992: 440) report widespread displacement of African-American janitors in Los Angeles, but the only evidence they offer is an interview with a local African-American union representative. Moreover, they do not seem to be aware of the rapid expansion of L.A. janitorial employment during this period.

9 Because this section focuses on industries where de-unionization drove the shift from U.S.- to foreign-born labor, it does not explore the poultry industry, which was never extensively unionized. However, as Schwartzman (2013) has documented, poultry also underwent a shift from African-American to Latinx labor in the late twentieth century.

10 In addition to the historical evidence discussed in the text, a study of the North Carolina labor market in the 1990s found that, while in poultry processing African-American workers were (involuntarily) displaced by Latinx immigrants, as Schwartzman (2013) also argues, that was not the case in meatpacking, where instead African Americans and whites moved up within the industry or moved on to (presumably) better employment opportunities elsewhere (Skaggs et al. 2000).

11 "Right-to-work" laws prohibit union contracts that require workers to become union members as a condition of employment.

12 Champlin and Hake (2006: 54) suggest that these companies had always intended to recruit immigrants to fill their payrolls. "It is unlikely that any company would open a new multi-million dollar facility with no thought to labor supply … it is reasonable to conclude that these plants were built with the recognition that labor would have to be brought in." They offer no direct evidence to support this argument, however.

13 A critic of Ribas's book points out that the timing of her research – conducted in 2008 when immigration enforcement was being ramped up – may have shaped this lack of concern with immigrant competition (Marrow 2017); another factor may have been that the meat-processing industry was a recent presence in the region and thus had employed African Americans only briefly. In the poultry industry, with its longstanding tradition of African-American employment in the South, as Schwarzman (2013) has shown, the perception was different.

14 Other forms of regulation affecting this industry expanded in the 1980s, such as rules limiting driving hours and ensuring highway safety (Belzer

2000: 68–75). But such changes had far less impact on truckers than the 1980 legislation described in the text.

Chapter 4 Growing Inequality and Immigrant Employment in Paid Domestic Labor and Service Industry Jobs

1 In 2018 care.com alone was reported to have registered 14 million consumers and 11 million workers for eldercare, child care, pet care, and housekeeping (Kim 2018).
2 Although this survey used a convenience sample, the respondents had a demographic profile similar to the representative sample of domestic workers in the same fourteen metropolitan areas who were included in the U.S. Census Bureau's American Community Survey (Burnham and Theodore 2012: 14–15, 41).

References

Abrajano, M., and Hajnal, S. L. (2015) *White Backlash: Immigration, Race, and American Politics*. Princeton, NJ: Princeton University Press.

Allen, S. G. (1994) Developments in Collective Bargaining in Construction in the 1980s and 1990s, in P. B. Voos (ed.), *Contemporary Collective Bargaining in the Private Sector*. Madison: Industrial Relations Research Association, pp. 411–45.

Andrias, K. (2016) The New Labor Law, *Yale Law Journal* 126(1): 2–100.

Bacon, D. (2001) Labor Fights for Immigrants, *The Nation*, May 21: 15–22.

——— (2008) Unions Come to Smithfield, *American Prospect*, December 17, https://prospect.org/article/unions-come-smithfield.

——— (1987) *Immigrants and Native Workers: Contrasts and Competition*. Boulder, CO: Westview Press.

Barber, L. (2017) *Latino City: Immigration and Urban Crisis in Lawrence, Massachusetts, 1945–2000*. Chapel Hill: University of North Carolina Press.

Barboza, D., and Sorkin, A. R. (2001) Tyson to Acquire IBP in $3.2 Billion Deal, *New York Times*, January 2: A13.

Bardacke, F. (1988) Watsonville: A Mexican Community on Strike, in M. Davis and M. Sprinker (eds), *Reshaping the U.S. Left: Popular Struggles in the 1980s*. New York: Verso.

——— (2011) *Trampling Out the Vintage: Cesar Chavez and the Two Souls of the United Farm Workers*. New York: Verso.

Barrett, J. R. (1987) *Work and Community in the Jungle: Chicago's Packinghouse Workers, 1894–1922*. Urbana: University of Illinois Press.

Batlan, F. (2015) *Women and Justice for the Poor: A History of Legal Aid, 1863–1945*. New York: Cambridge University Press.

Batt, R., Lee, J. E., and Lakhani, T. (2014) *A National Study of Human Resource Practices, Turnover, and Customer Service in the Restaurant Industry*. New York: Restaurant Opportunities Center United, https://rocunited.org/publications/a-national-study-of-human-resource-practices-turnover-and-customer-service-in-the-restaurant-industry/.

References

Belman, D. L., and Monaco, K. A. (2001) The Effects of Deregulation, De-unionization, Technology, and Human Capital on the Work and Work Lives of Truck Drivers, *Industrial and Labor Relations Review* 54: 502–24.

Belzer, M. H. (2000) *Sweatshops on Wheels: Winners and Losers in Trucking Deregulation.* New York: Oxford University Press.

Berezin, M. (2017) On the Construction Sites of History: Where did Donald Trump Come From? *American Journal of Cultural Sociology* 5(3): 322–37.

Bernhardt, A., Milkman, R., Theodore, N., Heckathorn, D., Auer, M., DeFilippis, J., González, A. L., Narro, V., Perelshteyn, J., Polson, D., and Spiller, M. (2009) *Broken Laws, Unprotected Workers: Violations of Employment and Labor Laws in America's Cities,* http://docs.wixstatic.com/ugd/90d188_3bee1 e0d979fd2b11f1ed9c74d4ba791.pdf.

Bjerklie, S. (1996) On the Outskirts of Town: Meat, Employment and the Struggle for Community in Storm Lake, Iowa, *Culture & Agriculture* 18(1): 9–13.

Blau, F. D., and Beller, A. H. (1992) Black–White Earnings Over the 1970s and 1980s: Gender Differences in Trends, *Review of Economics and Statistics* 74(2): 276–86.

Blau, F. D., and Mackie, C. (eds) (2017) *The Economic and Fiscal Consequences of Immigration.* Washington, DC: National Academies Press.

Blau, F. D., Brummund, P., and Liu, A. Y. (2013) Trends in Occupational Segregation by Gender 1970–2009: Adjusting for the Impact of Changes in the Occupational Coding System, *Demography* 50(2): 471–92.

Bloemraad, I., and Voss, K. (2019) Movement or Moment? Lessons from the Pro-Immigrant Movement in the United States and Contemporary Challenges, *Journal of Ethnic and Migration Studies,* https://doi.org/10.1080/136 9183X.2018.1556447.

Bloemraad, I., Voss, K., and Lee, T. (2011) The Protests of 2006: What Were They, How Do We Understand Them, Where Do We Go?, in K. Voss and I. Bloemraad (eds), *Rallying for Immigrant Rights: The Fight for Inclusion in 21st Century America.* Berkeley: University of California Press, pp. 44–62.

Bloemraad, I., Silva F., and Voss, K. (2016) Rights, Economics, or Family? Frame Resonance, Political Ideology, and the Immigrant Rights Movement, *Social Forces* 94(4): 1647–74.

Bluestone, B., and Harrison, B. (1982) *The Deindustrialization of America.* New York: Basic Books.

Bonacich, E. (1972) A Theory of Ethnic Antagonism: The Split Labor Market, *American Sociological Review* 37(5): 547–59.

Bonacich, E., and Wilson, J. B. (2008) *Getting the Goods: Ports, Labor, and the Logistics Revolution.* Ithaca, NY: Cornell University Press.

Brady, M. (2014) An Appetite for Justice: The Restaurant Opportunities Center of New York, in Ruth Milkman and Ed Ott (eds), *New Labor in New York: Precarious Workers and the Future of the Labor Movement.* Ithaca, NY: Cornell University Press.

References

Branch, E. H. (2011) *Opportunity Denied: Limiting Black Women to Devalued Work*. New Brunswick, NJ; Rutgers University Press.

Briggs, V. M. (2001) *Immigration and American Unionism*. Ithaca, NY: Cornell University Press.

Brody, D. (1960) *Steelworkers in America: The Nonunion Era*. New York: Harper & Row.

Bronfenbrenner, K. (2009) *No Holds Barred: The Intensification of Employer Opposition to Organizing*, Economic Policy Institute, Briefing Paper #235, www.epi.org/files/page/-/pdf/bp235.pdf.

Brooks, D. (2008) Hora de que los pequeños nos pongamos de pie, *La Jornada*, December 9, www.jornada.unam.mx/2008/12/09/index.php?section=economi a&article=052n1eco.

Brownell, P. B. (2009) Sanctions for Whom? The Immigration Reform and Control Act's "Employer Sanctions" Provisions and the Wages of Mexican Immigrants, PhD dissertation, University of California, Berkeley.

Brueggemann, J., and Brown, C. (2003) The Decline of Industrial Unionism in the Meatpacking Industry, *Work and Occupations* 30(3): 327–60.

Burnham, L., and Theodore, N. (2012) *Home Economics: The Invisible and Unregulated World of Domestic Work*. New York: National Domestic Workers Alliance.

Burtless, G. (1999) Effects of Growing Wage Disparities and Changing Family Composition on the U.S. Income Distribution, *European Economic Review* 43(4–6): 853–65.

Calavita, K. ([1992] 2010) *Inside the State: The Bracero Program, Immigration, and the I.N.S.* New Orleans: Quid Pro Books.

Capps, R., Chishti, M., Gelatt, J., Bolter, J., and Soto, A. G. R. (2018) *Revving Up the Deportation Machinery: Enforcement and Pushback under Trump*. Washington, DC: Migration Policy Institute, www.migrationpolicy.org/research/revving-deportation-machinery-under-trump-and-pushback.

Carter, S. B. (2006) Labor Force, in S. B. Carter, S. S. Gartner, M. R. Haines, A. L. Olmstead R. Sutch, and G. Wright (eds), *Historical Statistics of the United States*. New York: Cambridge University Press, chap. Ba, https://hsus.cambridge.org/HSUSWeb/toc/showChapter.do?id=Ba.

Carter, S. B., and Sutch, R. (2007) Labor Market Flooding? Migrant Destination and Wage Change during America's Age of Mass Migration, *Border Battles: The U.S. Immigration Debates*, Social Science Research Council, http://essays.ssrc.org/acrossborders/wp-content/uploads/2009/08/ch7.pdf.

Catanzarite, L. (2002) Dynamics of Segregation and Earnings in Brown-Collar Occupations, *Work and Occupations* 29(3): 300–45.

Champlin, D., and Hake, E. (2006) Immigration as Industrial Strategy in American Meatpacking, *Review of Political Economy* 18(1): 49–70.

Chaplin, D. (1978) Domestic Service and Industrialization, *Comparative Studies in Sociology* 1: 97–127.

References

Chiquiar, D., and Hanson, G. (2005) International Migration, Self-Selection, and the Distribution of Wages: Evidence from Mexico and the United States, *Journal of Political Economy* 113(2): 239–81.

Cleeland, N. (2000) Heartache on Aisle 3: Sweatshop for Janitors, *Los Angeles Times*, July 2.

Cobble, D. S. (1991) Organizing the Postindustrial Work Force: Lessons from the History of Waitress Unionism, *Industrial and Labor Relations Review* 44(3): 419–36.

Cobble, D. S., and Merrill, M. (1994) Collective Bargaining in the Hospitality Industry in the 1980s, in P. B. Voos (ed.), *Contemporary Collective Bargaining in the Private Sector*. Madison: Industrial Relations Research Association, pp. 447–89.

Cohen, L. (1990) *Making a New Deal: Industrial Workers in Chicago, 1919–1939*. New York: Cambridge University Press.

Cohen, P. (2019) Country Is Full? It's News to Us, Employers Say, *New York Times*, August 23, p. 1.

Cohn, D., Passel J. S., and Bialik, K. (2019) Many Immigrants with Temporary Protected Status Face Uncertain Future in U.S., Pew Research Center, March 8, www.pewresearch.org/fact-tank/2019/03/08/immigrants-temporary-protected-status-in-us/.

Colen, S. (1986) "With Respect and Feelings": Voices of West Indian Child Care and Domestic Workers in New York City, in J. B. Cole (ed.), *All American Women: Lines That Divide, Ties That Bind*. New York: Free Press, pp. 46–70.

Corchado, A. (2018) Even as Trump Tightens Immigration, the U.S. Labor Shortage is Becoming a Crisis, *Dallas Morning News*, May 17.

Cornelius, W. A., and Salehyan, I. (2007) Does Border Enforcement Deter Unauthorized Immigration? The Case of Mexican Migration to the United States of America, *Regulation & Governance* 1(2): 139–53.

Cortes, P. (2008) The Effect of Low-Skilled Immigration on U.S. Prices: Evidence from CPI Data, *Journal of Political Economy* 116(3): 381–422.

Coser, L. A. (1973) Servants: The Obsolescence of an Occupational Role, *Social Forces* 52(1): 31–40.

Cowie, J. (2016) *The Great Exception: The New Deal & the Limits of American Politics*. Princeton, NJ: Princeton University Press.

Cramer, K. J. (2016) *The Politics of Resentment*. Chicago: University of Chicago Press.

Craypo, C. (1994) Meatpacking: Industry Restructuring and Union Decline, in P. B. Voos (ed.), *Contemporary Collective Bargaining in the Private Sector*. Madison: Industrial Relations Research Association, pp. 63–96.

Currid-Halkett, E. (2017) *The Sum of Small Things: A Theory of the Aspirational Class*. Princeton, NJ: Princeton University Press.

Damaske, S. (2011) *For the Family? How Class and Gender Shape Women's Work*. New York: Oxford University Press.

References

Dangl, B. (2009) Firing the Boss: An Interview with Mark Meinster, Organizer of the Chicago Factory Occupation, *MR Zine*, January 15, http://monthlyreview.org/mrzine/dangl150109.html.

Daniel, C. E. (1981) *Bitter Harvest: A History of California Farmworkers, 1870–1941*. Ithaca, NY: Cornell University Press.

Davis, J. H., and Shear, M. D. (2019) *Border Wars: Inside Trump's Assault on Immigration*. New York: Simon & Schuster.

De Genova, N. P. (2002) Migrant "Illegality" and Deportability in Everyday Life, *Annual Review of Anthropology* 31: 419–47.

Delgado, H. (1993) *New Immigrants, Old Unions: Organizing Undocumented Workers in Los Angeles*. Philadelphia: Temple University Press.

de Peuter, G. (2007) Universities, Intellectuals and Multitudes: An Interview with Stuart Hall, in M. Cote, J. F. Day, and G. de Peuter (eds), *Utopian Pedagogy: Radical Experiments Against Neoliberal Globalization*. Toronto: University of Toronto Press, pp. 108–28.

DeSilver, D. (2017) Immigrants Don't Make Up a Majority of Workers in any U.S. Industry, Pew Research Center, March 16, www.pewresearch.org/fact-tank/2017/03/16/immigrants-dont-make-up-a-majority-of-workers-in-any-u-s-industry/.

Dew, B. (2018) *Union Membership Byte 2018*. Washington, DC: Center for Economic and Policy Research, http://cepr.net/images/stories/reports/union-byte-2018-01.pdf.

Donovan, S. A., and Bradley, D. H. (2018) *Real Wage Trends, 1979 to 2017*. Washington, DC: Congressional Research Service, March 15, https://fas.org/sgp/crs/misc/R45090.pdf.

Dreier, P., and Maier, M. (2016) Day Laborers Leader on Right-Wing Hostility: "So Far, We Have Won This Fight," *In These Times*, August 9, http://inthesetimes.com/working/entry/19366/day_laborers_leader_on_right_wing_hostility_so_far_we_have_won_this_fi.

Dwyer, R. (2013) The Care Economy? Gender, Economic Restructuring and Job Polarization in the U.S. Labor Market, *American Sociological Review* 78(3): 390–416.

Easterlin, R. A. (1968) *Population, Labor Force, and Long Swings in Economic Growth*. Cambridge, MA: National Bureau of Economic Research.

Eckstein, S., and Nguyen, T. N. (2011) The Making and Transnationalization of an Ethnic Niche: Vietnamese Manicurists, *International Migration Review* 45(3): 639–74.

Economic Policy Institute, State of Working America Data Library (2019) "Median/Average Hourly Wages," https://www.epi.org/data/#/?subject=wage-avg&g=*.

Elk, M. (2018) U.S. Meatpacking Workers Face New Hazard: Threat of Deportation by ICE, *The Guardian*, June 29, www.theguardian.com/environment/2018/jun/29/ohio-ice-meatpacking-industry-deportations.

References

England, P. (2010) The Gender Revolution: Uneven and Stalled, *Gender & Society* 24(2): 149–66.

Enos, R. (2017) *The Space between Us: Social Geography and Politics.* New York: Cambridge University Press.

Erickson, E. (1935) *Employment Conditions in Beauty Shops: A Study of Four Cities.* Washington, DC: U.S. Department of Labor, Women's Bureau.

Estlund, C. (2002) The Ossification of American Labor Law, *Columbia Law Review* 102(6): 1527–612.

Fairchild, S. K. (2018) Urban Farm Workers: A History of the Justice for Janitors Campaign as an Adaptive Response to Neoliberal Restructuring and Union Decline, PhD dissertation, University of California, San Diego.

Federman, M. N., Harrington, D. E., and Krynski, K. J. (2006) Vietnamese Manicurists: Are Immigrants Displacing Natives or Finding New Nails to Polish? *Industrial and Labor Relations Review* 59(2): 302–18.

Figueroa, H., and Jiménez Moreta, C. (2018) Immigrants and Unions Make America Great, *American Prospect*, July 6, https://prospect.org/article/immigrants-and-unions-make-america-great.

Fine, J. (2006) *Worker Centers: Organizing Communities at the Edge of the Dream.* Ithaca, NY: Cornell University Press.

——— (2007) A Marriage Made in Heaven? Mismatches and Misunderstandings between Worker Centers and Unions, *British Journal of Industrial Relations* 45(2): 335–60.

Fine, J., and Tichenor, D. (2009) A Movement Wrestling: American Labor's Enduring Struggle with Immigration, 1866–2007, *Studies in American Political Development* 23(1): 84–113.

Fine, J., Narro, V., and Barnes, J. (2018) Understanding Worker Center Trajectories, in J. Fine, L. Burnham, K. Griffith, M. Ji, V. Narro and S. Pitts (eds), *No One Size Fits All: Worker Organization, Policy, and Movement in a New Economic Age.* Champaign, IL: Labor and Employment Relations Association.

Fink, D. (1998) *Cutting into the Meatpacking Line.* Chapel Hill: University of North Carolina Press.

Fink, L. (2003) *The Maya of Morganton: Work and Community in the Nuevo New South.* Chapel Hill: University of North Carolina Press.

Fisk, C. L., Mitchell, D. J. B., and Erickson, C. L. (2000) Union Representation of Immigrant Janitors in Southern California: Economic and Legal Challenges, in R. Milkman (ed.), *Organizing Immigrants.* Ithaca, NY: Cornell University Press, pp. 199–224.

Freeman, R. B. (2002) *The Road to Union Renascence in the US*, paper presented at TUC Internet and Unions Conference, London, 2001, http://citeseerx.ist.psu.edu/viewdoc/download?doi=10.1.1.202.8096&rep=rep1&type=pdf.

Freeman, R. B., and Medoff, J. L. (1984) *What Do Unions Do?* New York: Basic Books.

References

Frum, D. (2019) If Liberals Won't Enforce Borders, Fascists Will, *The Atlantic*, April, pp. 64–74, www.theatlantic.com/magazine/archive/2019/04/david-frum-how-much-immigration-is-too-much/583252/.

Fuller, V. (1991) *Hired Hands in California's Farm Fields*. Davis: University of California, Giannini Foundation.

Gabriel, J. (2006) Organizing *The Jungle:* Industrial Restructuring and Immigrant Unionization in the American Meatpacking Industry, *WorkingUSA: The Journal of Labor and Society* 9(3): 337–59.

Galarza, E. (1964) *Merchants of Labor: The Mexican Bracero Story*. Santa Barbara, CA: McNally & Loftin.

Gallup (2018a) Immigration, https://news.gallup.com/poll/1660/immigration.aspx.

——— (2018b) Immigration/Border Security, www.pollingreport.com/immigration.htm.

Ganz, M. (2009) *Why David Sometimes Wins: Leadership, Organization, and Strategy in the California Farm Worker Movement*. New York: Oxford University Press.

Garea, S., and Stern, S. A. (2010) From Legal Advocacy to Organizing: Progressive Lawyering and the Los Angeles Car Wash Campaign, in R. Milkman, J. Bloom and V. Narro (eds), *Working for Justice: The L.A. Model of Organizing and Advocacy*. Ithaca, NY: Cornell University Press, pp. 125–40.

Garrick, J. (2014) Repurposing American Labor Law: Immigrant Workers, Worker Centers, and the National Labor Relations Act, *Politics & Society* 42(4): 489–512.

Gest, J. (2016) *The New Minority: White Working Class Politics in an Age of Immigration and Inequality*. New York: Oxford University Press.

Gies, H. (2018) Unions Can Protect Workers from Deportation, *In These Times "Working" Blog*, October 18, https://inthesetimes.com/working/entry/21516/immigrants-rights-workers-teamsters-tps-working-families-united.

Gimpel, J. G., and Edwards, J. R. (1999) *The Congressional Politics of Immigration Reform*. Boston: Allyn & Bacon.

Gleeson, S. (2016) *Precarious Claims: The Promise and Failure of Workplace Protections in the United States*. Berkeley: University of California Press.

Glenn, E. N. (1992) From Servitude to Service Work: Historical Continuities in the Racial Division of Paid Reproductive Labor, *Signs* 18(1): 1–43.

Glenn, S. A. (1990) *Daughters of the Shtetl: Life and Labor in the Immigrant Generation.*, Ithaca, NY: Cornell University Press.

Goldin, C. (1994) The Political Economy of Immigration Restriction in the United States, 1890 to 1921, in C. Goldin and G. D. Libecap (eds), *The Regulated Economy: A Historical Approach to Political Economy*. Chicago: University of Chicago Press, pp. 223–58.

Goldin, C., and Margo, R. A. (1992) The Great Compression: The Wage Structure in the United States at Mid-Century, *Quarterly Journal of Economics* 107(1): 1–34.

Goldstein, D. (2018) Schools Fill Low-Pay Jobs from Abroad, *New York Times*, May 3, p. 1.

Gompers, S. (1910) Mr. Hunter's Dilemma Proven, *American Federationist* 17(6): 484–91.

—— (1925) *Seventy Years of Life and Labor*, 2 vols. New York: E. P. Dutton.

Gordon, J. (2005) *Suburban Sweatshops: The Fight for Immigrant Rights*. Cambridge, MA: Harvard University Press.

—— (2017) Regulating the Human Supply Chain, *Iowa Law Review* 102(2): 445–504.

Gordon, J., and Lenhardt, R. A. (2007) *Conflict and Solidarity between African American and Latino Immigrant Workers*. University of California, Berkeley Law School, www.law.berkeley.edu/files/GordonLenhardtpaperNov30. pdf.

Gordon, L. (2017) *The Second Coming of the KKK: The Ku Klux Klan of the 1920s and the American Political Tradition*. New York: W. W. Norton.

Gouveia, L., and Stull, D. D. (1997) *Latino Immigrants, Meatpacking, and Rural Communities: A Case Study of Lexington, Nebraska*. East Lansing: Michigan State University, Julian Samora Research Institute, https://jsri.msu.edu/upload/ research-reports/rr26.pdf.

Greenberg, M. (2018) In the Valley of Fear, *New York Review of Books*, December 20, pp. 91–3.

Greenberg, S. B. (2018) Trump is Beginning to Lose His Grip, *New York Times*, November 17, www.nytimes.com/2018/11/17/opinion/sunday/trump-is-beginning-to-lose-his-grip.html?searchResultPosition=2.

Grey, M. A. (1995) Turning the Pork Industry Upside Down: Storm Lake's Hygrade Work Force and the Impact of the 1981 Plant Closure, *Annals of Iowa* 54(3): 244–59.

—— (1996) Patronage, Kinship, and Recruitment of Lao and Mennonite Labor to Storm Lake, Iowa, *Culture & Agriculture* 18(1): 14–18.

—— (1997) Storm Lake, Iowa, and the Meatpacking Revolution, in S. Stromquist and M. Bergman (eds), *Unionizing the Jungles*. Ames: University of Iowa Press, pp. 242–61.

—— (1999) Immigrants, Migration, and Worker Turnover at the Hog Pride Pork Packing Plant, *Human Organization* 58(1): 16–27.

Grieco, E. (2004) Immigrant Union Members: Numbers and Trends, Migration Policy Institute, Fact Sheet no. 7, www.migrationpolicy.org/research/ immigrant-union-members-numbers-and-trends.

Griffith, K. L. (2015) Worker Centers and Labor Law Protections: Why Aren't They Having Their Cake? *Berkeley Journal of Employment & Labor Law* 36(2): 331–49.

Grindy, B. (2016) How Does Household-Income Growth Affect Restaurants? Washington Hospitality Association, September 14, https://wahospitality.org/ blog/how-does-household-income-growth-affect-restaurants/.

References

Guglielmo, T. A. (2003) *White on Arrival: Italians, Race, Color, and Power in Chicago, 1890–1945*. New York: Oxford University Press.

Gulasekaram, P., and Ramakrishnan, S. K. (2015) *The New Immigration Federalism*. New York: Cambridge University Press.

Gutiérrez, D. G. (1995) *Walls and Mirrors: Mexican Americans, Mexican Immigrants, and the Politics of Ethnicity*. Berkeley: University of California Press.

―――― (1998) Ethnic Mexicans and the Transformation of "American" Social Space: Reflections on Recent History, in M. M. Suárez-Orozco (ed.), *Crossings: Mexican Immigration in Interdisciplinary Perspective*. Cambridge, MA: Harvard University, David Rockefeller Center for Latin American Studies, pp. 307–35.

Hahamovitch, C. (1997) *The Fruits of Their Labor: Atlantic Coast Farmworkers and the Making of Migrant Poverty, 1870–1945*. Chapel Hill: University of North Carolina Press.

Hainmueller, J., and Hopkins, D. J. (2014) Public Attitudes Toward Immigration, *Annual Review of Political Science* 17: 225–49.

Haney López, I. (2019) *Merge Left: Fusing Race and Class, Winning Elections, and Saving America*. New York: New Press.

Harrison, J. L., and Lloyd, S. E. (2013) New Jobs, New Workers, and New Inequalities: Explaining Employers' Roses in Occupational Segregation by Nativity and Race, *Social Problems* 60(3): 281–301.

Harrison, R., Hutson, N., West, J., and Wilke, J. (2007) Characteristics of Drayage Operations at the Port of Houston, Texas, *Transportation Research Record* 2033: 31–7.

Harvey, D. (2005) *A Brief History of Neoliberalism*. New York: Oxford University Press.

Hatton, T. J., and Williamson, J. G. (2005) *Global Migration and the World Economy: Two Centuries of Policy and Performance*. Cambridge, MA: MIT Press.

Haus, L. A. (2002) *Unions, Immigration, and Internationalization: New Challenges and Changing Coalitions in the United States and France*. New York: Palgrave Macmillan.

Hegewisch, A., Williams, C., Hartmann, H., and Aaronson, S. (2014) The Gender Wage Gap: 2013, Fact Sheet C413. Washington, DC: Institute for Women's Policy Research, March, https://iwpr.org/publications/the-gender-wage-gap-2013-differences-by-race-and-ethnicity-no-growth-in-real-wages-for-women/.

Higham, J. ([1955] 1968) *Strangers in the Land: Patterns of American Nativism 1860–1925*. New York: Atheneum.

Hirsch, B. T., and Macpherson, D. A. (2019) *Union Membership and Earnings Data Book*. Arlington, VA: Bureau of National Affairs.

Hirschman, A. O. (1971) *Exit, Voice and Loyalty*. Cambridge, MA: Harvard University Press.

References

Hirschman, C., and Mogford, E. (2009) Immigration and the American Industrial Revolution from 1880 to 1920, *Social Science Research* 38: 897–920.

Hoang, K. K. (2015) Nailing Race and Labor Relations: Vietnamese Nail Salons in Majority–Minority Neighborhoods, *Journal of Asian American Studies* 18(2): 113–39.

Hochschild, A. (2016) *Strangers in Their Own Land*. New York: New Press.

Hondagneu-Sotelo, P. (2001) *Doméstica: Immigrant Workers Cleaning and Caring in the Shadows of Affluence*. Berkeley: University of California Press.

Horowitz, R. (2002) The Decline of Unionism in America's Meatpacking Industry, *Social Policy* 32(3): 32–6.

Hourwich, I. A. (1912) *Immigration and Labor: The Economic Aspects of European Immigration to the United States*. New York: Putnam.

Human Rights Watch (2004) *Blood, Sweat, and Fear: Workers' Rights in U.S. Meat and Poultry Plants*, www.hrw.org/reports/2005/usa0105/usa0105.pdf.

Jacobs, K. (2018) Governing the Market from Below: Settling Labor Standards at the State and Local Levels, in J. Fine, L. Burnham, K. Griffith, M. Ji, V. Narro and S. Pitts (eds), *No One Size Fits All: Worker Organization, Policy, and Movement in a New Economic Age*. Champaign, IL: Labor and Employment Relations Association.

Jaffee, D., and Bensman, D. (2016) Draying and Picking: Precarious Work and Labor Action in the Logistics Sector, *WorkingUSA: The Journal of Labor and Society* 19(1): 57–79.

Jaffee, D., and Rowley, A. (2009) Hauling Containers: Port Drayage Drivers in the Logistics Supply Chain, paper presented at the Annual Meeting of the Southern Sociological Society, April 2010, www.unf.edu/~djaffee/hauling%20 containers-SSS.doc.

Jamieson, D. (2013) Car Wash Workers Ratify First Union Contract in New York City, *Huffpost*, May 28, www.huffpost.com/entry/ car-wash-new-york-contract_n_3348685.

——— (2017) Unions Are Stepping Up to Fight Deportations, *Huffpost*, September 12, www.huffpost.com/entry/organized-labor-steps-up-to-fight-deportations_ n_59b6df97e4b03e6197afea7c.

Jencks, C., Smith, M., Acland, H., Bane, M. J., Cohen, D., Gintis, H., Heyns, B., and Michelson, S. (1972) *Inequality: A Reassessment of the Effect of Family and Schooling in America*. New York: Basic Books.

Jenkins, J. C. (1978) The Demand for Immigrant Workers: Labor Scarcity or Labor Control? *International Migration Review* 12(4): 514–535.

Jenkins, S. (2002) Organizing, Advocacy, and Member Power: A Critical Reflection, *WorkingUSA: The Journal of Labor and Society* 6(2): 56–89.

Johnson, S. (2019) Union Leaders: Keep Protection for TPS and Dreamers Permanent! *New York Amsterdam News*, March 7, http://amsterdamnews. com/news/2019/mar/07/union-leaders-keep-protection-tps-and-dreamers-per/.

Johnson-Webb, K. D. (2002) Employer Recruitment and Hispanic Labor

Migration: North Carolina Urban Areas at the End of the Millennium, *Professional Geographer* 54(3): 406–21.

Jokela, M. (2015) Macro-Level Determinants of Paid Domestic Labor Prevalence: A Cross-National Analysis of Seventy-Four Countries, *Social Policy and Society* 14(3): 385–405.

Jordan, M. (2018) ICE Came for a Tennessee Town's Immigrants: The Town Fought Back, *New York Times*, June 8.

——— (2019) ICE Arrests Hundreds in Mississippi Raids Targeting Immigrant Workers, *New York Times*, August 7.

Judis, J. B. (2016) *The Populist Explosion: How the Great Recession Transformed American and European Politics*. New York: Columbia Global Reports.

——— (2018) *The Nationalist Revival: Trade, Immigration, and the Revolt against Globalization*. New York: Columbia Global Reports.

Kalleberg, A. (2011) *Good Jobs, Bad Jobs*. New York: Russell Sage Foundation.

Kandel, W., and Parrado, E. A. (2005) Restructuring of the US Meat Processing Industry and New Hispanic Migrant Destinations, *Population and Development Review* 31(3): 447–71.

Kang, M. (2010) *The Managed Hand: Race, Gender, and the Body in Beauty Service Work*. Berkeley: University of California Press.

Katzman, D. (1978) *Seven Days a Week: Women and Domestic Service in Industrializing America*. New York: Oxford University Press.

Kaufmann, E. (2019) *Whiteshift: Populism, Immigration and the Future of White Majorities*. New York: Abrams Press.

Kaushal, N. J. (2019) *Blaming Immigrants: Nationalism and the Economics of Global Movement*. New York: Columbia University Press.

Kazin, M. (2013) How Labor Learned to Love Immigration, *New Republic*, May 13, https://newrepublic.com/article/113203/labor-and-immigration-how-unions-got-board-immigration-reform.

Keck, M. E., and Sikkink, K. (1998) *Activists beyond Borders: Advocacy Networks in International Politics*. Ithaca, NY: Cornell University Press.

Kim, D.-O., and Kim, S. (1997) The Effects on Union Membership of Race and Immigration Status: Focusing on Asian Americans, *Journal of Applied Behavioral Science* 33(3): 378–96.

Kim, E. T. (2018) Americans Will Struggle to Grow Old at Home, *Bloomberg Businessweek*, February 9, www.bloomberg.com/news/features/2018-02-09/americans-will-struggle-to-grow-old-at-home.

King, M. C. (1992) Occupational Segregation by Race and Sex, 1940–88, *Monthly Labor Review* 115(4): 30–6.

Kitroeff, N. (2017) Immigrants Flooded California Construction: Worker Pay Sank. Here's Why, *Los Angeles Times*, April 22, www.latimes.com/projects/la-fi-construction-trump/.

Kitroeff, N., and Mohan, G. (2017) Wages Rise on California Farms: Americans

References

Still Don't Want the Job, *Los Angeles Times*, March 17, www.latimes.com/projects/la-fi-farms-immigration/.

Kochan, T. A., Yang, D., Kimball, W. T., and Kelly, E. L. (2019) Worker Voice in America: Is There a Gap between What Workers Expect and What They Experience? *ILR Review* 72(1): 3–38.

Kornrich, S. (2012) Hiring Help for the Home: Household Services in the Twentieth Century, *Journal of Family History* 37(2): 197–212.

Koziara, E. C., and Koziara, K. S. (1968) *The Negro in the Hotel Industry*. Philadelphia: Industrial Research Unit, Wharton School of Finance and Commerce, University of Pennsylvania.

Krissman, F. (2005) Sin Coyote Ni Patrón: Why the "Migrant Network" Fails to Explain International Migration, *International Migration Review* 39(1): 4–44.

Krugman, P. (2002) For Richer, *New York Times Magazine*, October 20.

Lafer, G. (2017) *The One Percent Solution: How Corporations Are Remaking America One State at a Time*. Ithaca, NY: Cornell University Press.

Lauck, J. K. (1998) Competition in the Grain Belt Meatpacking Sector after World War II, *Annals of Iowa* 57(2): 135–59.

Lee, S. (2019) The Case for Open Borders, *Catalyst* 2(4), https://catalyst-journal.com/vol2/no4/the-case-for-open-borders.

Leiter, J., Hossfield, L., and Tomaskovic-Devey, D. (2001) North Carolina Employers Look at Latino Workers, paper presented at the Annual Meeting of the Southern Sociological Society.

Lester, T. W. (2019) Restructuring Restaurant Work: Employer Responses to Local Labor Standards in the Full-Service Restaurant Industry, *Urban Affairs Review*, https://doi.org/10.1177/1078087418773907.

Levitz, E. (2018) Mass Immigration Creates Problems for the Left: Tighter Borders Can't Be the Solution, *New York Magazine: Intelligencer*, November 30, http://nymag.com/intelligencer/2018/11/immigration-open-borders-hillary-clinton-angela-nagle-the-left.html.

Lieberson, S. (1980) *A Piece of the Pie: Blacks and White Immigrants since 1880*. Berkeley: University of California Press.

Lind, D. (2016) The Disastrous, Forgotten 1996 Law that Created Today's Immigration Problem, *Vox*, April 28, www.vox.com/2016/4/28/11515132/iirira-clinton-immigration.

Linder, M. (1987) Farm Workers and the Fair Labor Standards Act: Racial Discrimination in the New Deal, *Texas Law Review* 65: 1335–92.

———— (2000) *Wars of Attrition: Vietnam, the Business Roundtable, and the Decline of Construction Unions*. 2nd edn, Iowa City: Fanpihua Press.

López-Sanders, L. (2009) *Trapped at the Bottom: Racialized and Gendered Labor Queues in New Immigrant Destinations*, Working Paper, Center for Comparative Immigration Studies, University of California, San Diego, https://escholarship.org/uc/item/1r39d099.

References

Manjoo, F. (2019) There's Nothing Wrong with Open Borders, *New York Times*, January 16.

Marculewicz, S., and Thomas, J. (2012) *Labor Organizations by Another Name: The Worker Center Movement and its Evolution into Coverage under the NLRA and LMRDA*. Washington, DC: Federalist Society, https://fedsoc.org/commentary/publications/labor-organizations-by-another-name-the-worker-center-movement-and-its-evolution-into-coverage-under-the-nlra-and-lmrda.

Marquis, S. L. (2017) *I Am Not a Tractor! How Florida Farmworkers Took on the Fast Food Giants and Won*. Ithaca, NY: Cornell University Press.

Marrow, H. B. (2017) On the Line: Latino Life in New Immigrant Destinations after 2005, *Contemporary Sociology* 46(3): 265–73.

Martin, P. L. (2003) *Promise Unfulfilled: Unions, Immigration and the Farm Workers*. Ithaca, NY: Cornell University Press.

———— (2018) Immigration and Farm Labor: Challenges and Opportunities, in *California Agriculture: Dimensions and Issues*. 3rd edn, University of California Giannini Foundation of Agricultural Economics, https://giannini.ucop.edu/publications/cal-ag-book/.

Massey, D. S., and Magaly Sánchez, R. (2010) *Brokered Boundaries: Creating Immigrant Identity in Anti-Immigrant Times*. New York: Russell Sage Foundation.

Massey, D. S., Durand, J., and Malone, N. J. (2002) *Beyond Smoke and Mirrors: Mexican Immigration in an Era of Economic Integration*. New York: Russell Sage Foundation.

Matthews, D. (2013) North Carolina Needed 6,500 Farm Workers: Only 7 Americans Stuck it Out, *Washington Post*, May 15, www.washingtonpost.com/news/wonk/wp/2013/05/15/north-carolina-needed-6500-farm-workers-only-7-americans-stuck-it-out/?utm_term=.77ff2da7b1a1.

McCall, L. (2008) What Does Class Inequality among Women Look Like? A Comparison with Men and Families, 1970 to 2000, in A. Lareau and D. Conley (eds), *Social Class: How Does it Work?* New York: Russell Sage Foundation, pp. 293–325.

McCartin, J. (2018) Innovative Unions Strategies and the Struggle to Reinvent Collective Bargaining, in J. Fine, L. Burnham, K. Griffith, M. Ji, V. Narro and S. Pitts (eds), *No One Size Fits All: Worker Organization, Policy, and Movement in a New Economic Age*. Champaign, IL: Labor and Employment Relations Association.

McElmurry, S. (2017) *Heartland Hospitality: Serving the Needs of the Midwest Economy through Immigration*, Chicago Council on Global Affairs, www.thechicagocouncil.org/sites/default/files/report_immigration_hospitality_170824.pdf.

McWilliams, C. (1939) *Factories in the Field: The Story of Migratory Farm Labor in California*. Boston: Little, Brown.

References

——— ([1948] 1990) *North from Mexico: The Spanish-Speaking People of the United States*. 3rd edn, Santa Barbara, CA: Praeger.

Merton, R. K. (1959) Notes on Problem-Finding in Sociology, in R. K. Merton, L. Broom and L. S. Cottrell (eds), *Sociology Today: Problems and Prospects*. New York: Basic Books.

Migration Policy Institute (2018) Profile of the Unauthorized Population: United States, www.migrationpolicy.org/data/unauthorized-immigrant-population/state/US.

Milkman, R. (2006) *L.A. Story: Immigrant Workers and the Future of the U.S. Labor Movement*. New York: Russell Sage Foundation.

——— (2011) L.A.'s Past, America's Future? The 2006 Immigrant Rights Protests and their Antecedents, in K. Voss and I. Bloemraad (eds), *Rallying for Immigrant Rights: The Fight for Inclusion in 21st Century America*. Berkeley: University of California Press.

——— (2013) Back to the Future? US Labour in the New Gilded Age, *British Journal of Industrial Relations* 51(4): 645–65.

——— (2018) *Making Paid Care Work Visible*. New York City Department of Consumer Affairs, Office of Labor Policy and Standards, www1.nyc.gov/assets/dca/downloads/pdf/workers/Making-Paid-Care-Work-Visible.pdf.

Milkman, R., and Luce, S. (2019) *The State of the Unions 2019: A Profile of Organized Labor in New York City, New York State, and the United States*. City University of New York School of Labor and Urban Studies, https://docs.wixstatic.com/ugd/90d188_8213e15a8d79402eaba03f392d899f2c.pdf.

Milkman, R., and Terriquez, V. (2012) "We Are the Ones Who Are Out in Front": Women's Leadership in the Immigrant Rights Movement, *Feminist Studies* 38(3): 723–52.

Milkman, R., and Wong, K. (2000) Organizing the Wicked City: The 1992 Southern California Drywall Strike, in R. Milkman (ed.), *Organizing Immigrants*. Ithaca, NY: Cornell University Press, pp. 169–98.

Milkman, R., Reese, E., and Roth, B. (1998) The Macrosociology of Paid Domestic Labor, *Work and Occupations* 25(4): 483–510.

Miller, S. V. (2018) *Economic Anxiety or Racial Resentment? An Evaluation of Attitudes toward Immigration in the U.S. from 1992 to 2016*, working paper, http://svmiller.com/research/economic-anxiety-racial-resentment-immigration-1992-2016/.

Mines, R., and Avina, J. (1992) Immigrants and Labor Standards: The Case of California Janitors, in J. A. Bustamante, C. W. Reynolds, and R. A. Hinojosa Ojeda (eds), *U.S.–Mexico Relations: Labor Market Interdependence*. Stanford, CA: Stanford University Press, pp. 429–48.

Minian, A. R. (2018) *Undocumented Lives: The Untold Story of Mexican Migration*. Cambridge, MA: Harvard University Press.

Mink, G. (1986) *Old Labor and New Immigrants in American Political Development*. Ithaca, NY: Cornell University Press.

References

Mins, L. E. (1938) Unpublished Letters of Karl Marx and Friedrich Engels to Americans, *Science & Society* 2(2): 218–31.

Miraftab, F. (2016) *Global Heartland: Displaced Labor, Transnational Lives and Local Place-Making*. Bloomington: Indiana University Press.

Montgomery, D. (1986) Nationalism, American Patriotism, and Class Consciousness among Immigrants in the United States in the Epoch of World War I, in D. Hoerder (ed.), *"Struggle a Hard Battle": Essays on Working-Class Immigrants*. DeKalb: Northern Illinois University Press, pp. 327–51.

Moore, T. G. (1986) Rail and Trucking Deregulation, in L. W. Weiss and M. W. Klass (eds), *Regulatory Reform: What Actually Happened*. Boston: Little, Brown.

Mora, G. C. (2014) *Making Hispanics: How Activists, Bureaucrats, and Media Constructed a New American*. Chicago: University of Chicago Press.

Morales, R. A. (1992) Contending Tradeoffs: IRCA, Immigrants, and the Southern California Restaurant Industry, *Review of Policy Research* 11(2): 143–51.

Morawska, E. (1990) The Sociology and Historiography of Immigration, in V. Yans-McLaughlin (ed.), *Immigration Reconsidered: History, Sociology, and Politics*. New York: Oxford University Press, pp. 187–238.

Moss, P., and Tilly, C. (2001) *Stories Employers Tell: Race, Skill, and Hiring in America*. New York: Russell Sage Foundation.

Mouffe, C. (2018) *For A Left Populism*. New York: Verso.

Murphy, B. (2017) Forced into Debt. Worked Past Exhaustion. Left with Nothing, *USA Today Network Investigative Report*. June 16, www.usatoday.com/pages/interactives/news/rigged-forced-into-debt-worked-past-exhaustion-left-with-nothing/.

Nadler, R. (2019) At What Cost? *National Review*, February, pp. 23, 28–30.

Nagle, A. (2018) The Left Case Against Open Borders, *American Affairs* 2(4), https://americanaffairsjournal.org/2018/11/the-left-case-against-open-borders/.

Nails magazine (2018) Industry Statistics, 2017–18, The Big Book, https://files.nailsmag.com/Handouts/NABB2017-18stats-LR.pdf.

Narro, V., and Fine, J. (2018) Labor Unions/Worker Center Relationships, Joint Efforts, Experiences, in J. Fine, L. Burnham, K. Griffith, M. Ji, V. Narro and S. Pitts (eds), *No One Size Fits All: Worker Organization, Policy, and Movement in a New Economic Age*. Champaign, IL: Labor and Employment Relations Association.

National Conference of State Legislators (2015) Tuition Benefits for Immigrants, July 21, www.ncsl.org/documents/immig/InStateTuition_july212015.pdf.

Ness, I. (2005) *Immigrants, Unions and the New U.S. Labor Market*. Philadelphia: Temple University Press.

Ngai, M. (1999) The Architecture of Race in American Immigration Law: A Reexamination of the Immigration Act of 1924, *Journal of American History* 86(1): 67–92.

References

———— (2004) *Impossible Subjects: Illegal Aliens and the Making of Modern America*. Princeton, NJ: Princeton University Press.

———— (2006) How Grandma Got Legal, in *Border Battles: The U.S. Immigration Debates*, Social Science Research Council, July 28, https://items.ssrc.org/border-battles/how-grandma-got-legal/.

Nicholls, W. J. (2013) *The Dreamers: How the Undocumented Youth Movement Transformed the Immigrant Rights Debate*. Stanford, CA: Stanford University Press.

———— (2019) *The Immigrant Rights Movement: The Battle Over National Citizenship*. Stanford, CA: Stanford University Press.

Nir, S. M. (2015) The Price of Nice Nails, *New York Times*, May 7.

Nolan, H. (2019) AFL-CIO Budget Is a Stark Illustration of the Decline of Organizing, *Splinter*, May 16, https://splinternews.com/afl-cio-budget-is-a-stark-illustration-of-the-decline-o-1834793722.

Oestreicher, R. J. (1986) *Solidarity and Fragmentation: Working People and Class Consciousness in Detroit, 1875–1900*. Urbana: University of Illinois Press.

Olmstead, A. L., and Rhode, P. W. (2006) Farms and Farm Structure, in S. B. Carter, S. S. Gartner, M. R. Haines, A. L. Olmstead, R. Sutch, and G. Wright (eds), *Historical Statistics of the United States*. New York: Cambridge University Press, chap. Da, https://hsus.cambridge.org/HSUSWeb/toc/showChapter.do?id=Da.

———— (2018) A History of California Agriculture, in *California Agriculture: Dimensions and Issues*. 3rd edn, University of California Giannini Foundation of Agricultural Economics, https://giannini.ucop.edu/publications/cal-ag-book/.

Orrenius, P. M., and Zavodny, M. (2009) Do Immigrants Work in Riskier Jobs? *Demography* 46(3): 535–51.

Ozimek, A. (2017) No Sign of a Bubble for the U.S. Restaurant Industry, *Moody's Analytics*, March 13, www.economy.com/dismal/analysis/datapoints/294288/No-Sign-of-a-Bubble-for-the-US-Restaurant-Industry/.

Palladino, G. (2005) *Skilled Hand, Strong Spirits: A Century of Building Trades History*. Ithaca, NY: Cornell University Press.

Palmer, P. (1989) *Domesticity and Dirt: Housewives and Domestic Servants in the United States, 1920–1945*. Philadelphia: Temple University Press.

Parrenas, R. (2015) *Servants of Globalization: Migration and Domestic Work*. 2nd edn, Stanford, CA: Stanford University Press.

Passel, J. S. (2006) *The Size and Characteristics of the Unauthorized Migrant Population in the U.S.*, Pew Hispanic Center, March 7, www.pewresearch.org/wp-content/uploads/sites/5/reports/61.pdf.

Passel, J. S., and Cohn, D. (2016) Size of U.S. Unauthorized Workforce Stable after the Great Recession, Pew Research Center, November 3, www.pewresearch.org/hispanic/wp-content/uploads/sites/5/2016/11/LaborForce2016_FINAL_11.2.16-1.pdf.

——— (2018) U.S. Unauthorized Immigrant Total Dips to Lowest Level in a Decade, Pew Research Center, November 27, www.pewhispanic. org/2018/11/27/u-s-unauthorized-immigrant-total-dips-to-lowest-level-in-a-decade/.

——— (2019) Mexicans Decline to Less Than Half the U.S. Unauthorized Immigrant Population for the First Time, Pew Research Center, June 12, www.pewresearch.org/fact-tank/2019/06/12/us-unauthorized-immigrant-population-2017/.

Peri, G., and Sparber, C. (2009) Task Specialization, Immigration, and Wages, *American Economic Journal: Applied Economics* 1(3): 135–69.

Perlman, S. (1928) *A Theory of the Labor Movement.* New York: Macmillan.

Perry, C. R. (1986) *Deregulation and the Decline of the Unionized Trucking Industry.* Philadelphia: Wharton School, Industrial Relations Unit.

Pew Research Center (2016) How Americans Assess the Job Situation Today and Prospects for the Future, October 6, www.pewsocialtrends.org/2016/10/06/2-how-americans-assess-the-job-situation-today-and-prospects-for-the-future/.

Phillips, J. A., and Massey, D. S. (1999) The New Labor Market: Immigrants and Wages after IRCA, Demography 36(2): 233–46.

Phillips, S. (2016) *Brown is the New White.* New York: New Press.

Pidgeon, M. E., and Mitchell, A. W. (1956) *Employment Opportunities for Women in Beauty Service.* Washington, DC: U.S. Department of Labor, Women's Bureau.

Pierce, S., and Selee, A. (2017) *Immigration under Trump: A Review of Policy Shifts in the Year since the Election*, Migration Policy Institute Policy Brief, December, www.migrationpolicy.org/research/immigration-under-trump-review-policy-shifts.

Piketty, T., and Saez, E. (2014) Inequality in the Long Run, *Science* 344: 838–43.

Piore, M. J. (1975) Restrictions Aren't the Answer – The Illegals, in *Illegal Aliens*, Testimony at Hearings before the Subcommittee on Immigration, Citizenship, and International Law of the Committee on the Judiciary, U.S. House of Representatives, H.R. 982, Serial No. 8: 424–6.

——— (1979) *Birds of Passage: Migrant Labor and Industrial Societies.* New York: Cambridge University Press.

Port Jobs (2006) *Big Rig, Short Haul: A Study of Port Truckers in Seattle*, www. portjobs.org/storage/documents/bigrig_shorthaul_exec.pdf.

Postrel, V. (1998) The Acrylic Sector, *Forbes*, November 1.

Preston, J. (2006a) Immigrants' Families Figuring Out What to Do After Federal Raids, *New York Times*, December 16.

——— (2006b) U.S. Raids 6 Meat Plants in ID Case, *New York Times*, December 13.

Prince, T. (2005) Endangered Species, *Journal of Commerce*, May 9, pp. 12–16.

Rabourn, M. (2008) Organized Labor in Residential Construction, *Labor Studies Journal* 33(1): 9–26.

References

Rachleff, P. (1993) *Hard Pressed in the Heartland: The Hormel Strike and the Future of the American Labor Movement*. Boston: South End Press.

Radford, J. (2019) Key Findings about U.S. Immigrants, Pew Research Center, June 17, www.pewresearch.org/fact-tank/2019/06/17/key-findings-about-u-s-immigrants/.

Reeves, R. (2017) *Dream Hoarders*. Washington, DC: Brookings Institution Press.

Reskin, B., and Padavic, I. (2002) *Women and Men at Work*. 2nd edn, Thousand Oaks, CA: Pine Forge Press.

Reskin, B., and Roos, P. (1990) *Job Queues, Gender Queues*. Philadelphia: Temple University Press.

Rho, H. J., and Brown, H. (2019) Union Membership Byte 2019, Center for Economic and Policy Research, March, http://cepr.net/data-bytes/union-membership-bytes/union-byte-2019-01.

Ribas, V. (2016) *On the Line: Slaughterhouse Lives and the Making of the New South*. Oakland: University of California Press.

Roca-Servat, D. (2010) Justice for Roofers: Toward a Comprehensive Union Organizing Campaign Involving Latino Construction Workers in Arizona, *Labor Studies Journal* 35(3): 343–63.

Rolf, D. (2013) Labor: Building a New Future, *Democracy: A Journal of Ideas*, no. 29, https://democracyjournal.org/magazine/29/labor-building-a-new-future/.

Rollins, J. (1985) *Between Women: Domestics and Their Employers*. Philadelphia: Temple University Press.

Romero, M. (1992) *Maid in the U.S.A.* New York: Routledge.

Rosado Marzán, C. F. (2017) Worker Centers and the Moral Economy: Disrupting through Brokerage, Prestige and Moral Framing, *University of Chicago Legal Forum*, Article 16.

Rose, N. L. (1987) Labor Rent Sharing and Regulation: Evidence from the Trucking Industry, *Journal of Political Economy* 95(6): 1146–78.

Sánchez, G. J. (1993) *Becoming Mexican-American: Ethnicity, Culture, and Identity in Chicano Los Angeles, 1900–1945*. New York: Oxford University Press.

Sandoval-Strausz, A. K. (2019) *Barrio America: How Latino Immigrants Saved the American City*. New York: Basic Books.

Sassen, S. (2001) *The Global City: New York, London, Tokyo*. Princeton, NJ: Princeton University Press.

Saulny, S. (2008) Hundreds are Arrested in U.S. Sweep of Meat Plant, *New York Times*, May 13.

Schierholz, H. (2013) *Low Wages and Scant Benefits Leave Many In-Home Workers Unable to Make Ends Meet*. Washington, DC: Economic Policy Institute.

—— (2014) *Low Wages and Few Benefits Mean Many Restaurant Workers Can't Make Ends Meet*, Briefing Paper 383. Washington, DC: Economic Policy Institute.

References

Schlosser, E. (2001) *Fast Food Nation*. Boston: Houghton Mifflin.

Schneider, D., and Hastings, O. P. (2017) Income Inequality and Household Labor, *Social Forces* 96(2): 481–505.

Schuck, P. H. (2007) The Disconnect between Public Attitudes and Policy Outcomes in Immigration, in C. Swain (ed.), *Debating Immigration*. New York: Cambridge University Press, pp. 17–31.

Schwartzman, K. C. (2013) *The Chicken Trail*. Ithaca, NY: Cornell University Press.

Sessions, J. (2014) Amnesty Won't Work, *National Review*, March 24.

Shaw, R. (2008) *Beyond the Fields: Cesar Chavez, the UFW, and the Struggle for Justice in the 21st Century*. Berkeley: University of California Press.

Sherman, R. (2017) *Uneasy Street: The Anxieties of Affluence*. Princeton, NJ: Princeton University Press.

Sherman, R., and Voss, K. (2000) "Organize or Die": Labor's New Tactics and Immigrant Workers, in R. Milkman (ed.), *Organizing Immigrants*. Ithaca, NY: Cornell University Press, pp. 81–108.

Sides, J., Tesler, M., and Vavreck, L. (2018) *Identity Crisis: The 2016 Presidential Campaign and the Battle for the Meaning of America*. Princeton, NJ: Princeton University Press.

Silver, B. (2003) *Forces of Labor: Workers' Movements and Globalization since 1870*. New York: Cambridge University Press.

Singer, A. (2012) Appendix to Immigrant Workers in the U.S. Labor Force, Brookings, www.brookings.edu/wp-content/uploads/2016/06/0315_immigrant_workers_appendix.pdf.

Skaggs, S., Tomaskovic-Devey, D., and Leiter, J. (2000) Latino/a Employment Growth in North Carolina: Ethnic Displacement or Replacement? Unpublished Working Paper, North Carolina State University.

Smith, R., Marvy, P. A., and Zerolnick, J. (2014) *The Big Rig Overhaul: Restoring Middle-Class Jobs at America's Ports through Labor Law Enforcement*, National Employment Law Project, https://nelp.org/wp-content/uploads/2015/03/Big-Rig-Overhaul-Misclassification-Port-Truck-Drivers-Labor-Law-Enforcement.pdf.

Sorokin, P. A., Hanna, G. C., Israel, C., McKibben, L. L., Parten, M., Rothem, M. B., Tanquit, M., and Eddy, E. N. (1927) Leaders of Labor and Radical Movements in the United States and Foreign Countries, *American Journal of Sociology* 33(3): 382–411.

Standing, G. (2011) *The Precariat: The New Dangerous Classes*. London: Bloomsbury.

Stanley, K. (1992) Immigrant and Refugee Workers in the Midwestern Meatpacking Industry: Industrial Restructuring and the Transformation of Rural Labor Markets, *Policy Studies Review* 11(2): 106–17.

Stigler, G. J. (1946) *Domestic Servants in the United States, 1900–1940*, Occasional Paper 24. New York: National Bureau of Economic Research.

References

Streeck, W. (2018) Between Charity and Justice: Remarks on the Social Construction of Immigration Policy in Rich Democracies, *Culture, Practice & Europeanization* 3(2): 3–22.

Tavernise, S. (2018) Growing Share of U.S. Is Born on Foreign Soil, *New York Times*, September 13.

Terriquez, V. (2015) Intersectional Mobilization, Social Movement Spillover, and Queer Youth Leadership in the Immigrant Rights Movement, *Social Problems* 62(3): 343–62.

Thomas, R. J. (1981) The Social Organization of Industrial Agriculture, *Insurgent Sociologist* 10(winter): 5–20.

—— (1985) *Citizenship, Gender, and Work: Social Organization of Industrial Agriculture.* Berkeley: University of California Press.

Thompson, D. (2017) The Paradox of American Restaurants, *The Atlantic*, June 20, www.theatlantic.com/business/archive/2017/06/its-the-golden-age-of-restaurants-in-america/530955/.

U.S. Bureau of Labor Statistics (2017) National Industry-Specific Occupational Employment and Wage Estimates, NAICS 722500 – Restaurants and Other Eating Places, www.bls.gov/oes/2017/may/naics4_722500.htm.

—— (2018) Occupational Employment and Wages, Manicurists and Pedicurists, www.bls.gov/ooh/personal-care-and-service/manicurists-and-pedicurists.htm.

—— (2019) Foreign-Born Workers: Labor Force Characteristics – 2018, www.bls.gov/news.release/pdf/forbrn.pdf.

U.S. Immigration and Customs Enforcement (2018) ICE Worksite Enforcement Investigations in FY18 Surge, News Release, December 11, https www.ice.gov/news/releases/ice-worksite-enforcement-investigations-fy18-surge.

U.S. Women's Bureau (1964) *Negro Women Workers in 1960.* Washington, DC: U.S. Government Printing Office.

Verhovek, S. H. (1999) The New Language of American Labor, *New York Times*, June 26.

Viscelli, S. (2016) *The Big Rig: Trucking and the Decline of the American Dream.* Oakland: University of California Press.

Waldinger, R., and Der-Martirosian, C. (2000) Immigrant Workers and American Labor: Challenge … or Disaster?, in R. Milkman (ed.), *Organizing Immigrants.* Ithaca, NY: Cornell University Press.

Waldinger, R., and Lichter, M. (2003) *How the Other Half Works: Immigration and the Social Organization of Labor.* Berkeley: University of California Press.

Waldinger, R., Erickson, C., Milkman, R., Mitchell, D. J. B., Valenzuela, A., Wong, K., and Zeitlin, M. (1998) Helots No More: A Case Study of the Justice for Janitors Campaign in Los Angeles, in K. Bronfenbrenner, S. Friedman, R. W. Hurd, R. A. Oswald and R. L. Seeber (eds), *Organizing to Win: New Research on Union Strategies.* Ithaca, NY: Cornell University Press, pp. 102–20.

Waltz, L. (2018) *Hog Wild: The Battle for Rights at the World's Largest Slaughterhouse.* Iowa City: University of Iowa Press.

References

Warren, R. (2017) US Undocumented Population Continued to Fall from 2016 to 2017, and Visa Overstays Significantly Exceeded Illegal Crossings for the Seventh Consecutive Year, Center for Migration Studies, https://cmsny.org/publications/essay-2017-undocumented-and-overstays/.

Weil, D. (2014) *The Fissured Workplace*. Cambridge, MA: Harvard University Press.

Weir, M. (2002) *Income Polarization and California's Social Contract*, https://sociology.berkeley.edu/sites/default/files/faculty/weir/Income%20Polarization%20and%20California%27s%20Social%20Contract.pdf.

Wells, M. J. (2000) Immigration and Unionization in the San Francisco Hotel Industry, in R. Milkman (ed.), *Organizing Immigrants*. Ithaca, NY: Cornell University Press.

Western, B., and Rosenfeld, J. (2011) Unions, Norms, and the Rise in U.S. Wage Inequality, *American Sociological Review* 76(4): 513–37.

Willett, J. A. (2005) "Hands across the Table": A Short History of the Manicurist in the Twentieth Century, *Journal of Women's History* 17(3): 59–80.

Wong, T. K. (2017) *The Politics of Immigration*. New York: Oxford University Press.

Wright, G. (1988) American Agriculture and the Labor Market: What Happened to Proletarianization? *Agricultural History* 62(3): 182–209.

Wuthnow, R. (2018) *The Left Behind*. Princeton, NJ: Princeton University Press.

Zabin, C. (2000) Organizing Latino Workers in the Los Angeles Manufacturing Sector: The Case of American Racing Equipment, in R. Milkman (ed.), *Organizing Immigrants*. Ithaca, NY: Cornell University Press.

Zamorano, N. D., Perez, J., Guitierrez, J., and Meza, N. (2010) DREAM Activists: Rejecting the Passivity of the Nonprofit, Industrial Complex, https://truthout.org/articles/dream-activists-rejecting-the-passivity-of-the-nonprofit-industrial-complex/.

Zavodny, M., and Jacoby, T. (2013) *Filling the Gap: Less-Skilled Immigrants in a Changing Economy*. Washington, DC: Immigration Works USA and American Enterprise Institute, www.aei.org/wp-content/uploads/2013/06/-zavodny-filling-the-gap-immigration-report_140631709214.pdf.

Zepeda-Millán, C. (2017) *Latino Mass Mobilization: Immigration, Racialization, and Activism*. New York: Cambridge University Press.

Zolberg, A. (2006) *A Nation by Design: Immigration Policy in the Fashioning of America*. Cambridge, MA: Harvard University Press.

Zong, J., Batalova, J., and Burrows, M. (2019) Frequently Requested Statistics on immigrants and Immigration in the United States, March 14, www.migrationpolicy.org/article/frequently-requested-statistics-immigrants-and-immigration-united-states#Demographic.

Index

Index

Index

Index

Index

H.R. 4437 (2005) 151, 155–6
Johnson–Reed Act (1924) 55, 56, 63
Ribas, V. 84, 95
Rollins, J. 109–10, 114, 117
Roosevelt, F. D. 62
Roosevelt, T. 41
Rustbelt 7, 71, 72, 73

Sanchéz, G. 56
Schlosser, E. 90, 93, 94–5
Service Employees International Union (SEIU) 81, 82–3, 138, 140, 151
Sessions, J. 10–12
Sherman, R. 107–8, 117
   and Voss, K. 136
Sides, J., et al. 6, 9, 10
social networks 37, 78–9, 134–5
Stanley, K. 85, 91–2
stigmatization 136–7
Streeck, W. 166
subcontracting and deregulation 96–101
Sunbelt 71, 72

Teamsters' union 57, 59, 97
textile industry 71–2
Thomas, R. J. 59, 60
transnational advocacy networks (TANs) 148
trucking industry 96–101
Trump, D. 2, 3, 4, 6–13, 19, 73, 96, 127, 144, 159–60, 161, 164, 165, 167–8

unauthorized/undocumented immigrants 1–2, 3, 23, 25–7
   domestic workers 115
   immigrant rights movement 152–3, 154, 157, 158–9
   labor activism 148, 151
   labor "unorganizability" 130, 131, 132
   Latinx 8, 25–6

Mexican 48–50, 51, 56–7, 59–60, 69–70
   restaurant work 120–1
   see also deportations
union decline see labor degradation and union decline
union organizing see labor organizing and advocacy
unionization rates 30, 165
UNITE HERE 140, 141
United Farm Workers (UFW) 57–61, 141, 150
United Food and Commercial Workers (UFCW) 87–8
U.S. Immigration Commission 39, 40

voting behaviour 8–10, 156, 168

Walker, F. A. 37
Weil, D. 68, 101
whites
   "diploma divide" 8, 10
   European migration 37
   non-college educated/low income workers 6–7, 9–10, 12, 16, 73
   women 108–9, 111–12
women 15–16, 23
   African American 105, 111–13, 116, 118, 123
   Asian 123–4, 125
   white 108–9, 111–12
   see also domestic workers
worker centers 144–51
Worker Representation and Participation Survey (WRPS) 133
Working Families United coalition 165
workplace raids 28–9, 95–6, 131, 155–6, 164, 165

Youngstown, Ohio 72–3

Zavodny, M., and Jacoby, T. 22–3, 25, 26–7, 28

200